SIR WALTER SCOTT:

the formative years

Some other books by Arthur Melville Clark

The Realistic Revolt in Modern Poetry
Thomas Heywood, Playwright and Miscellanist
Autobiography, its Genesis and Phases
Studies in Literary Modes
Spoken English : An Idiomatic Grammar for Foreign Students
Sonnets from the French, and Other Verses

WALTER SCOTT, aged about 12

SIR WALTER SCOTT:
the formative years

Arthur Melville Clark

WILLIAM BLACKWOOD
Edinburgh and London
1969

William Blackwood & Sons Ltd
45 George Street
Edinburgh 2

Printed at the Press of the Publisher
William Blackwood & Sons Ltd, Edinburgh
SBN: 85158 015 7

CONTENTS

ILLUSTRATIONS

PREFACE

The aim of this book is to present in a manner between narration and comment the educational phase of Scott's life. I use that phrase to cover not only schooling, tutoring, university instruction, legal apprenticeship, and preparation for the Bar, but also (and quite as much) Scott's haphazard and ranging self-education by a very miscellaneous reading of all kinds of printed matter from *belles lettres* downwards, in English and in four other modern languages, with dabblings in two or three more. And I have likewise regarded as educational Scott's eager attention to the conversation and anecdotes of his elders; his pursuit of social graces and accomplishments; his endeavour to equal or surpass his fellows in physical activity despite his disabilities; his rambles and excursions on foot or on horseback; and his attempt through his membership of various clubs and societies, especially the Speculative Society, to make good some defects in his background by associating with more knowledgeable contemporaries. The only side of his preparation for life on which I have said but little is his *éducation sentimentale*. At appropriate points I have noticed Scott's versifying in his boyhood and in his adolescence, his first essays in prose, and his commencing as a man of letters by translating and imitating German models. Some attention also is paid to Scott's concern in the education of his own children to make them happier than he had been himself at their age; to his interesting and unrecognised role as an educational innovator; and to his attitude to university reform and his unwilling involvement in Rectorial campaigns.

Scott was given to the autobiographical, or at least the reminiscential about his past and the persons belonging to it, not egotistically but, on the contrary, in a modest and self-depreciatory way. I have quoted Scott himself freely because his own turns of phrase are so apt and racy, and in so doing have drawn not merely on passages in which he speaks overtly of himself but also on others in which he echoes personal details and situations in the course of a fiction.

Naturally I have made a considerable use of Lockhart and the other early biographers of Scott, but always with caution. As Scott's education was not their main theme, but as it is mine, I have gone into much greater detail; and I have tried to throw light as well on all the persons with whom Scott was on terms of pupilage, friendship, or mere acquaintance during the first twenty-five years of his life. My aim has been to interest and (I would hope) amuse those who love and admire Scott the man, as well as Scott the poet and novelist, by presenting him more fully than he has hitherto been made to appear during the time when he was still amaking.

It is with pleasure that I take the opportunity of this Preface to acknowledge the generous help I have received and the facilities I have been so readily accorded. By the great kindness of Mrs Patricia and Miss Jean Maxwell-Scott, who have interested themselves warmly in my work, I have been able to consult important material in the Abbotsford Library and to reproduce four particularly appropriate portraits. The bold and effective design by the late Professor Otto Schlapp on the dust-cover of the book appears by the kind consent of my old friend, Dr Robert Schlapp. As will be seen from the list of Illustrations, other owners to give similar permission were Edinburgh Booksellers' Society Limited (Mr Ian Grant, Praeses; Mr A. L. Russell, Secretary; and Mr Thomas G. Clark, Treasurer), the Trustees of the late Adrian Henry Cook, W.S. (Mrs A. H. Cook and Mr H. J. D. Cook), and the Faculty of Advocates (Mr D. A. O. Edward, Clerk of Faculty). Mr Charles H. Stewart, Secretary to the University of Edinburgh, supplied me with one of the photographs used. About all the illustrations I was helpfully and patiently advised by Mr R. E. Hutchison, Keeper of the Scottish National Portrait Gallery; he arranged for excellent photographs for most of them to be made, and he and Mr Duncan Thomson, Assistant Keeper, helped me in checking the details. Mr D. A. O. Edward kindly gave me access to the Faculty of Advocates' minutes; Mr Nigel Pearson to the minutes of the Speculative Society; and Mr Baillie T. Ruthven, Rector, and two of my former students on his staff, Mr James Noble and Mr Alexander Forsyth, to the records of the Royal High School. Another old student who made my way smoother was Mr William Park, Keeper of Manuscripts in the National Library of Scotland. Dr J. C. Corson, Honorary Librarian of Abbotsford, whose *Bibliography of Sir Walter Scott* is masterly and invaluable, and Mr W. M. Parker, than whom nobody knows better Scott's Letters, were ever ready for consultation and with information. Mr Douglas Grant and Professor Neil Campbell gave me such friendly advice and encouragement as I shall not forget. And another of my former students, Dr Isabel M. Brown, whom I consulted on various points, read the proofs of this book with her unfailing care and accuracy. To all of these kind helpers I extend my cordial thanks. I should be indeed blameworthy if I did not conclude with a special word of thanks to Mr Douglas Blackwood and his two aides, Mr David Fletcher and Mr Trevor Royle, for their expert professional guidance, skill, and care on the one hand, and for their very human kindness and consideration on the other.

ARTHUR MELVILLE CLARK

Edinburgh, 1969

I have tagged with rhyme and blank verse the subdivisions of this important narrative, in order to seduce your continued attention by powers of composition of stronger attraction than my own.

Rob Roy, *Chapter III.*

ABBREVIATIONS

Allan
George Allan (continuing work begun by William Weir), *Life of Sir Walter Scott, Baronet; with Critical Notices of his Writings.* 1834.

Bower
Alexander Bower, *The History of the University of Edinburgh.* 3 vols 1817.

Burns
Sir Walter Scott, 1809 review of R. H. Cromek's *Reliques of Robert Burns in Prose* (q.v.).

Carlyle
Alexander Carlyle, *The Autobiography of Dr Alexander Carlyle of Inveresk, 1722-1805.* Edited by John Hill Burton. 1910.

C.B.E.L.
The Cambridge Bibliography of English Literature. Edited by F. W. Bateson. 4 vols 1940.

Chambers
Robert Chambers, *Life of Sir Walter Scott.* Revised by William Chambers. 1871.

Chivalry
Sir Walter Scott, *Essay on Chivalry* in *Prose* (q.v.).

Cockburn
Lord Cockburn, *Memorials of his Times.* Edited by Harry A. Cockburn. 1910.

Cook
New Love-Poems by Sir Walter Scott, Discovered in the Narrative of an Unknown Love Episode with Jessie —— of Kelso. Edited by Davidson Cook. 1932.

Corson
J. C. Corson, *A Bibliography of Sir Walter Scott. A Classified and Annotated List of Books and Articles relating to his Life and Works, 1797-1940.* 1943.

Demonology
Sir Walter Scott, *Letters on Demonology and Witchcraft.* Edited by Henry Morley. 1884.

D.N.B.
Dictionary of National Biography. Edited by Sir Leslie Stephen.

Drama	Sir Walter Scott, *Essay on the Drama* in *Prose* (q.v.).
Essays	Sir Walter Scott, *Essays on Chivalry, Romance, and the Drama* (The Chandos Classics). n.d.
Fasti	*Fasti Ecclesiae Scoticanae. The Succession of Ministers in the Church of Scotland from the Reformation.* Edited by Hew Scott, J. A. Lamb, etc. 9 vols 1915-61.
General Preface	Sir Walter Scott, *General Preface* to the Waverley Novels. 1829.
G. Ballads	Sir Walter Scott, *Ballads from the German* in *P.W.* (q.v.).
Gillies	R. P. Gillies, *Recollections of Sir Walter Scott, Bart.* 1837.
Graham, *Soc. Life*	Henry Grey Graham, *The Social Life of Scotland in the Eighteenth Century.* 2 vols 1899.
Graham	Henry Grey Graham, *Scottish Men of Letters in the Eighteenth Century.* 1901.
Grandfather	Sir Walter Scott, *Tales of a Grandfather.* History of Scotland. 3 vols 1840. History of France. 1854.
Grant	Sir Alexander Grant, *The Story of the University of Edinburgh during its first Three Hundred Years.* 2 vols 1884.
Grierson	Sir Herbert Grierson, *Sir Walter Scott, Bart.* 1938.
Hogg	James Hogg, *The Domestic Manners and Private Life of Sir Walter Scott. With a Memoir of the Author, Notes,* etc. 1834.
Home	Sir Walter Scott, 1827 review of Henry Mackenzie's *Life and Works of the Author of 'Douglas'* in *Prose* (q.v.).
Imitations	Sir Walter Scott, *Essay on Imitations of the Ancient Ballads* and Appendix in *Minstrelsy* (q.v.).

Intro. Note	Sir Walter Scott, *Introductory Note to Ballads from the German* in *P.W.* (q.v.).
Irving	John Irving, manuscript letters to J. G. Lockhart in the National Library of Scotland.
Journal	Sir Walter Scott, *The Journal of Sir Walter Scott*, 1825-32. Edited by J. G. Tait. 3 vols 1939-46.
Lay	Sir Walter Scott, *The Lay of the Last Minstrel* in *P.W.* (q.v.).
Letters	Sir Walter Scott, *The Letters of Sir Walter Scott*, 1787-1832. Edited by Sir Herbert Grierson, assisted by Davidson Cook, W. M. Parker, and others. 12 vols 1932-37.
Letter-Books	*The Private Letter-Books of Sir Walter Scott. Selections from the Abbotsford Manuscripts. With a Letter to the Reader from Hugh Walpole.* Edited by Wilfred Partington. 1930.
Lockhart	John Gibson Lockhart, *Memoirs of the Life of Sir Walter Scott, Bart.* 2 vols 1878.
Lockhart(abr.)	John Gibson Lockhart, *The Life of Sir Walter Scott, Bart.* Abridged from the larger work. 2 vols 1898.
Mrs Cockburn	Mrs Cockburn, *Letters and Memoir of her own Life.* By Mrs Alison Rutherford or Cockburn. Also *Felix*, a Biographical Sketch, and Various Songs. Edited by T. Craig-Brown. 1900.
Mrs Hughes	Mrs Hughes of Uffington, *Letters and Recollections of Sir Walter Scott.* Edited by Horace G. Hutchinson. n.d.
Memoir	Sir Walter Scott, *Memoir of the Early Life of Sir Walter Scott, written by Himself* in Lockhart (q.v.)
Minstrelsy	Sir Walter Scott, *Minstrelsy of the Scottish*

Border. Edited by T. F. Henderson. 4 vols 1932.

Paton — Hugh Paton, *A Series of Original Portraits and Caricature Etchings, by the late John Kay, Miniature Painter, Edinburgh; with Biographical Sketches and Anecdotes.* 2 vols 1842.

Post-Bag — *Sir Walter's Post-Bag.* More Stories and Sidelights from his Unpublished Letter-Books. Edited by Wilfred Partington. Foreword by Hugh Walpole. 1932.

Prose — Sir Walter Scott, *The Miscellaneous Prose Works of Sir Walter Scott, Bart.* Containing Biographical Memoirs, Essays, Letters, with Notes. 1848.

P.W. — Sir Walter Scott, *The Poetical Works of Sir Walter Scott.* With the Author's Introductions and Notes. Edited by J. Logie Robertson. 1904.

Ruff — William Ruff, *A Bibliography of the Poetical Works of Sir Walter Scott, 1796–1832 in Edinburgh Bibliographical Society Transactions,* vol I. 1937–38.

Lord Sands — Sir C. N. Johnston (Lord Sands), *Sir Walter Scott's Congé.* 1930.

Spec. Soc. (1845) — *History of the Speculative Society of Edinburgh from its Institution in MDCCLXIV.* 1845.

Spec. Soc. (1905) — *The History of the Speculative Society, 1764–1904.* 1905.

Steven — William Steven, *The History of the High School of Edinburgh.* 1849.

van Antwerp — W. C. van Antwerp, *A Collector's Comment on his First Editions of the Works of Sir Walter Scott.* 1932.

Wilson — Sir Daniel Wilson, *Memorials of Edinburgh in the Olden Time.* 2 vols 1891.

IN PIAM MEMORIAM

J. C. ET M. M. C.

MCMLXIX

A.D.

CHAPTER I

THE DATE OF SCOTT'S BIRTH

An ancient Minstrel sagely said
" Where is the life which late we led? "
That motley clown in Arden wood,
Whom humorous Jaques with envy view'd,
Not even that clown could amplify
On this trite text so long as I.
                    Marmion, *Introduction to Canto Fourth.*

My birth was neither distinguished nor sordid.   According to
the prejudices of my country, it was esteemed gentle, *as I was*
connected, though remotely, with ancient families both by my
father's and my mother's side.
                              Memoir, *I, 1.*

SIR WALTER SCOTT was born within easy reach of the best in the way of education that his city afforded, but a stone's throw from its High School and in the very shadow of its University. His father's house was on the third storey of a venerable quadrangular building at the top of the gloomy College Wynd, on the east side thereof and only a few feet from the richly carved gateway of the College itself. It has since been pulled down to make room for the north side of the Old College. Hence the story, circulated among the simpler bajans,[1] that Scott was born in the Greek class-room.[2] But besides his birth and early nurture in such a learned quarter, Scott was a grandson of one Professor[3] and a nephew of another soon to be appointed,[4] and was perhaps christened by William Robertson who was both Principal of the University and one of the Ministers of Greyfriars of which parish Scott senior was an elder. More-over, though born an uncommonly sturdy infant and show-ing every sign of health and strength until he was some eighteen months old,[5] Scott became then and remained for long the peculiar care of the Medical Faculty, to say nothing 'of empirics,[6] or of ancient ladies or gentlemen who con-ceived themselves entitled to recommend various remedies, some of which were of a nature sufficiently singular.[7] Gossips, then, like his Ailsie Gourlay or his Meg Merrilies, 'keekin' in his loof,'[8] might have predicted for the infant Scott a career more distinguished for scholastic and academic success than his proved to be. For indeed his formal studies at school and at the University left comparatively little trace on the work he was born to do and bent his genius not at all.

If the accepted date for Scott's birth, 15th August 1771 (two years to the day after Napoleon's), be correct, he was only twelve years and three months at the time of his first matriculation at the University in 1783. This is not im-possible, for grammar- and high-school education was not as a rule so prolonged in Scotland as in England, and the average age of entrants to a Scottish University was less than at Oxford or Cambridge.[9] David Hume (1722) and

Henry Mackenzie (1746) were actually only eleven. Hugh Blair (1730), Principal William Robertson (1733), David Dickson the elder (1766),[10] and Principal George Husband Baird (1773) were twelve. John Erskine (1734),[11] Alexander ('Jupiter') Carlyle (1735), Sir John Sinclair (1767), Thomas Charles Hope (1779),[12] Sir John Leslie (1779), and David Dickson the younger (1793)[13] were thirteen. Adam Smith (1737) and Henry Cockburn (1793) were fourteen. But many entrants were eighteen or more, not a few (especially in the Medical Faculty) being in their twenties. Besides, it was not unusual for students to remain at a University for eight or ten years or even more. Scott's closest friend from 1788 for many years, William Clerk, attended classes continuously from 1783-84 to 1790-91. As will appear, Scott himself was a student during six of the same sessions, the first three and the last three.

But I am inclined to think that the accepted date for Scott's birth is wrong by a year, and that he was in fact thirteen years and three months on entering the University. In a miscellaneous memorandum he incidentally gave 1771, without qualification, as the year of his birth[14]; and on the last leaf of a black-letter Bible of 1630 at Abbotsford he formally entered his own name at the beginning of a family register thus:

' Secundum Morem Majorum.

Haec de familia Gualteri Scott Jurisconsulti Edinensis in librum hunc sacrum manu sua conscripta sunt.

Gualterus Scott Filius Gualteri Scott et Annae Rutherford natus erat apud Edinam 15mo die Augusti A.D. 1771.'[15]

There is no hint of any doubt in this entry, which was presumably made with due deliberation. But any such hint would have been out of place in such a register. In two other passages, just as much deliberated, Scott clearly shows that he was uncertain about the year of his birth.

In his *Memoir*, where the birth-date was an important detail, he gives the accepted date, but with a somewhat doubtful 'as I believe';[16] and in the *Journal*, in a passage of speculation on how soon he could expect to be clear of debt, he says 'if I was born in 1771, I shall only be sixty in 1831'.[17] Two other pieces of evidence against the 1771 date are, first, that the tutor, James Mitchell who retained very affectionate and reliable memories of his pupil, reckoned him to have been in his twelfth or thirteenth year in 1782;[18] and, secondly, that John Irving, who was Scott's greatest friend in boyhood and who was born in November 1770, was convinced that Scott was his senior by three months. I have vainly searched all the Edinburgh baptismal registers to prove or disprove this. The absence of Scott's name from these registers is probably due to his having been baptised at home, not in the church or the minister's manse. His mother noted, apparently after 8th June 1787 when her son Robert was buried at sea, that 'none of my present family was born till some time' after 30th August 1766, when her first child called Walter was born.[19] The first of her children born after the date just mentioned was John, who was 'about three years older than' the second Walter.[20] However 'some time' and 'about three years' are both vague phrases and leave the date of the second Walter's birth open.

As Irving remarks, if the accepted date for Scott's birth be correct, he became an advocate on 11th July 1792 before he was of age and so contrary to the Faculty's regulations.[21] That may be why Scott makes Provost Crosbie in *Redgauntlet* say to the newly-fledged young advocate Alan Fairford, whose character and career were but slightly fictionised from Scott's own, " Were you a twelve-month aulder, we would make a burgess of you, man."[22] It has to be admitted, however, that Alan had already been described as 'now entitled, as arrived at the years of majority, and a member of the learned Faculty, to direct his own motions'.[23] It is also a fact that breaches of professional regulations as to age were not unknown. Alexander Wedderburn [24] and Henry Erskine were both admitted to the Faculty of Advocates when only nineteen;[25] Henry Mackenzie when twenty was likewise irregularly admitted attorney in the Court of the Exchequer in Scotland; and James Hall [26] was licensed to preach and James Struthers [27] was ordained to a charge at ages short of twenty-one.[28]

But the most conclusive piece of evidence in my opinion is a scrap of manuscript once at Abbotsford but now lost, which, so far as I am aware, has never been used by or known to any of the biographers of Scott and of which the significance was not realised on the only occasion on which it was on view. This was at the Exhibition in Edinburgh in 1871 to commemorate the accepted centenary of Scott's birth. It is of course not surprising that one manuscript item in a case with many others should not be very carefully scrutinised. But the illustrated catalogue which was published the following year [29] as a more lasting souvenir of the Exhibition fortunately includes among its many plates a facsimile of the item in question. It is a 'remit'[30] written and signed by Henry Erskine, Dean of the Faculty of Advocates, in connection with Scott's application for examination; and it runs as follows:

' Edinburgh 14 June 1791—

The Dean of Faculty remits the Petitioner to the private Examinators on the Civil Law to assign him a day for his trial thereon he having promised on his honor to give no treat or entertainment on account thereof and producing to the Examinators proper Certificates of his being twenty years of age—

Henry Erskine D.F.'

As Scott was duly examined, he must have produced the necessary certificates. There were probably two, one from his father, and one from his minister. Since there is no question as to the month and the day of Scott's birth, but only as to the year, it would therefore appear that on 14th June 1791 he was already twenty years of age, having had his twentieth birthday on 15th August 1790, and that he was, despite the biographers and the works of reference, actually born on the corresponding day in 1770. The birth or baptismal certificates suffered, I suspect, the all-too-common fate of such documents when they get into official hands.

NOTES ON REFERENCES

1   First-year students in a Scottish university (from Fr. *bec jaune*).

2   What was the Greek classroom till a few years ago is probably nearer the site than is the unworthy tablet in Guthrie Street which is supposed to mark it.

3   John Rutherford, Professor of Medicine and one of the founders of the Medical School.

4   Daniel Rutherford, Professor of Botany from 1786.

5   Twenty-two months, according to Allan, who quotes a nurse as saying that till the onset of infantile paralysis he was ' as fine sonsy [= plump, good-natured] a bairn as ever woman held in her arms ' (5).

6   Including Dr James Graham, founder and hierophant of the Temple of Health and Hymen. He lectured in his native city first in 1781 and again in 1783 and treated many whose cases had not yielded to the regular practitioners. Scott was subjected to the ' earth-bath ' and to applications of electricity and ' magnetism '. His parents had enough faith in the electrical treatment to continue it till he was in his 'teens when John Irving helped to apply it.

7   *Memoir*, I, 5.

8   Burns, *There was a Lad*.

9   Scott's brother-Romantics, Wordsworth, Coleridge and Southey, were respectively eighteen, nineteen, and twenty when they first matriculated.

10   Minister first of College Church and then of New North Church.

11   One of the Ministers of Greyfriars Church and an intimate friend of the Scott family.

12   Professor of Chemistry, Edinburgh.

13   Senior Minister of St Cuthbert's Church.

14   *The Letters of Sir Walter Scott and Charles Kirkpatrick Sharpe to Robert Chambers, 1821-45. With Original Memoranda of Sir Walter Scott*, 59. Scott was supplying Chambers with notes for *Traditions of Edinburgh*, 1825.

15   On the verso of the leaf the second Sir Walter entered the deaths of his father and mother. The entry for his father is: 'Died at Abbotsford upon Friday the 21st day of September 1832 at Twenty-five minutes past one pm. Sir Walter Scott, aged 61 years and 22 days.'

16   I, 4.

17   III, 114 (2nd July 1830).

18   Cf. Lockhart, I, 30.

19   Lockhart, I, 22 note 2. Like Major Bridgenorth and his wife, the Scotts 'lost successively a family of no less than six children, apparently through a delicacy of constitution, which cut off the little prattlers at the early age when they most wind themselves around the hearts of the parents' (*Peveril of the Peak*, Chapter I). Cf. *Letters*, IX, 59 (to Henry Mackenzie, 2nd April 1825).

20   *Memoir*, I, 4; cf. *infra*, 15.

21   Hence Gillies's remark that Scott assumed the gown 'in his twenty-first year' (55).

22   Chapter X. Scott himself was made a burgess of Aberdeen (of which his father was the law agent) when attending the Court there in 1796.

23   Chapter II.

24   Lord Chancellor Loughborough and Earl of Rosslyn.

25   Erskine was the Dean of the Faculty when Scott was admitted in 1792.

26   Minister of Lesmahagow.

27   Minister of College Street Relief Church, Edinburgh.

28   Scott notes that for special reasons a squire could be knighted while still a minor (*Chivalry*, 540).

29   *The Scott Exhibition. MDCCCLXXI. Catalogue of the Exhibition held in Edinburgh, in July and August 1871, on occasion of the Commemoration of the Centenary of the Birth of Sir Walter Scott* (1872), 150, 163.

30   I.e. direction to a committee or an individual to take certain steps and report thereon.

CHAPTER II

SCHOOLING AND TUTORING

I used to think [Philipp Emanuel von Fellenberg] something of a quack in proposing to discover how a boy's natural genius lies, with a view to his education. How would they have made me a scholar, is a curious question. Whatever was forced on me as a task I should have detested.

Journal III, 105 (15th June 1830).

[A]lthough at a more advanced period of life I have enjoyed considerable facility in acquiring languages, I did not make any great figure at the High School—or, at least, any exertions which I made were desultory and little to be depended on.

Memoir, I, 8.

You call this education, do you not?
Why, 'tis the forced march of a herd of bullocks
Before a shouting drover. The glad van
Move on at ease, and pause a while to snatch
A passing morsel from the dewy greensward;
While all the blows, the oaths, the indignation,
Falls on the croupe of the ill-fated laggard
That cripples in the rear.

The Monastery, *Motto for Chapter XI.*

IN the eighteenth century there were no entrance examinations for any of the Scottish Universities. Scott, however, had qualifications at least equal to those of the many who, by the hard persuasion of schoolmasters skilled in the preparation of tabloid knowledge, are thrust into a University with a Certificate of Education, or who, without such a talisman, struggle painfully past a series of ' Prelims '.

What, then, had Scott in fact learned by the time he was twelve or thirteen? I shall begin with what he learned, not always very willingly, by way of regular instruction in the recognised school subjects in his day. By his own account in the *Memoir*, he got the rudiments of reading at a dame's school in Bath which he attended as a three- or four-year-old for about a quarter; ' and I never had a more regular teacher. . . . An occasional lesson from my aunt supplied the rest '.[1] His aunt's lessons probably began even before the sojourn of about a year at Bath (where he benefited much more in mind than in body) and continued off and on so long as he was in her charge. Tibby Hunter, who had been a domestic at Sandy-knowe, remembered that, though Walter was ' very gleg [2] at the uptake ', he was not particularly fond of his book and used every pretext to be instead out-of-doors with Sandy Ormistoun, the cowbailie. But ' Miss Jenny was a grand hand at keeping him to the bit, and by degrees he came to read brawly '.[3] To continue Scott's own account from the point at which I broke off above: ' Afterwards, when grown a big boy, I had a few lessons from Mr Stalker of Edinburgh,[4] and finally from the Rev. Mr Cleeve.[5] But I never acquired a just pronunciation, nor could I read with much propriety.'[6] This passage must be taken as referring to Scott below the age of six or seven. As usual, he underestimates himself. He had made extraordinary progress intellectually at Bath, and the process continued as prosperously on his return. Moreover Mrs Cockburn, who pronounced the six-year-old Scott ' the most extraordinary genius of a boy I ever saw ', declared that he had ' acquired the perfect English accent . . . and . . . reads like a Garrick '.[7]

By this time, the winter of 1777, George Square had become his ' most established place of residence '.[8] His adjustment to it and the brothers and sister he had scarcely known before may be regarded as part of his education, and not the most agreeable part, his eldest brother Robert exercising his seniority of seven or eight years in no very merciful manner. ' I felt the change,' says Scott, ' from being a single indulged brat, to becoming a member of a large family, very severely; for under the gentle government of my kind grandmother, and of my aunt, who, though of an higher temper, was exceedingly attached to me, I had acquired a degree of licence which could not be permitted in a large family.'[9] He was apparently more amenable than his brothers to parental discipline,[10] and more gentle and refined in manners from having lived so long among adults, most of them women;[11] but against fraternal bullying he put up such a fight as his physical condition allowed, often keeping ' the nursery in an uproar, [and] using his crutch upon his brothers with good effect '.[12] He resented, too, the impatience of servants and nursery-maids, from whom his disability required (without always getting) a little extra care. I am inclined to doubt, however, the story that, in order to punish an offending cook-maid, he drowned a litter of puppies in the water-cistern, and that the phenomenon of his refusing his dinner thereafter from remorse and sulks led to inquiry and discovery.[13] But there can be no doubt that an incident which Scott tells in a fictional way in *My Aunt Margaret's Mirror* is genuinely autobiographical: ' There is the stile at which I can recollect a cross child's maid [14] upbraiding me with my infirmity as she lifted me coarsely and carelessly over the flinty steps, which my brothers traversed with shout and bound. I remember the suppressed bitterness of the moment, and, conscious of my own inferiority, the feeling of envy with which I regarded the easy movements and elastic steps of my more happily formed brethren. Alas ! ' he goes on with a characteristic shift from emotion past to emotion present, ' these goodly barks have all perished on life's wide ocean, and only that which seemed so little seaworthy, as the naval phrase goes, has reached the port when the tempest is over '.[15] The child Scott certainly had the spirit to resent bullying and unkindness, but the over-all impression we get on all hands is ' of a child of extraordinary sweetness and charm ',[16] winning every heart by his openness, his good-nature and placability, his intelligence, his enthusiasm in his special interests and his readiness to talk of them with an engaging eagerness, ' and his wonderful dutifulness . . . a readiness to admit and give full value to the claims—the rights and the wishes—of others '.[17] It was his uncle, Thomas Scott, who once said, ' God bless thee, Walter, my man ! thou hast risen to be great, but thou wast always good ',[18] meaning by ' good ', not a Sunday-school paradigm, but an unfailing kindness and consideration. And quite as remarkable, and indeed more so in the circumstances, is the sagacity with which he accepted his situation when restored to the family circle, and the wise lesson he drew from it. ' I had sense enough, however,' he says, ' to bend my temper to my new circumstances; but such was the agony which I internally experienced, that I have guarded against nothing more in the education of my own family, than against their acquiring habits of self-willed caprice and domination.'[19]

The time was now approaching for Scott to enter the High School of Edinburgh; and he would no doubt have joined its ' petulant brood '[20] in ' the tumult of the Gytes' Class ',[21] had he not been thought rather backward by school standards, at least for the class for which he was probably designed. He was accordingly sent to the private school of John Leechman in Hamilton's Entry, Bristo Port, to be brought on in the subjects he had missed through illness while he laid up a store of less usual information. Leechman, who was so much esteemed by Scott's father that ' for many years he was a weekly guest of the family ',[22] was an English master.[23] But apparently neither he nor anyone else gave Scott much grounding in English grammar and orthography.[24] His spelling retained a refreshing originality to the end; and when Lockhart pointed out some of his linguistic solecisms in 1826, he wrote, 'Well! I will try to remember all this, but after all I write grammar as I speak, to make my meaning known, and a solecism in point of composition, like a Scotch word in speaking, is indifferent to me. I never learned grammar; and not only Sir Hugh Evans but even Mrs Quickly might puzzle me about Jinnie's case and horum harum horum.[25] I believe the Bailiff in *The Good-natured Man*[26] is not far wrong when he says, " One man has one way of expressing himself, and another another, and that is all the difference between them ".'[27] Apparently the schooling under Leechman did not answer as well as had been expected; and for the remainder of the period of preparation Scott was entrusted to a tutor at home, James French,[28] who was a divinity student and the son of one of the High School masters.

It might be inferred from this record of varied teaching that Scott's parents were puzzled to know what to do with a boy of unusual gifts whose wandering attention could not easily be secured for the slow and dry routine of education as it was then practised. Nor, as will be seen, did the parents' anxiety to do their best for their son end with his admission to the High School.

Unfortunately the date of that admission, like some other dates in Scott's boyhood and youth, has been variously given by his biographers, none of whom seems to have taken much trouble to get at the facts. Scott's own statement in his *Memoir* was, I believe, as follows: 'In 1779 I was sent to the second class of the Grammar School, or High School of Edinburgh,[29] then taught by Mr Luke Fraser.'[30] But the manuscript of the *Memoir*, which was at one time at Abbotsford and was lent by J. R. Hope-Scott to the Scott Exhibition of 1871,[31] has disappeared; and we have to rely on Lockhart's version of it printed as the first chapter of his biography of Scott. Lockhart prints the above passage thus: ' In [1778] I was sent,' etc.[32] Indeed he prints nine or ten of the dates in the *Memoir* in square brackets, indicating thereby (one would conclude) either that Scott himself had left blanks or that Lockhart as editor had corrected what he believed to be mistakes. Be that as it may, Scott's entry of the High School was certainly in 1779, not in 1778. The year is established by the contemporary authority of the High School records. If there ever was any admission roll for the School, it has been lost, but the names of all the boys and their subscriptions were entered in the March of each year in a Library register under their respective masters and classes.[33] Scott's name appears for the first time in the March 1780 list as one of the 1779-80 class under Luke Fraser.[34] On this evidence and this alone the first historian of the High School dates Scott's entry in October 1779,[35] though in fact the session began on 20th September. But here is the difficulty: Scott was not, as he averred, ' three years under Mr Fraser ',[36] before passing on to the Rector's class, but only two (that is to say, if ' years ' be taken to mean ' sessions or parts thereof'). The explanation may be that Scott entered the School in 1779, but between March when the Library register was made up and the end of the session in August. He could thus have been one of Fraser's pupils during part of one session, 1778-79, and throughout the two following sessions 1779-80 and 1780-81, which is near enough to ' three years '. Certainly boys did enter High School classes at other times than the openings of sessions;[37] and Scott might well have regarded a few weeks in the summer of 1779 as not a regular entry.

According to Scott himself, he was still ' rather behind ' the other boys ' both in years and in progress '.[38] What he means by the phrase ' behind in years ' is ' younger than the average age of the class '. His being ' behind in progress ' was simply the natural consequence. I think that he was

put into too advanced a class (only one behind his elder
brother John, who was ' about three years older '[39]), probably at the request of his parents because the lower class
in session 1779-80 was under the savage William Nicol,
whom Scott describes as ' worthless, drunken, and in-
humanly cruel to the boys under his charge ',[40] insulting
the Rector's [41] person and authority and carrying his feud
within an inch of assassination by waylaying and felling
Dr Adam in the dark,[42] very much as the brutal Bonthron
poleaxed poor Oliver Proudfute in *The Fair Maid of Perth*.[43]

It should perhaps be explained that the four classical
under-masters at the High School were on a footing of
equality among themselves. One in rotation opened the
first or elementary class in October yearly, and carried forward the same pupils during four sessions, at the end of
which they were transferred to the Rector's instruction.
The following table gives the roster of masters and the
number of pupils each had during the four (or five) sessions
of Scott's attendance:

1778-79		1779-80	
The Rector	96	The Rector	111
William Nicol	73	James French	69
James French	66	William Cruickshank	66
William Cruickshank	74	Luke Fraser	87
Luke Fraser	76	William Nicol	89

1780-81		1781-82	
The Rector	95	The Rector	95
William Cruickshank	66	Luke Fraser	94
Luke Fraser	91	William Nicol	101
William Nicol	103	James French	86
James French	71	William Cruickshank	94

1782-83

The Rector	106
William Nicol	92
James French	94
William Cruickshank	103
Luke Fraser	115

Modern educationists will be horrified at the sizes of the classes, and may not unreasonably conclude that such teaching as there was must have been effected for the most part *vi et armis*.

Scott speaks feelingly of the 'real disadvantage' he felt, at least at first, in Fraser's class as 'one to which a boy of lively temper and talents ought to be as little exposed as one who might be less expected to make up his lee-way, as it is called. The situation has the unfortunate effect of reconciling a boy of the former character (which in a posthumous work I may claim for my own) to holding a subordinate station among his class-fellows—to which he would otherwise affix disgrace. There is also, from the constitution of the High School, a certain danger not sufficiently attended to. The boys take precedence in their *places*, as they are called, according to their merit,[44] and it requires a long while, in general, before even a clever boy, if he falls behind the class, or is put into one for which he is not quite ready,[45] can force his way to the situation which his abilities really entitle him to hold. But, in the meanwhile, he is necessarily led to be the associate and companion of those inferior spirits with whom he is placed; for the system of precedence, though it does not limit the general intercourse among the boys, has nevertheless the effect of throwing them into clubs and coteries, according to the vicinity of the seats they hold. A boy of good talents, therefore, placed even for a time among his inferiors, especially if they be also his elders, learns to participate in their pursuits and objects of ambition, which are usually very distinct from the acquisition of learning; and it will be well if he does not also imitate them in that indifference which is contented with bustling over a lesson so as to avoid punishment, without affecting superiority or aiming at reward '.[46]

Such a frustration was indeed galling to this boy of parts; and Scott as a schoolboy felt keenly at first his real or his imagined inferiority and was eager to excel, not only in the class (though perhaps somewhat erratically there), but also, as will be seen, in the playground. It was probably while he was still under Fraser that the incident occurred which he told thus to Samuel Rogers, with amusement and regret at the prank

'in that wayward mood of mind,
When various feelings are combined ':[47]

' There was a boy in my class at school, who stood always at the top,[48] nor could I with all my efforts supplant him. Day came after day, and still he kept his place, do what I would; till at length I observed that, when a question was asked him, he always fumbled with his fingers at a particular button in the lower part of his waistcoat. To remove it, therefore, became expedient in my eyes; and in an evil moment it was removed with a knife. Great was my anxiety to know the success of my measure; and it succeeded too well. When the boy was again questioned, his fingers sought again for the button, but it was not to be found. In his distress he looked down for it; it was to be seen no more than to be felt. He stood confounded, and I took possession of his place; nor did he ever recover it, or ever, I believe, suspect who was the author of his wrong. Often in after-life has the sight of him smote me as I passed by him; and often have I resolved to make him some reparation; but it ended in good resolutions. Though I never renewed my acquaintance with him, I often saw him, for he filled some inferior office in one of the courts of law at Edinburgh. Poor fellow! I believe he is dead; he took early to drinking.'[49]

Scott calls Fraser ' a good Latin scholar and a very worthy man '.[50] But pupil and teacher had little in common intellectually. Scott had no aptitude for small details of grammar and syntax (then or later), and his school exercises in consequence bristled with errors and solecisms.[51] Fraser, on the other hand, conscientious and painstaking and anxious to clear every verbal difficulty from the path of his pupils, rarely or never rose above the letter of the text that was being read. His whole emphasis was on the linguistic and grammatical technicalities of Latin, not on exciting ' curiosity about historical facts, or imagination to strain after the flights of a poet ',[52] to both of which Scott would so readily have responded. According to Scott's friend Gillies, who was a High School boy nearly twenty years later, the first task Fraser imposed ' was to get by heart the Latin rudiments.[53] But in the case of one whose intellect and feelings had already been roused, where there existed, even in childhood, a fondness for books, of which the sense was understood, it was no easy matter to force lessons that were to be learned merely by rote, without one iota of intelligence thence derived; and without even any adequate explanation why it was necessary that the task should be encountered '.[54] When the pupils had been thoroughly grounded in the declensions and conjugations, they were made to learn and repeat a daily assignment of words from Ruddiman's vocabulary and to get by heart the greater part of his *Grammatica Minora* in Latin. From such stern preliminaries Fraser took his pupils on to Corderius's uninspiring *Colloquia*, four or five lives from the *De Viris Illustribus* of Cornelius Nepos, and the first four books of Caesar's commentaries *De Bello Gallico*. In the fourth year of his course Fraser introduced his pupils to Latin poetry in selections from Ovid's *Metamorphoses* and Virgil's *Eclogues* and in the first book of the *Aeneid*.

For three years,[55] Scott tells us in a significant and revealing sentence, ' I glanced like a meteor from one end of the class to the other, and commonly disgusted my kind master as much by negligence and frivolity as I occasionally pleased him by flashes of intellect and talent.'[56]   The joint testimony of Scott's mother and of an old domestic at George Square to the effect that he was 'a careless boy about his lessons' and 'no one ever knew when he got them'[57] probably refers to this period of his schooling in particular.   The fact is that Scott was generally bored by schoolwork at a school's pace.   To a boy with such quickness of mind and such a richly stored memory it was easy on an occasion to shine and for the rest of the time to rub along 'in a decent place about the middle of the class', as he once put it to James Skene of Rubislaw.[58]   But his skipping Fraser's fourth or 1781-82 class and passing straight from Fraser's third class to the Rector's indicates that he had made better progress than he himself realised.   Though Fraser was 'one of the severest flagellators of the *old school*',[59] Scott later regretted that he had been treated too leniently; 'I am an enemy to corporal punishment,' he said, 'but there are many boys who will not attend without it.   It is an instant and irresistible motive, and I love boys' heads too much to spoil them at the expense of their opposite extremity.   Then, when children feel an emancipation on this point, we may justly fear they will loosen the bonds of discipline altogether.   The master, I fear, must be something of a despot at the risque of his becoming something of a tyrant.   He governs subjects whose keen sense of the present is not easily ruled by any considerations that are not pressing and immediate.   I was indifferently well beaten at school; but I am now quite certain that twice as much discipline would have been well bestowed'.[60]

It was Dr Alexander Adam,[61] the Rector of the High School, who induced Scott to put a higher value on the knowledge which he had hitherto regarded as only a burdensome task.   'It was the fashion,' says Scott, 'to remain two years at his class, where we read Caesar, and Livy, and Sallust in prose; Virgil, Horace, and Terence in verse.'[62] In point of fact Scott was in the class for only one full

session, 1781-82, and about six months of another, 1782-83.
The benevolent and well-loved Adam was a distinguished
Latin scholar, as is proved by his still useful *Roman Antiquities*,[63] and an instructor of a much more enlightened kind
than the plodding Fraser. Chambers describes him as ' one
of the . . . most eminent teachers Scotland has ever produced ',[64] and Gillies does not hesitate to pronounce his old
Rector ' a man of genius '.[65] But perhaps the best tribute
to Adam is Lord Cockburn's: ' Never was a man more
fortunate in the choice of a vocation. He was born to
teach Latin, some Greek, and all virtue. In doing so he
was generally patient, though not, when intolerably provoked, without due fits of gentle wrath; inspiring to his
boys, especially the timid and backward; enthusiastically
delighted with every appearance of talent or goodness; a
warm encourager by praise, play, and kindness; and
constantly under the strongest sense of duty. The art of
teaching has been so immeasurably improved in good Scotch
schools since his time, that we can scarcely estimate his
merits now. He had most of the usual peculiarities of a
schoolmaster; but was so amiable and so artless that no
sensible friend would have wished one of them to be even
softened. His private industry was appalling.'[66] He was
an indefatigable reader, at least in classical fields, rising all
the year round at four o'clock to put in several hours of
study before his schoolwork began and he was by nature
communicative of his scholarship, stimulating interest by
illustration and parallel passage and anecdote, and comment-
ing freely on whatever topic might arise in the course of
a lesson. By his variety and breadth he inspired his pupils
with something more like a real love of learning than any
of his assistants could. He was as interested in his pupils
personally as in his subject, not merely in school but on holiday rambles with those who had gained his good opinion.

If under Dr Adam's stimulating influence Scott still
wavered in diligence and failed to excel as he might well

have done, nevertheless his talents and potentialities did not escape the Rector's discerning eye. 'I had by this time mastered, in some degree,' he says, 'the difficulties of the language, and began to be sensible of its beauties. This was really gathering grapes from thistles; nor shall I soon forget the swelling of my little pride when the Rector pronounced, that though many of my school-fellows understood the Latin better, *Gualterus Scott* was behind few in following and enjoying the author's meaning.'[67] The Rector was in the habit of inviting his pupils to translate from Virgil and Horace into English verse, without however setting such eassys as tasks; and by his praise Scott was encouraged to submit several, by which he 'gained some distinction'.[68] One of the translations from Virgil, the well-known description of Aetna in eruption,[69] has been preserved, as have also lines *On a Thunderstorm* [70] and *On the Setting Sun* of approximately the same date. Scott himself says that *On a Thunderstorm* was 'much approved of, until . . . an apothecary's blue-buskined wife . . . affirmed that my most sweet poetry was stolen from an old magazine'. The accusation was unjust and rankled even as late as 1830, though Scott admitted that 'like most premature poets' he had 'copied all the words and ideas' without having stolen the poem ready-made.[71] One or two other essays in verse about this time were, on the advice of friends, consigned to the fire. The result of Scott's verse translations was that 'the Rector in future took much notice of me; and his judicious mixture of censure and praise went far to counterbalance my habits of indolence and inattention. I saw I was expected to do well, and I was piqued in honour to vindicate my master's favourable opinion. I climbed, therefore, to the first form; and, though I never made a first rate Latinist, my school-fellows, and what was of more consequence, I myself, considered that I had a character for learning to maintain'.[72] Adam came to call Scott the Historian of the class and frequently consulted him on dates, battles, and other events alluded to in the classical authors read. Nor did the Rector's interest cease at the end of Scott's pupillage. 'Dr Adam, to whom I owe so much,' he said, 'never failed to remind me of my obligations when I had made some figure in the literary world. He was, indeed, deeply imbued with that fortunate vanity which alone could induce a man who has arms to pare and burn a muir,[73] to submit to the yet more toilsome task of cultivating youth. As Catholics confide in the imputed righteousness of their saints, so did the good old Doctor plume himself upon the success of his scholars in life, all of which he never failed (and often justly) to claim as the creation, or at least the fruits, of his early instructions. He remembered the fate of every boy at his school during the fifty years he had superintended it, and always traced their success or misfortunes entirely to their attention or negligence when under his care.'[74]

The following letter, written by Scott on 18th August 1806 after he 'had made some figure in the literary world '[75] and addressed *per incuriam* to 'Dr Adams', has never been printed, so far as I know, except in the Royal High School magazine.[76] It shows the retention by Scott the man of a feeling warmer than mere respect for his old headmaster:

'My dear Sir

Will you permit me to request your assistance in a matter where I know no person better qualified than yourself to afford it. It has perhaps come to your knowledge that I have been for some time busy on an entire edition of Drydens works which to the shame of the passd century has not been undertaken by one better qualified for the task. I observe that Johnson criticizes the title which Dryden has to his lamentation or elegy for Charles the Second as not being classical.[77] Threnodia *Augustalis* is you know the phrase employed. As a good Editor I will not if I can help it leave this blot in the poets scutcheon unless

the criticism is confirmed by you after you have considered the authorities [78]   if any occurs for the
epithet Augustalis. I have turned over the few classics
I have with me at this farm but to no purpose &
therefore use this freedom of an old disciple to request
your assistance & that you will forgive this trouble
from Dear Sir

Your affectionate humble Servant

Walter Scott.

My address is Ashesteil by Selkirk.'[79]

But despite the Rector's encouragement and approval,
Scott 'made a brighter figure in the *yards* [80] than in the
class',[81] and by such exploits in the city and its environs
as the boys thought of greater distinction than a reputation
for learning. If, according to one report, the lame, delicate-
looking boy was thrust about to begin with and regarded
as of little consequence, he had the spirit to fight his way
manfully to speedy recognition and to teach aggressors their
lesson.[82] 'I will call none man,' he was to say through his
Halbert Glendinning, 'but he that can bear himself manlike
and masterful.'[83] He may have been precluded by his lameness from running and such games as required smart foot-
work. But he tried, as he says, 'to supply that disadvantage
by making up in address what I wanted in activity';[84] and,
as he told Mrs Hughes, 'his lameness had never prevented
his active habits, for that he had resolved to do everything
that other boys accomplished [85] and had even a pride in
outdoing his school-fellows in feats of agility'.[86] Precarious
as his health was, he probably had even at school a frame
not easily tired and, with that, muscular strength and a
formidable grip; and he was what in Scotland is admiringly
called 'a bonny fechter', able to give a hearty blow without
rancour and to take one without flinching. He told Lockhart once, when they were walking through the Yards forty

years later, how 'he had scarcely made his first appearance there, before, some dispute arising, his opponent remarked that " there was no use to hargle-bargle [87] with a cripple "; upon which he replied, that if he might fight *mounted*, he would try his hand with any of his inches. " An elder boy," said he, ". . . suggested that the two little tinklers [88] might be lashed front to front upon a deal board—and . . . the proposal being forthwith agreed to, I received my first bloody nose in an attitude which would have entitled me, in the blessed days of personal cognizances, to assume that of a *lioncel seiant gules*. My pugilistic trophies here," he continued, " were all the results of such *sittings in banco*." '[89] He participated with zest in any ' bicker '[90] or mischief [91] and accepted any challenge to his manliness with a reckless courage and disregard for danger. Not the least of his daring was, as ' a desperate climber ',[92] to scramble about and over the old city walls and gateways and up the precipitous cliffs in the King's Park or at the Castle. ' I once thought,' he wrote to Mrs Hughes, ' there were few not slaters or sailors by profession who could have boasted more steadiness of brain where such feats were in question ';[93] and ' even in my age ', he told her on another occasion, ' I can climb like a cat and in my boyhood was one of the boldest *craigs-men* in the High School, as the Cats-neck on Salisbury Crags & the Kittle Nine Steps [94] on the Castle rock could tell if they would speak '.[95] His lameness so gamely borne, then, his boldness as a ringleader and ' juvenile dreadnought ',[96] his sunny temper and good nature, his flow of things remembered and things imagined which made him ' the inexhaustible narrator '[97] for an admiring circle round Lucky Brown's hearth, his willingness to help others in their tasks while he neglected his own—these were some of the things that gave him great popularity with his fellows and bound to him ' a little party of staunch partisans and adherents, stout of hand and heart, though somewhat dull of head—the very tools for raising a hero to eminence '.[98]

In spite of this social success, however, Scott was not a happy schoolboy. 'Did I ever pass unhappy years any-where?' he asked himself and replied 'None that I re-member, save those at the High School, which I thoroughly detested on account of the confinement'.[99] Nor was the confinement the sole reason for his dislike. When his son Walter was ready for the High School in 1809, he wrote to Mrs Clephane ' my imagination like that of Leontes in *The Winter's Tale* is running thirty years back and recollect-ing when I first crept swinging my satchel through George Square with Robert Dundas [100] to learn tasks to which I could annex neither idea nor utility'.[101] I suspect also that he suffered, without being fully aware of its nature, from a spiritual and intellectual loneliness (many and kind as his adult encouragers and mentors were)—a loneliness which, I think, haunted Scott all his days.[102]

Scott's father, like Milton's, did not entrust his children's education solely to their ordinary day-school; and the High School curriculum, which was nothing if not classical,[103] was supplemented for Scott by other tuition. For some unspecified time he attended for an hour a day a writing-and-arithmetic school [104] run by John Morton in Merlin's or Marlin's Wynd [105] and subsequently in Carrubber's Close. I venture to identify this Morton with 'a stout Whig and a very worthy man, a writing-master by occupation, who [when a volunteer for the defence of Edinburgh against the Jacobite army in 1745] ensconced his bosom beneath a professional cuirass, consisting of two quires of long foolscap writing-paper; and, doubtful that even this defence might be unable to protect his valiant heart from the claymores, amongst which its impulses might carry him, had written on the outside, in his best flourish, " This is the body of J— M—;[106] pray give it Christian burial." Even this hero, prepared as one practised how to die, could not find it in his heart to accompany the devoted battalion farther than the door of his own house, which stood conveniently open about the head of the Lawnmarket'.[107]

In 1782 and probably in 1783 Walter and some of the other Scott children had the assistance of a resident tutor, James Mitchell,[108] 'a young man of an excellent disposition, and a laborious student'[109] of divinity. He was of the strictest Evangelical and Sabbatarian persuasion, which no doubt recommended him to the elder Scott. He 'thought it almost a sin', says his pupil, 'to open a profane play or poem';[110] and, though his manuscript memoirs which were made available to Lockhart show him proud of having once tutored the great Sir Walter, it is pretty clear that Mitchell had never read any of the poems and novels; and it is certain that he was scandalised by Scott's collecting 'ancient ballads and traditional stories about fairies, witches, and ghosts' when on the Northern Circuit and devoting so much 'precious time . . . to the *dulce*, rather than to the *utile*, of composition'.[111] In addition to tutoring, he appears to have acted also as a kind of domestic chaplain to the household, assisting at the religious exercises and the Sunday-evening catechising. He tells us that, though Walter had 'a very soporific tendency' in church, he was always able to answer the questions about the sermons better than any of the other children. 'The only way that I could account for this,' he says, 'was, that when he heard the text, and divisions of the subject, his good sense, memory, and genius supplied the thoughts which would occur to the preacher.'[112] From this 'faithful and active instructor'[113] it was that Scott 'chiefly . . . learned writing and arithmetic. I repeated to him my French lessons,[114] and studied with him my themes in the classics, but not classically'.[115] It is not clear what the last phrase means, for Mitchell's classical attainments were of a high order. From him Scott also picked up in the course of friendly debates, tutor and pupil being on the best of terms though on opposite sides, 'some knowledge of school-divinity and church-history,[116] and a great acquaintance in particular with the old books describing the early history of the Church of Scotland, the wars and sufferings of the Covenanters, and so forth. I, with a head on fire for chivalry', Scott continues, 'was a Cavalier; my friend was a Roundhead: I was a Tory, and he was a Whig. I hated Presbyterians, and admired Montrose with his victorious Highlanders; he liked the Presbyterian Ulysses, the dark and politic Argyle: so that we never wanted subjects of dispute; but our disputes were always amicable. In all these tenets there was no real conviction on my part, arising out of acquaintance with the views or principles of either party; nor had my antagonist address enough to turn the debate on such topics. I took up my politics at that period, as King Charles did his religion, from an idea that the Cavalier creed was the more gentlemanlike persuasion of the two '.[117]

Another subject on which pupil and tutor are likely to have disagreed was the theatre. As it happened, an innovation began during Scott's schooldays, of the High School boys going in a body to the play under their Rector and masters. The first occasion was in 1781, when the new school buildings begun in 1777 were still incomplete. *The Edinburgh Courant* for 19th February informed the public that *Henry IV* [118] would be presented at the Theatre Royal on 21st February ' by appointment of the Committee for erecting the new High Schoolhouse in this city the profits to be applied for finishing this useful work '. The schoolboys filling the pit ' will exhibit ', the *Courant* foretold, ' as pleasing an appearance as any that has been seen in this city, whether we consider the delighted countenances of so great a number of charming boys, or the expressive looks of those parents who may chuse to be present '. The next year on 9th May *The Revenge* by Edward Young was given in similar circumstances; and this time six rows of the first gallery as well as the pit were to be reserved ' till six o'clock, for the accommodation of the young gentlemen from the School, who are requested to come early '.

The Highfliers or Wild Party, as the Moderates in the Church of Scotland called their puritanical opponents, was the one to which Mitchell adhered and of whose condemnation of such frivolous amusements as the theatre he approved. In 1756 the Highfliers had been outraged by a minister, John Home, writing his play of *Douglas* and having it performed with the support of several fellow-Moderates. The theatrophobes scored an early success by forcing Home to resign his living at Athelstaneford [119] and by carrying in the General Assembly of 1757 a Declaratory Act forbidding the clergy to countenance the theatre. 'But,' says that stalwart of the Moderates, Dr Alexander Carlyle '. . . manners are stronger than laws; and this Act, which was made on recent provocation, was the only Act of the Church of Scotland against the theatre—and so was it totally neglected,'[120] by laity and clergy except among the irreconcilables. The fact that High School boys were being taken in the seventeen-eighties, not individually by their parents, but in a body by their preceptors is a measure of the general recognition of the theatre as something more than a profane pastime. And a little later, as Carlyle tells us, 'in the year 1784, when the great actress Mrs Siddons first appeared in Edinburgh, during the sitting of the General Assembly, that court was obliged to fix all its important business for the alternate days when she did not act, as all the younger members, clergy as well as laity, took their stations in the theatre on those days by three in the afternoon'.[121]

The good Mitchell, who did not become an inmate at George Square till 1782, could not have confirmed such anti-theatrical scruples as the Scott parents, especially the stricter father, may have had in 1781; but by May 1782 his strictures may have fallen on ears half-disposed to accept them. In any case there is a circumstantial story to the effect that for Scott senior 'The theatre was a forbidden place. It was then customary for the High School boys to desire a play once a year. Attendance on the occasion was not compulsory, but payment of the ticket was. Old Scott duly paid the 3s. for each of his boys, but refused to permit them to enter the unholy precincts, winding up the whole

transaction with the remark, " that he would rather give
it to a charity sermon " '.[122]   Nevertheless, I have a sus-
picion that, ban or no ban, Walter contrived to attend one
or both of the school occasions, perhaps with the con-
nivance of his mother, who like all mothers could stretch
a point for a favourite son, and like all wives could keep a
family secret from her husband.

However wayward [123] Scott may have been at the High
School, Mitchell found that tutoring him ' cost . . . but
little trouble ', for ' by the quickness of his intellect, tenacity
of memory, and diligent application to his studies ' the pupil
was generally able on his own to cope with his tasks.
' Master Walter ' indeed was ' not so much . . . a pupil
. . . as a friend and companion, and I may add, as an
assistant also; for, by his example and admonitions, he
greatly strengthened my hands, and stimulated my other
pupils to industry and good behaviour.'[124]

Another tutor, not as a resident but as a visitor, was
summoned to George Square in the same period, Mrs Scott
wanting her younger children to have music lessons or at
least instruction in psalmody.   The psalm-singing may have
been stressed to reconcile Mr Scott to an expenditure he
may have disliked.   In any case Walter had neither a tunable
voice nor any great desire to improve it.   The ' incurable
defects of . . . voice and ear ',[125] which he shared with all
his brothers but Robert,[126] drove his sensitive singing-master
to despair and Lady Cumming, the Scotts' neighbour in
George Square, to beg that ' the boys might not be all
flogged precisely at the same hour, as, though she had no
doubt the punishment was deserved, the noise of the concord
was really dreadful '.[127]

The unfortunate tutor was the warm-hearted, handsome,
and romantic Alexander or Allister Campbell, a pupil of
the great Tenducci and a musician, singer (especially of
Scottish songs of which he was a passionate lover and
collector), and musicologist of note.[128]   Though he could
make nothing of Scott musically, the two, who were only

six or seven years apart in age, may have discovered that they had much in common. For Campbell, in spite of his clanship, was an Episcopalian and organist in a non-juring chapel, and an ardent Jacobite and nationalist with a taste for literature, landscape, and antiquities. He and Scott were to remain on terms of friendship. I think it is likely to have been Campbell from whom Scott got information about and transcriptions of Gaelic music.[129] Certainly Scott came to Campbell's help in his financial difficulties, employed him as an amanuensis, and contributed to his *Albyn's Anthology; or, A Select Collection of the Melodies and Vocal Poetry peculiar to Scotland and the Isles*, 1816-18.[130] These and perhaps other obligations Campbell did not forget. ' His sense of gratitude,' says Scott, ' was very strong, and showed itself oddly in one respect. He would never allow that I had a bad ear; but contended, that if I did not understand music, it was because I did not choose to learn it.'[131] This, however, was but Gaelic *suairceas* or politeness to Scott himself. To third parties Campbell admitted that ' he never made any progress [with his pupil], owing, as he used to say, to the total destitution of that great man in the requisite of an *ear*'.[132]

It was only in fact by long practice and attention that Scott, as he grew older, learned to select and distinguish melodies. And the utmost of his musical taste, as distinct from his attempts to sing, did not go beyond the appreciation of a simple tune, more for the words it accompanied and for the feeling and expression of the singer than for the music alone; but it is fair to add that few things delighted or moved him more than good singing of a good song in a language he understood.[133] He puts it thus in his *Journal*: ' complicated harmonies seem to me a babble of confused though pleasing sounds. Yet songs and simple melodies, especially if connected with words and ideas, have as much effect on me as on most people. But then I hate to hear a young person sing without feeling and expression suited to the song. I cannot bear a voice that has no more life

in it than a pianoforte or a bugle-horn '.[134]   Instrumental
music really bored him; and so did singing when he did
not get every word.[135]   He got nothing, he said, from
Italian music.[136]   *The Marriage of Figaro* in Italian ' was all
caviare ' to him.[137]   When his young friend, William Forbes,
sang nothing but songs in foreign languages, even though
' with a feeling and taste indescribably fine ', Scott's ' ears
were not much gratified. I have no sense ', he continues,
' beyond Mungo:[138] " What signify me hear if me no
understand " '.[139]   And when he attended a grand recital
in London, he slept soundly through a long concerto and
an Italian bravura piece, greatly to the disappointment of a
lady who had asked to have the great man pointed out to
her.[140]   Perhaps it should be added that Scott in his own
opinion was usually unsuccessful in writing verses for existing melodies and he attributed this to his musical limita-
tions.[141]

As for his singing, however poor his voice, he would
strike up (' with perfect correctness ', says one reporter;[142]
' in unmusical vehemence ', says another [143]) a song, generally
grotesque or comic, for the entertainment of a company
when the wine was in a brisk circulation. Among his
special favourites were the following: *Tarry Woo, Auld Lang
Syne, Bannocks o' Bear Meal, Bannocks o' Barley*, and *Kenmure's
On and Awa*.

As for the other social accomplishment of dancing and
deportment, Lockhart rejects a story in print to the effect that
Scott had dancing lessons at home along with his brothers.[144]
The name of the visiting dancing master was said to be
Wilson. Naturally one's first impulse in this reference is
to agree with Lockhart and to dismiss as absurd the following passage in Allan which is presumably what Lockhart
had read: ' One spectator of their performances insists upon
it, that Walter was the best dancer among them. Nor will
our readers be astonished at this apparently strange decision,
when they recollect that the *gude wives* of Scotland care
less for grace, or exact observance of the measure, than the

hearty good-will shewn by strenuous thumping of the floor.'[145] Scott is as unlikely to have learned, as the dancing master to have taught, the gambols of ploughmen. But it is at least conceivable that he was taught how to make his bow at an assembly and perhaps how to walk through a minuet. His lameness in boyhood did not prevent his activity and he always did his best to keep up with other boys or outdo them. There is a passage in *Redgauntlet*, in which novel occur so many reminiscences of Scott's youth, that may lend support to the story Lockhart refused to believe. 'The dance to be performed,' writes Darsie Latimer to Alan Fairford, ' was the old Scots jig, in which you are aware I used to play no sorry figure at La Pique's, when thy clumsy movements used to be rebuked by raps over the knuckles with that great professor's fiddlestick.'[146] That Scott did not regularly take the floor when he was a young man we can well believe, and appreciate the remark, made to Lockhart ' with an arch simplicity of look and tone ': ' It was a proud night with me when I first found that a pretty young woman could think it worth her while to sit and talk with me, hour after hour, in a corner of the ball-room, while all the world were capering in our view.'[147]

In the normal course of things Scott would have gone straight from Dr Adam's charge to the University after the summer holidays. But, rather fortunately in his own opinion, the state of his health sent him for a change of air to his aunt Janet Scott's house in Kelso in the summer of 1783.[148] He was left to his own devices except for four hours a day, during which he attended the Grammar School[149] to keep his Latin from rusting. The Rector, Lancelot Whale, is described by James Ballantyne as ' an absent, grotesque being, betwixt six and seven feet high ',[150] and by Scott himself as ' a humourist, and worthy man ', with a great dislike of the inevitable puns on his name.[151] He was, moreover, ' an excellent classical scholar ',[151] much too good for the office he filled and for the elementary grind to which it condemned him. He was only too pleased to take time off from his duties and 'escape to Persius and Tacitus from the eternal Rudiments and Cornelius Nepos; and', says Scott who was a very grateful pupil, 'as perusing these authors with one who began to understand them was to him a labour of love, I made considerable progress under his instructions'.[151] The star from Edinburgh was treated with great respect both by the master and by the other pupils. Scott had his special bench; he was called on to act as usher or pupil-teacher and to hear the lessons of the lower classes; and he was chosen to impress the parents of Kelso by spouting the speech of Galgacus from Tacitus's *Agricola* at a public examination—the very speech which ran through Jonathan Oldbuck's mind as he lectured to Lovel on castrametation and pointed out the all-but-certainty that the Kaim of Kinprunes 'in conspectu classis' was no other than the battlefield of Mons Graupius.[152] Adapting the most famous tag in the speech, we may hope that the good people of Kelso, listening to the sonorous Latin, took 'omne ignotum pro magnifico'.

NOTES ON REFERENCES

1   I, 7.
2   I.e. quick.
3   Lockhart, I, 23.
4   A James Stalker was Assistant Chaplain at Fort George and later Minister of Lilliesleaf. A Hugh Stalker was Minister of Kirkwall and St Ola.
5   An Episcopal parson. He was one of the three ministers of different denominations who attended at the execution of Deacon William Brodie in 1788.
6   *Memoir*, I, 7.
7   Mrs Cockburn, 124-26.
8   *Memoir*, I, 8: The Scotts had moved from College Wynd to George Square in 1774. A passage in *Redgauntlet*, Letter II, was no doubt suggested by this removal: 'I ought to recollect, and, Darsie, I do recollect, that my

father, upon various important occasions, has shown that he can be indulgent as well as strict. The leaving his old apartments in the Luckenbooths was to him like divorcing the soul from the body; yet Dr R——— did but hint that the better air of this new district was more favourable to my health, as I was then suffering under the penalties of too rapid a growth, when he exchanged his old and beloved quarters, adjacent to the very Heart of Midlothian, for one of those new tenements [entire within themselves] which modern taste has so lately introduced.' By Dr R——— Scott probably meant his grandfather Dr John Rutherford, who had certainly recommended his stay at Sandy-knowe (cf. *Memoir*, I, 5).

9   *Memoir*, I, 8.

10   Cf. Allan, 25.

11   An old George Square servant described him as ever ' regardful and polite', unlike his brothers, and unlike them, too, in never swearing, using no stronger asseveration than ' Faith' (Allan, 24-5).

12   Allan, 6.

13   Cf. Allan, 6.

14   Perhaps the one who described him long after as ' a wearie laddie' (Allan, 20).

15   Introductory chapter.

16   Grierson, 13.

17   Grierson, 13-14.

18   Lockhart, I, 21.

19   *Memoir*, I, 8. Cf. *Kenilworth*, Chapter XXV: ' the mistaken kindness that had spared [Amy Robsart's] childhood the painful but most necessary lesson of submission and self-control'.

20   *The Heart of Midlothian*, Chapter III.

21   *Redgauntlet*, Letter I. The *gytes* were the small boys in the lowest class—as might now be said, the *kids*. It may indeed be that *gyte* is a variant of *gait*, a Scots form of *goat*; and not derived, as the *N.E.D.* has it, from the same root as *get* and *beget*. At least it has been said that at the High School all the classes were at one time commonly designated by the names of various animals, *gytes* being the only one still in use.

22 Steven, 128, note 2.

23 In 1792 he was appointed one of the four English masters on the city's establishment.

24 Unless his uncle Robert Scott had some pedagogic intention in giving him in 1783 or later Archibald Campbell's *Lexiphanes*, a Lucianic dialogue ' suited to the present Times. Being An Attempt to restore the English Tongue to its ancient Purity, And to correct, as well as expose, the affected Style, hard Words, and absurd Phraseology of many late Writers, and particularly of Our English Lexiphanes, the Rambler'. *Lexiphanes* is one of a number of books still to be mentioned which Scott had been given or had bought up to the early seventeen-nineties. I have not named every book known to have been in his early library. And it can be taken for granted that there were many more than we have evidence for. My friend, Dr J. C. Corson, who is the Honorary Librarian at Abbotsford, has supplied me with a list of such books as the young Scott certainly possessed; but Dr Corson is also my authority for saying that Scott gave books away generously and weeded out from his collection early acquisitions as he obtained better copies or later editions.

25 Cf. *The Merry Wives of Windsor*, IV, 1.

26 III, 1.

27 *Journal*, I, 158-9 (22nd April 1826).

28 Minister successively of Carmunnock and of East Kilbride and Torrens. He published one sermon, *The Effectual and Universal Influence of the Cross of Christ*, 1796.

29 The new school-buildings were barely two years old and not yet complete.

30 *Memoir*, I, 8. Chambers wrongly states that Scott entered the High School in Fraser's third class (16).

31 The volume, ' collected and bound by me, in December 1848, J. G. L.', contained the 50 leaves of the *Memoir* (headed ' Memoirs ' by Scott himself), the 1791 petition of Scott as a candidate for the Bar, the certificate of his marriage, and other personal documents.

32 In his own narrative of Scott's life, Lockhart gives the more specific date of ' October 1778 ' for the school admission (I, 25).

33 The completeness of the lists is proved by the fact that the names were entered of boys exempted from the levy or absent when it was received and of boys whose parents were unwilling or slow to pay. Scott, like most of the boys, contributed a shilling; but a fair number gave two shillings or half-a-crown.

34 He is named again in the March 1781 list as still under Fraser, and in the March lists of 1782 and 1783 as under the Rector.

35 Steven, 128-29, note 2. I do not think that Steven founded on Allan's statement that Scott's 'name appears for the first time in the register of the High School in October 1779' (15). Steven quotes: 'In 1779 I was sent,' etc., without square brackets (129). In the list of distinguished pupils, Steven gives Scott as under 'Fraser, 1779-81; Adam, R., 1782' (Appendix, 211), though Scott was in Adam's class in 1783 also. 1779 is accepted as the admission year by J. J. Trotter, *The Royal High School, Edinburgh*, 162 ('[In 1779] I was sent,' etc., with square brackets restored), 188; and by W. C. A. Ross, *Royal High School*, 145. Gillies, who was at the High School nearly twenty years after Scott and whose *Recollections* came out shortly before Lockhart's biography, gives 1779 as the admission year, but December as the month (26).

36 *Memoir*, I, 9.

37 Likewise they dropped out at other times than the ends; and it is perhaps worth noting that in the March 1783 list of the Rector's class Scott's name with ten others is added at the end, the reason being his withdrawal from the School on account of his health.

38 *Memoir*, I, 8.

39 *Memoir*, I, 4; cf. *supra*, 4. The statement by Chambers (17) that Walter was put into the same class as John is disproved by the High School records. Equally unacceptable are Allan's statements to the effect that Scott was at first regularly carried to school by a servant (15, 20) and that he was entrusted to the care of his brother Tom (15). Walter was quite able to walk and also to fend for himself; and Tom, who despite his many failings and misdemeanours was Walter's favourite brother, was born in 1774

and not old enough to attend the High School till 1780-81. Walter, too, would have resented the idea that he needed any moral or physical support in the rough-and-tumble of a strange school.

40   *Memoir*, I, 10.

41   I.e. Headmaster's.

42   Scott admits that Nicol was ' an excellent classical scholar, and an admirable convivial humourist (which latter quality recommended him to the friendship of Burns) ' (*Memoir*, I, 10).

43   Chapter XVI.

44   But not according to rank or nationality. ' Several circumstances ... seemed ... to distinguish the High School, and ... could not fail to give a peculiar character to many of its scholars in after life. For instance, the variety of ranks: for I used to sit between a youth of a ducal family and the son of a poor cobbler. Again, the variety of nations: for in our class, under Mr Pillans [appointed Rector in 1810] there were boys from Russia, Germany, Switzerland, the United States, Barbadoes, St Vincent's, Demerara, the East Indies, England, and Ireland ' (Steven, 191-92).

45   As in his own case.

46   *Memoir*, I, 8.

47   *Rokeby*, Canto Third.

48   Irving thought ' that the boy referred to sat at the top, not of the *class*, but of Scott's own bench or division of the class ' (Lockhart, I, 27, note 3).

49   Lockhart, I, 26.

50   *Memoir*, I, 8.

51   Cf. *Letters*, I, 15 (to William Clerk, 3rd September 1790): ' Well—I was never able in my life to do anything with what is called gravity and deliberation.'

52   Lockhart, I, 26.

53   The standard textbook was Thomas Ruddiman's *Rudiments of the Latin Tongue*, 1714, which was frequently republished under different editors and titles. But Dr Adam introduced his own Latin grammar (cf. *infra*, 38 note 63), at least in his own class, not without opposition from the other masters, and even from the Town Council.

54 26-27.

55 Not two, as Allan says (17).

56 *Memoir*, I, 9.

57 Allan, 19.

58 Lockhart, I, 26.

59 Chambers, 17.

60 *Journal*, I, 290-1 (13th December 1826).

61 Cf. *Memoir*, I, 10, for a character sketch. The degree of LL.D. was conferred on Adam in 1780 by Edinburgh University.

62 *Memoir*, I, 9.

63 1791 and frequently reprinted. Adam's other works were: *The Principles of Latin and English Grammar*, 1772; *A Geographical Index . . . being a Supplement to the Summary of Ancient and Modern Geography*, 1795; *Classical Biography*, 1800; and *A Compendious Dictionary of the Latin Tongue*, 1805.

64 18-19.

65 36.

66 4-5. Allan's judgement is much less favourable to Adam as a teacher (18-19).

67 *Memoir*, I, 9.

68 *Memoir*, I, 9.

69 *Aeneid*, III, 571-77.

70 Cf. Lockhart, I, 23, for the infant Scott's fearless delight at the flashing of lightning, when at Sandy-knowe. Allan tells the same story, but is probably wrong in giving George Square as the setting (6-7). Cf. Chambers, 20-1, for the occasion of the poem and the mother's pleasure and pride at it.

71 *Intro. Note*, 650.

72 *Memoir*, I, 9.

73 This unusual phrase appears to have been originated by Scott and to be neither a quotation nor a proverbial expression.

74 *Memoir*, I, 9-10.

75 Especially by *Minstrelsy of the Scottish Border*, 1802-3; his edition of *Sir Tristrem*; *The Lay of the Last Minstrel*, 1805; and *Ballads and Lyrical Pieces*, 1806.

76 *Schola Regia*, XXIX, No. 84 (summer 1932), 128.

77 In his *Life of Dryden* Johnson calls *Augustalis* ' a term I

am afraid neither authorized nor analogical' (*Works*, ed. 1792, IX, 415).

78 One or more words after 'authorities' have been stroked out and rendered illegible.

79 Scott's edition of Dryden was published in eighteen volumes in 1808 and again in 1821. He quotes at some length the defence of Dryden's phrase by 'My learned friend, Dr Adam', who 'making allowance for the taste of the times and the licence of poets in framing names' saw 'no just foundation for Johnson's criticism on the epithet *Augustalis*' (X, 60).

80 I.e. the High School playground.

81 *Memoir*, I, 9-10. Cf. Lockhart, I, 27-28.

82 Cf. Allan, 20.

83 *The Monastery*, Chapter XI.

84 *Memoir*, I, 9.

85 Including the thrusting of his head through the George Square railings, from which a blacksmith had to release him (cf. Allan, 20).

86 Mrs Hughes, 165.

87 I.e. wrangle, squabble.

88 I.e. urchins.

89 Lockhart, I, 27.

90 A 'bicker' is a free fight or running brawl between groups, not individuals, in which sticks and stones as well as fists are the weapons. The High School boys in Scott's day no doubt bickered among themselves; but their continuing warfare was with outsiders. Cf. *General Preface* for the famous *Greenbreeks* bicker.

91 Such as harrying the veterans of the City Guard (cf. *The Heart of Midlothian*, Chapter III), tormenting 'the hucksters in the High School Wynd', and 'manning the Cowgate Port in snowball time' (*Redgauntlet*, Letter I note).

92 Mrs Hughes, 165.

93 *Letters*, IX, 165 (2nd July 1825).

94 To reach and cross the steps was an achievement 'considered as equal to three battles' (Mrs Hughes, 165). 'This was so favourite a feat with the "hell and neck boys" of the higher classes, that at one time sentinels were

posted to prevent its repetition' (*Redgauntlet*, footnote to Letter I).

95   *Letters*, X, 348 (25th December 1827).

96   Cf. *Redgauntlet*, footnote to Letter I: 'To recollect that the author himself, however naturally disqualified, was one of those juvenile dreadnoughts, is a sad reflection to one who cannot now step over a brook without assistance.'

97   *Memoir*, I, 9. Cf. Lockhart, I, 32, for James Ballantyne's description of Scott when a schoolboy at Kelso as 'certainly the best story-teller I had ever heard, either then or since'. Gillies, writing of Scott as an adult raconteur, says, 'He had almost magical power . . . all materials derived from history, romance, or legend . . . became in the utmost degree *plastic*; so that, while the leading incidents remained, the general character of the narrative, and impressions it conveyed, were entirely new, and altogether his own' (42-43).

98   *Memoir*, I, 9.

99   *Journal*, I, 147 (4th April 1826). He adds, but not with quite the same force, 'I disliked serving in my father's office, too, from the same hatred of constraint' (cf. *infra*, 147).

100 Robert Saunders Dundas, later second Viscount Melville.

101 *Letters*, II, 261 (27th October 1809). Cf. *The Monastery*, Introductory Epistle: '[to] go to school and learn tasks, that last of evils in my estimation'. At the beginning of *Old Mortality* he shows his sympathy with the boredom, as great or still greater, experienced by the schoolmaster.

102 Cf. *infra*, 163-66.

103 Except for writing and book-keeping, which were taught till 1777 by John Maclure and from 1780 by Edmund Butterworth. A master for arithmetic and mathematics was not appointed till 1828.

104 Cf. *Rob Roy*, Chapter I: 'I wish, by the way, you would write a more distinct current hand—draw a score through the tops of your *t*s, and open the loops of your *l*s.'

105 Removed to make room for the South Bridge.

106 Graham gives as the name 'John Maxwell' (61). But Scott, who was the first to tell the story, has only the initials.

107   *Home*, 829.

108   After being for a time Chaplain to Lady Glenorchy, Mitchell ministered at South Shields, Montrose, and Wooler. He demitted office at Montrose because he could not convince his seafaring parishioners of ' the guilt of setting sail on the Sabbath' (*Fasti*, V, 414).

109   *Memoir*, I, 9.

110   *Memoir*, I, 10.

111   Lockhart, I, 31.

112   Lockhart, I, 31.

113   *Memoir*, I, 9.

114   There was no regular teaching of French at the High School, and probably no instruction at all in the language, till 1834. Scott must therefore have been grounded elsewhere. It is possible that he was a pupil of Louis Cauvin the younger, who taught French also to Burns during his stay in Edinburgh.

115   *Memoir*, I, 9.

116   Church-history was the favourite study of Scott's father.

117   *Memoir*, I, 9.

118   Almost certainly part I, part II being seldom produced anywhere till its London revival in 1784.

119   But not his play-writing.

120   338.

121   338-9.

122   Allan, 17. Allan does not mention the two occasions I have referred to; and I do not think that the play-going of the High School boys was annual and customary.

123   I think ' wayward' suits the case better than Gillies's ' very unmanageable' (28).

124   Lockhart, I, 30.

125   *Memoir*, I, 15. Cf. *Journal*, I, 35 (21st November 1825): ' I do not know and cannot utter a note of music.'

126   Who sang ' agreeably—(a virtue which was never seen in me) ' (*Memoir*, I, 4).

127   *Memoir*, I, 15, note 1.

128   Alexander Campbell's brother, John, likewise a pupil of Tenducci, taught music and also reading, writing, etc., and was the precentor of Canongate Church till 1795 when he was succeeded by his son Charles.

129   Cf. *Letters*, I, 403 (15th Dec. 1807); II, 67-68 (1st June 1808).

130   Campbell's other publications include: *Odes and Miscellaneous Poems*, 1796; *An Introduction to the History of Poetry
in Scotland . . . With a Conversation on Scottish Song . . .
To which are subjoined Sangs of the Lowlands of Scotland*,
1798-99; *A Journey from Edinburgh through Parts of North
Britain* (with aquatints from the author's sketches), 1802;
and *The Grampians Desolate. A Poem* (with voluminous
notes), 1804. The *Conversation on Scottish Song* was
received with praise on the Continent as giving the first
satisfactory explanation of the native pentatonic scale.

131   *Memoir*, I, 15, note 1. In 1824 Scott wrote an obituary
notice of Campbell for the *Edinburgh Weekly Journal*.

132   Robert Chambers, *A Biographical Dictionary of Eminent
Scotsmen* (1853-55), II, 467-68.

133   Cf. *Memoir*, I, 15; and Lockhart, I, 165: 'He delighted
to hear his daughters sing . . .; but, so the singer appeared
to feel the spirit of her ballad, he was not at all critical of
the technical execution.'

134   I, 5 (21st November 1825). Cf. *ibid.*, III, 103 (4th June
1830): 'Anne wants me to go to hear the Tyrolese
minstrels, but though no one more esteems that bold and
highspirited people, I cannot but think their *udalling*, if
this be the word, is a variation, or set of variations, upon
the tones of a Jack Ass.'

135   Cf. Mrs Hughes, 152.

136   *Journal*, III, 47 (4th April 1829).

137   *Journal*, I, 265 (2nd November 1826). Cf. Francis Osbaldistone's musical preferences: 'I see old Mabel, her head
slightly agitated by the palsy of age . . . as she concluded
with a sigh the favourite old ditty, which I then preferred,
and—why should I not tell the truth?—which I still prefer
to all the opera airs ever minted by the capricious brain of
an Italian Mus.D.—
    Oh, the oak, the ash, and the bonny ivy tree,
    They flourish best at home in the North Country!'
                                    (*Rob Roy*, Chapter IV).

138   A character in Isaac Bickerstaffe's *Padlock*.

139   *Journal*, III, 48 (6th April 1829).

140   Cf. Mrs Hughes, 152.

141 Cf. *Memoir*, I, 15.

142 Gillies, 45.

143 Chambers, 24.

144 I, 32.

145 24.

146 Letter XII. Captain Clutterbuck also refers to his attendance ' at Simon Lightfoot's weekly Practising ' and remembers the regret ' with which I went through the polite
ceremonial of presenting my partner with an orange '
that he would much rather have kept for himself (*The
Monastery*, Introductory Epistle).

147 I, 45.

148 Scott himself says for half a year (*Memoir*, I, 10). But
James Ballantyne, whose friendship with Scott dates from
this time, thought the period was only a few weeks during
the High School vacation. Lockhart suggests that Scott
may have thought his stay at Kelso longer than it was by
blending it with a visit made a year later (I, 32).

149 Allan states that Scott had been a pupil at Kelso at an
earlier period also and before going to the High School
(12-14); and indeed, on the strength of some information
he had received, he sends Scott to Bath after this alleged
Kelso schooling, although he admits his uncertainty as to
the date of the Bath residence (15). Neither Scott nor
Lockhart makes any reference to an earlier schooling at
Kelso.

150 Lockhart, I, 32.

151 *Memoir*, I, 10. One may discount entirely some of the
phrases used by Allan, who wrote from hearsay: ' the
worst-tempered man in Britain ', ' an awful pedagogue ',
' this Ogre turned schoolmaster ' (13). Ballantyne noted
Whale's strong resemblance to Dominie Sampson, adding,
however, that he had more gentlemanly manners with
equal classical learning and was altogether ' a much
superior sort of person ' (Lockhart, I, 32). The true
prototype of Dominie Sampson was the Rev. George
Thomson, who occasionally tutored Scott's two boys (cf.
infra, 83).

152 *The Antiquary*, Chapter IV.

CHAPTER III

BOYISH SELF-EDUCATION

[A] fond mother's care and joy
Were centred in her sickly boy.
Rokeby, Canto First.

Of ballads and romances I think I have held a longer
acquaintance than have I with any other kind of learning.
Letters, I, 7 (to Jessie ——, 1787).

[I]f memory goes, all is up with me, for that was always my
strong point.
Remark quoted by Lockhart, II, 683, note 6.

[I]t's a queer thing, I say, but I think the Hieland blude
o' me warms at thae daft tales, and whiles I like better to hear them
than a word o' profit, Gude forgie me!
Rob Roy, Chapter XXVI.

THE preceding chapter dealt with Scott's conventional schooling along the prescribed lines in his day. But during the years of his schooling, Scott's real education, as later at the University, proceeded alongside his regular studies and especially in the gaps in them due to illness, at his own rapid pace and in his own desultory manner; and his darling subjects were ballad and romance, poetry and drama, legend and history. He describes himself rightly as having been ' from infancy devoted to legendary lore ',[1] his enthusiasm being ' chiefly awakened by the wonderful and the terrible —the common taste of children, but in which I have remained a child even unto this day '.[2]

Lockhart speaks of ' that self-education which alone is of primary consequence to spirits ' of Scott's order.[3] Scott, he says a little later, was ' self-educated in every branch of knowledge which he ever turned to account in the works of his genius '.[4] And undoubtedly Scott, whose lameness, illnesses, and solitary habits had made him a reader, was under little or no direction as to his reading when he was in Edinburgh and under still less when he was at Sandy-knowe or Kelso. But if he had no direction in his self-education, the young Scott was exceptionally well supplied with friendly encouragers. His sunny eagerness, his winning ways, and his intelligent curiosity disposed his adult friends to interest themselves in what interested him and to suggest and discuss.

It is true that Scott's father,[5] kind as he was despite his strictness and austerity and obviously anxious according to his lights to give his children a good education, was certainly no great admirer of the literature that appealed to his son Walter and rather discouraged than otherwise that son's ' early devotion to the pursuits which led him to the heights of literary eminence '[6] and away from the paths of sedater distinction in the law. But Scott senior is said to have had a large library of miscellaneous books with the law, church-history (his favourite reading), and polemics specially well represented; and it was probably due to his father, more than to any one else, that Scott 'had his Bible, the Old Testament especially, by heart'.[7]

On the other hand, Mrs Walter Scott, who was as sincerely devout as her husband but with a religion, 'as became her sex, of a cast less austere',[8] and who had a cheerful and happy temper, had received the best kind of education then given in Scotland to girls and young gentlewomen. It was of a more liberal type than the uncompromisingly classical one bestowed on their young brothers, however strict as regards deportment and carriage. Mrs Scott indeed had acquired a strong turn for poetry and literature, 'a turn . . . quite uncommon among the ladies of the time'.[9] She 'had good natural taste and great feeling',[10] and she had about her such books as her son could read with zest. She had a partiality for her precocious and delicate boy, which consoled him particularly in the trying and mortifying period of adjustment to family life in George Square from Sandy-knowe where he had been

> 'wayward, bold, and wild,
> A self-will'd imp, a grandame's child;
> But half a plague, and half a jest,
> Was still endur'd, belov'd, caress'd'.[11]

Mrs Scott listened to her Walter reading aloud, evidently with attention; and, he tells us, 'she used to make me pause upon those passages which expressed generous and worthy sentiments, and if she could not divert me from those which were descriptions of battle and tumult, she contrived at least to divide my attention between them'.[12] Somewhat later in his schooldays, Mrs Scott had no longer the same opportunities of hearing Walter read; and she was to some extent inhibited as regards imaginative literature by the scruples of the puritanical James Mitchell when he was tutoring the Scott children.[13]

Among Mrs Scott's kin there were many active encouragers of Walter's tastes, including her father, Dr John Rutherford who till his death in 1779 interested himself much in his grandson's physical and intellectual wellbeing;[14] her half-brother, Dr Daniel Rutherford, in whose house the boy from his earliest days had some contact with scientists and literary men; her half-sisters, Mrs Jane or Jean Russell of Ashestiel (*née* Rutherford) and Janet and Christian Rutherford, especially the latter who was an unusually accomplished woman and who by reason of her juniority was more like an elder sister than an aunt to her nephew; Mrs Scott's maternal aunt, always known (though a spinster) as Mrs Margaret Swinton,[15] who provided Scott with the story he developed in *My Aunt Margaret's Mirror*; and another aunt of Mrs Scott but on the paternal side, Mrs Alison Cockburn (*née* Rutherford).[16]

Scott's paternal relatives likewise included several who interested themselves as keenly in his mental development and pursuits, including his grandmother, Mrs Barbara Scott; his aunt, Janet Scott; and his uncle, Captain Robert Scott. His grandfather, Robert Scott of Sandy-knowe, died when Scott was little more than an infant; but the grandson at least remembered

> 'the thatch'd mansion's grey-hair'd Sire,
> Wise without learning, plain and good,
> And sprung of Scotland's gentler blood;
> Whose eye, in age, quick, clear, and keen,
> Show'd what in youth its glance had been;
> Whose doom discording neighbours sought,
> Content with equity unbought'.[17]

Janet, who has already been mentioned as teaching Scott his letters, was ' a woman of tastes and acquirements very far above what could have been often found among Scotch ladies, of any but the highest class at least, in that day '.[18] She is said to have been ' clever but satirical ' and unwilling to ' pass a flaw without having a fling at it ', yet having ' great kindness of disposition '.[19] Certainly she was a most devoted aunt, as Scott generously recognised, never grudging the time and care she bestowed on him at Sandy-knowe,

Bath, and Kelso. 'She did all but bear him,' said one of her unnamed contemporaries to George Allan.[20] Captain Robert Scott, apart from Walter's own mother, was perhaps the relative most in his confidence, from the time when the Captain's arrival at Bath delighted the little boy. The uncle introduced the nephew to such amusements of the place as fitted his age and took him for the first time to a theatre. The Captain, who had none of the coldness for polite letters shown by Scott's father, entered with sympathy and zest into his nephew's pursuits and interests as a real companion. And he was consulted by Scott on all his early attempts in verse or in prose. In a letter of 1790 Walter, in submitting the scroll copy of one of his essays, pays his uncle this sincere tribute, 'There is none whose advice I prize so high, for there is none in whose judgment I can so much confide, or who has shown me so much kindness.'[21]

Scott's passion for anything with a story in it and his initiation into the studies that were to make him both poet and novelist antedated his ability to read for himself. They began with his arrival at conscious existence when he was scarcely more than an infant during his first sojourn at Sandy-knowe. His mind received a deep and indelible impression from the 'haunted ground'[22] on every side. He rightly says that 'The local information, which I conceive had some share in forming my future taste and pursuits, I derived from the old songs and tales which then formed the amusement of a retired country family'.[23] And in 1787 in one of his very first letters he tells his correspondent Jessie, whose surname is not known, 'that from the earliest period of my existence, ballads and other romantic poems I have read or heard as a favourite, and sometimes as an exclusive gratification'.[24]

It was for Scott the beginning of that 'period in youth when the mere power of numbers has a more strong effect on ear and imagination than in more advanced life'.[25] The two primary sources of balladry and anecdote for him were his Scott grandmother and Auld Sandy Ormistoun, the cow-bailie at Sandy-knowe. Scott says of his grandmother's recalls (and the same might have been said of Auld Sandy's), ' My grandmother, in whose youth the old Border depredations were matter of recent tradition, used to tell me many a tale of Watt of Harden, Wight Willie of Aikwood, Jamie Telfer of the fair Dodhead, and other heroes, merrymen all of the persuasion and calling of Robin Hood and little John. A more recent hero, but not of less note, was the celebrated Diel of Littledean, whom she well remembered, as he had married her mother's sister. Of this extraordinary person I learned many a story, grave and gay, comic and warlike '.[26] Aunt Jenny also is said (though not by Scott himself) to have had a great store of ballads and legendary tales, not to mention old songs.[27]

In some of his most heart-felt and memorable lines, Scott like Wordsworth expressed his belief in the power of early impressions and his recollections of some of the first things his imagination responded to:

> ' Thus while I ape the measure wild
> Of tales that charm'd me yet a child,
> Rude though they be, still with the chime
> Return the thoughts of early time;
> And feelings, rous'd in life's first day,
> Glow in the line, and prompt the lay.
> Then rise those crags, that mountain tower
> Which charm'd my fancy's wakening hour. . . .
> It was a barren scene, and wild,
> Where naked cliffs were rudely pil'd;
> But ever and anon between
> Lay velvet tufts of loveliest green;
> And well the lonely infant knew
> Recesses where the wall-flower grew,
> And honey-suckle lov'd to crawl
> Up the low crag and ruin'd wall.
> I deem'd such nooks the sweetest shade

The sun in all its round survey'd;
And still I thought that shatter'd tower
The mightiest work of human power;
And marvell'd as the aged hind
With some strange tale bewitch'd my mind,
Of forayers, who, with headlong force,
Down from that strength had spurr'd their horse,
Their southern rapine to renew,
Far in the distant Cheviots blue,
And, home returning, fill'd the hall
With revel, wassel-rout, and brawl.
Methought that still with trump and clang
The gateway's broken arches rang;
Methought grim features, seam'd with scars,
Glar'd through the window's rusty bars,
And ever, by the winter hearth,
Old tales I heard of woe or mirth,
Of lovers' slights, of ladies' charms,
Of witches' spells, of warriors' arms;
Of patriot battles, won of old
By Wallace wight and Bruce the bold;
Of later fields of feud and fight,
When, pouring from their Highland height,
The Scottish clans, in headlong sway,
Had swept the scarlet ranks away.
While stretch'd at length upon the floor,
Again I fought each combat o'er,
Pebbles and shells, in order laid,
The mimic ranks of war display'd;[28]
And onward still the Scottish Lion bore,
And still the scatter'd Southron fled before.'[29]

From hearing ballads to learning them by heart was for the three- or four-year-old Scott but a short step. And ' the first poem I ever learnt—the last I shall ever forget '[30] was *Hardyknute*,[31] taught to him before he could read out of his grandfather's copy at Sandy-knowe of Allan Ramsay's

Tea-Table Miscellany. Such was his enthusiasm that he
recited it only too vociferously for the visiting parish
minister, Dr Alexander Duncan. " One may as well speak,"
said the exasperated victim, " in the mouth of a cannon as
where that child is."[32] It is to this and other misdemeanours
that Scott refers in these lines:

> ' the venerable Priest,
> Our frequent and familiar guest,
> Whose life and manners well could paint
> Alike the student and the saint;
> Alas! whose speech too oft I broke,
> With gambol rude and timeless joke '.[33]

Another ballad he picked up a month or two later from a
single recitation of it by an Irish servant-girl at Bath and
could repeat most of it, poor as the verses were, years after.[34]

Scott's memory was remarkably retentive and ' reached
to an earlier period of childhood than that of almost any
other person '.[35] Without thinking it in any way out of
the ordinary, he makes Darsie Latimer's memory run back
' Perhaps . . . to the age of three years, or a little farther '.[36]
His own certainly went quite as far. He came to ' the
first consciousness of existence ' at Sandy-knowe;[37] and he
remembered the circumstances distinctly—his helplessness,
his being swathed by way of remedy for his lameness in
the just-flayed and still warm fleece of a sheep, his grandfather and Sir George MacDougal using every induce-
ment to make him crawl (Sir George's watch pulled along
the carpet being the chief lure), and even the very clothes
Sir George wore. He dates the incident about his third
year, meaning thereby before his third birthday.[37] He
remembered as distinctly his grandfather's funeral, early in
his fourth year.[38] Very shortly after, while still under four,
he spent a few days in London on his way to Bath and
was taken to see the sights, including Westminster Abbey
and the Tower. When twenty-five years later he paid his
second visit to London, he was himself astonished by the

accuracy of his memory; 'and I have ever since,' he said, 'trusted more implicitly to my juvenile reminiscences'.[39] Of Bath, too, and his life there he retained impressions as vivid. So he continued throughout his life to retain circumstantial memories of countless places, persons, and incidents, some no doubt striking but others quite unremarkable in themselves.

It was, however, Scott's verbal memory that was specially interesting. 'I had always,' he tells us, 'a wonderful facility in retaining in my memory whatever verses pleased me,'[40] and, it would appear, passages of prose also. 'But,' he adds, 'this memory of mine was a very fickle ally, and has through my whole life acted merely upon its own capricious motion . . . it seldom failed to preserve most tenaciously a favourite passage of poetry, a playhouse ditty, or, above all, a Border-raid ballad; but names, dates, and the other technicalities of history escaped me in a most melancholy degree.'[40] The technicalities to which he was referring were, I think, the unwillingly learned data of his schooling; since his memory for such details obtained otherwise was by no means leaky.

At Sandy-knowe 'Two or three old books which lay in a window-seat,' he says, 'were explored for my amusement in the tedious winter-days. *Automathes*[41] and Ramsay's *Tea-Table Miscellany* were my favourites, although at a later period an odd volume of Josephus's *Wars of the Jews* divided my partiality. My kind and affectionate aunt, Miss Janet Scott, whose memory will ever be dear to me, used to read these works to me with admirable patience till I could repeat long passages by heart.'[42] It was the same when he returned to his home in George Square, where, he tells us, 'I got by heart, not as a task, but almost without intending it, the passages with which I was most pleased, and used to recite them aloud, both when alone and to others—more willingly, however, in my hours of solitude, for I had observed some auditors smile, and I dreaded ridicule at that time of life more than I have ever done since.'[43]

Some other facts about his boyish readiness in memorising will be noticed later. But I may perhaps refer here to two extraordinary feats of memory when Scott was no longer young, since the *terminus a quo* in each case belongs to his youth. The first was his ability, until the crisis of 1826, to recite every letter he had written from the beginning of his correspondence at the age of fifteen, on getting the first line as his cue. The second is the sad evidence provided by *The Siege of Malta*, which he began in December 1831 and which his failing powers led him to think one of his best works; whereas in fact the more coherent parts are 'an almost verbatim reproduction'[44] of Vertot's *Knights of Malta*, read by him about fifty years before.

The tricksiness of Scott's memory is illustrated by what it so arbitrarily retained. 'Strange as it may seem,' says Gillies, 'he . . . stored up dross and rubbish, as well as better materials, and yet without the slightest confusion, so that a friend once compared his mind to a kaleidoscope, which retains and displays its symmetrical powers, however coarse may be the substances placed within it.'[45] So at parties he would often help out, through every comic stanza if necessary, a singer who had forgotten his words, rendering them himself in an appropriately ludicrous style. On one such occasion towards midnight, the singer of a favourite song having gone, Scott offered to give the words without the music, if that would be acceptable. Then without missing a line and 'with an accurate adherence to the forecastle style of recitativo'[46] he supplied the whole ballad:

'I courted Molly of Spithead,
　And asked her to be marri-ed;
At first she vas most cruel kind,
　But she proved valse, as you shall find;
　　With a chip chow, fal lal de ray.'

Of course, while he was still being read to, Scott had become a reader for himself, an inveterate and indefatigable reader. What may have been the very first book of verses the child read was the curious and rare *True History of Several Honourable Families of the Name of Scot*, written by Captain (as he called himself) Walter Scot and published in 1688. For he remembered 'spelling' the lines of old Satchells, as the author was generally called from his property. '[N]or did he conceal his belief that he owed much to the influence exerted over his juvenile mind by the rude but enthusiastic clan-poetry.'[47] But, according to Scott's own reckoning, which does not really contradict what has been said, 'the first poetry which I perused' was 'a few traditionary ballads, and the songs in Allan Ramsay's *Evergreen*', followed by Pope's Homer.[48]

But once he had acquired the ability to read, he soon went on to much else, reading in bed for hours morning and evening, or lying on his back on the carpet with his lame right leg bent over his left to make a book-rest, or poring over a book 'even at breakfast . . . while sipping his coffee, like his own Oldbuck in *The Antiquary*',[49] in spite of his uncle Daniel's protests. We hear, for example, of his reading before his going to the High School (and I give only the authors or books mentioned by name by Scott himself or by Lockhart) Ramsay's *Tea-Table Miscellany*, *The Arabian Nights*, Bunyan's *Pilgrim's Progress*, Gessner's *Death of Abel*,[50] Mrs Elizabeth Rowe's *Letters from the Dead to the Living*, Falconer's *Shipwreck*, Milton's *Paradise Lost*, and Shakespeare. That his reading included a great deal more may be taken for granted. Items 4, 5, and 6 in the above list, with some others unnamed, were permitted 'to relieve the gloom of one dull sermon succeeding to another' on Sundays at George Square;[51] and for that reason Scott retained a regard for them.[52] As for Falconer's *Shipwreck*, 'the most extraordinary genius of a boy I ever saw', then aged six, read it to Mrs Cockburn and his mother, his excitement rising with the storm and his imaginative recreation of the scene agitating him so much that he had to break off.[53] Mrs Cockburn, to whom he took because she was 'a virtuoso' like himself—'one who wishes and will

know everything ',[54] records his not unnatural observation:
' How strange it is that Adam, just new come into the world,
should know everything—that must be the poet's fancy.'[55]
He instantly yielded, however, when he was told that God
had created Adam perfect.

He must have been about the same age, when a servant
at the house of Mrs Keith of Ravelston ' remarked to
Walter that he ought to be thankful to Providence for
having placed him above the want and misery ' of an old
beggar who had just received an alms. ' The child looked
up with a half-wistful, half-incredulous expression, and said
"Homer was a beggar!" "How do you know that?"
said the other. "Why, don't you remember," answered
the little Virtuoso, " that:

> Seven *Roman* cities strove for Homer dead,
> Through which the living Homer begged his bread?"

The lady [who told the incident to Lockhart] smiled at the
"*Roman* cities,"—but already

> Each blank, in faithless memory void,
> The poet's glowing thought supplied.'[56]

Of all his early reading by far the most important for
Scott, more important even than the ballads, was Shakespeare, who for him first and last was the author of authors
and of whose plays he had a knowledge ' extensive and
peculiar ', like Mr Weller's knowledge of London.[57] He
had been introduced to Shakespeare at Bath, when he was
taken to a theatre for the first time, by his uncle Robert,
the play being *As You Like It.* Lockhart thinks that probably
this performance ' first tempted him to open the pages of
Shakespeare '.[58] Quite certainly, he was deeply impressed
by the occasion; ' the witchery of the whole scene is alive
in my mind at this moment ', he says in the *Memoir* [59];
and in a *Quarterly Review* article [60] he recalls it again with
eloquent detail as lovingly and vividly as did Charles Lamb
his parallel experience in *My First Play.* At a rather later

date he found some odd volumes of Shakespeare in his mother's dressing-room, in which he slept at the time; 'nor can I easily forget', he says, 'the rapture with which I sate up in my shirt reading them by the light of the fire in her apartment, until the bustle of the family rising from supper warned me it was time to creep back to my bed, where I was supposed to have been safely deposited since nine o'clock'.[61] Scott's passion for Shakespeare was encouraged by his mother and his aunt Christian Rutherford and by an elderly friend of his father and admirer of his aunt Janet Scott. This was George Constable, who was at Prestonpans during Scott's stay there for sea-bathing when he was aged seven, and whose peculiarities of temper were long after developed in the character of Jonathan Oldbuck.[62] Constable 'was the first person who told me about Falstaff and Hotspur, and other characters in Shakespeare. What idea I annexed to them I know not, but I must have annexed some, for I remember quite well being interested on [sic] the subject'.[63] And, as it happened, *Henry IV* continued to be perhaps his favourite play, certainly his favourite among Shakespeare's histories. I would even suggest that its lacing of history with fiction provided the general model for the Waverley Novels. We know, too, that Shakespeare's plays were among the literature 'often read aloud in the family circle by Walter', and that 'many a happy evening hour' was so spent at George Square. Moreover, 'however good Mitchell [64] may have frowned at such a suggestion, even Mr Scott made little objection [65] to his children, and some of their young friends, getting up private theatricals occasionally in the dining-room, after the lessons of the day were over. . . . Walter was always the manager, and had the whole charge of the affair'.[66] Curiously enough, the favourite play (probably, however, not Scott's favourite) was Nicholas Rowe's *Jane Shore*, in which he played Hastings and his sister Anne played Alicia. In Shakespeare's *Richard III* Walter took the chief role, observing that 'the limp would do well enough to represent the hump'.[67]

Before his acting days and while he was still a small boy, he had begun to make manuscript collections of poems and ballads,[68] to which he continued to add [69] and which may be regarded as the germ of *Minstrelsy of the Scottish Border*.

Quite as early or earlier he had become ' a great collector of . . . chapbooks ',[70] such as itinerant packmen since Shakespeare's day and before had carried among their wares and distributed all over the country; and of these, unsuitable as some of them were for the young, he was as devout a reader at a time when to read was to remember. Nor did his love of this homely culture cease in his youth: he continued to buy chapbooks until his library contained over two thousand items, one of the largest, if not quite the largest, collection of the kind in Britain.[71]

In 1810 Scott had bound in six volumes 114 chapbooks which he believed he had bought with his pennies ' before I was ten, comprehending most of the more rare and curious of our popular tracts '.[72] He wrote in the first volume of the collection: ' Untill put into its present decent binding it had such charms for the servants that it was repeatedly and with difficulty rescued from their clutches. It contains most of the pieces that were popular about 30 years since and I dare say many that could not now be purchased for any price.' They are mostly of Scottish origin as regards printing and, to a large extent, as regards authorship and contents also.

Lockhart describes Scott's early chapbooks as ' little humorous stories in prose '.[73] But in fact about fifty of them are in verse, mainly in batches of what the publishers somewhat laxly call ' excellent new songs ', which, whatever their merit or age, have a surprising range in theme and treatment. The dozen or so which Lockhart's description does fit are stories of middle- and lower-class contemporary life, generally on themes of courtship, wiving, and the married state and mostly with an offtaking or satirical slant. A typical specimen is *The Whole Proceedings of Jockey and Maggy*, which Scott's note on the title-page pronounces 'An excellent piece of low humour'. As can be well imagined, these stories and the already-mentioned songs are not infrequently broad in their humour. And as Scott came to realise, some chapbooks contained such 'sculduddery' as Thomas Trumbull in a drunken mistake thrust into Alan Fairford's hand, consisting of 'profligate tales and more profligate songs, ornamented with figures corresponding in infamy with the letterpress'.[74] It is but fair to add, however, that the bulk of chapbook literature is more respectable and a good deal of it is pious and edifying. Another dozen of Scott's early collecting might likewise be described as humorous stories in prose. But they belong to the jest-book class and give the jokes and japes of such persons as Lothian Tom, Paddy from Cork, John Falkirk the merry piper, George Buchanan the King's Fool, and a clerical wit 'the late Reverend Mr J. Pettegrew'.[75] One of Scott's boyhood jest-books he remembered more than forty years later when he was writing *Redgauntlet*.[76] It is the *History of Buckhaven* [77] and of its customs and worthies, including 'wise Eppie' the spaewife-alewife.

Contemporary stories of a serious or sensational kind are also well represented among Scott's early treasures. A good few are cautionary tales, 'strange and true', like *The Buckingham Wonder*, *The Oxfordshire Tragedy*, *The Bride's Burial*, and *A Dreadful Warning to Cruel Mothers*. Others are specimens of rogue-literature, recounting the lives of pirates and highwaymen or the adventures of *The Female Sailor*.

Probably more to Scott's boyhood taste would be the chapbooks which handed on legendary or traditional matter. At any rate he had many stall-tracts of this kind: fairy-tales and *Märchen* about Tom Thumb and Jack the Giant-killer, Dick Whittington and the Babes in the Wood; or 'sadly abridged and adulterated' [78] romances like *Rosewal and Lilian*, *Valentine and Orson*, *The Three Destructions of Troy*, and *The Seven Sages of Rome*; or quasi-historical narratives about Robin Hood and his men, Edward III and the Countess of Salisbury, Jane Shore, and Dr Faustus.

More strictly literary chapbooks by named authors of some reputation were fairly common; and Scott had a good selection of them. If, as is very likely, he once owned William Hamilton of Gilbertfield's abridgment of Blind Harry's *Wallace*, a chapbook [79] so popular as to have reached practically every cottage in Scotland, and the scarcely less popular selections from Sir David Lindsay, they must have been abstracted from his collection or thumbed out of existence by the domestics. But Scott did retain the following items of Scots literature: *Christ's Kirk on the Green*, ' Written by King James the First', Alexander Montgomerie's *The Cherry and the Slae*, and Allan Ramsay's *Gentle Shepherd* and *The Monk and the Miller's Wife*. Scott had in addition a number of chapbook versions of such English works as Thomas Deloney's *Gentle Craft*, Goldsmith's *Deserted Village*, and John Wesley's abridgment of Henry Brooke's *Fool of Quality*.

A collection of chapbooks without one or two of a prophetical character would not be representative. Scott as a boy bought several of such tracts, as for example *The Explication of Thomas Rymer's Prophecies*,[80] *The Cheshire Prophecy* of Robert Nixon who lived in the early seventeenth century, and *The Wonderful Prophecies* of Phebe Totterdale of Saratoga, N.Y., who was born an idiot and in 1774 became suddenly sane and surprisingly oracular.[81] Scott's lively interest in the American War [82] may have prompted his purchase of the last-mentioned pamphlet, as it did also his acquisition of *A Letter from a Scots Piper* upbraiding the French King for (among other things) ' encouraging the Americans to rebel against their lawful sovereign' and *Captain O'Blunder's Observations on the Bloody War in America*.

Two of Scott's religious chapbooks were: *Jerusalem's Captivities Lamented . . . To which is added A Full and True Account of the Life of St Peter the Apostle*; and *A New His-*

torical Catechism containing 'witty answers to several questions . . . both from Sacred Records, and the greatest Authors Ancient and Modern '.[83] These and other popular items not represented in Scott's early collection, such as the Scriptural paraphrases (often ' embellished with cuts ' of Joseph or Moses, Paul or Judas), or the devotional manuals, are so to speak undenominational. But many of the religious chapbooks are markedly sectarian and polemical, like one Scott acquired early, *The . . . History of the Buchanites; giving a particular Account of that old Jezebel, Mrs Buchan,*[84] or like the ' well-approved tracts ' against the Quakers which the elder Fairford recommended to Darsie Latimer, *The Snake in the Grass* and *The Foot out of the Snare.*[85] Many other tracts or sermons, with just such fanciful titles, were evidently in demand, *The Plant of Renown, A Choice Drop of Honey,* and so on. They were all by preachers of an ultra-Protestant and evangelical type and of a surprising range in date from such sixteenth-century divines as Thomas Wilcox down to Ebenezer Erskine, the founder of the Secession Church in 1733, and perhaps to others considerably later. Of this class of chapbook the boy Scott had: *Satan's Decoy; or, The Youth's Faith in Christ; The Surprising Miracle; or, A Seasonable Warning to all Sinners. Shewing the Wonderful Relation of one Mary Moor*; and *An Account of the Last Words of Christian Kerr,* who died in Edinburgh in her eleventh year.[86] The author of *Old Mortality,* too, knew in his boyhood some of the chapbooks which kept alive in the late eighteenth century the anti-prelatical and Covenanting animosities of the seventeenth and which indeed were still circulating in the middle of the nineteenth. Such is *The Life and Prophecies of the Reverend Mr Alexander Peden.*[87] But more interesting was the possession by the author-to-be of *Wandering Willie's Tale* of this chapbook, of which for obvious reasons I give the title in full: [88] *An Elegy in Memory of that Valiant Champion, Sir R. Grierson, Late Laird of Lag, Who died Dec. 23d, 1733. Wherein the Prince of Darkness Commends many of his best friends, who were the Chief*

Managers of the late Persecution.[89]

By the time Scott went to the High School, his ' totally unregulated and undirected '[90] reading had become more and more diversified and ranging. ' [M]y acquaintance with English literature,' he says, ' was gradually extending itself. In the intervals of my school hours I had always perused with avidity such books of history or poetry or voyages and travels as chance presented to me—not forgetting the usual, or rather ten times the usual, quantity of fairy-tales, eastern stories, romances, etc.'[91] He borrowed from the High School's well-stocked library one or several volumes of each of the following works: Edmund Burke and others' *Annual Register* for 1761; Goldsmith's *Grecian History, The Roman History* abridged by the younger Colin Maclaurin, and *The History of England*; William Robertson's *History of Scotland*; John and William Langhorne's *Plutarch's Lives*; the Duc de Sully's *Memoirs* translated by Charlotte Lennox; Awnsham and John Churchill's *Collection of Voyages and Travels* including Sir Thomas Roe's *Journal of his Voyage to the East Indies*; John Newbery's *World Displayed; or, A Curious Collection of Voyages and Travels*; a *History of the World*, probably *A General History of the World* for which Goldsmith wrote a preface; and Samuel Ward's *Modern System of Natural History*. His comment on his reading (part of which has already been quoted) is as follows: ' My memory . . . seldom failed to preserve most tenaciously a favourite passage of poetry, a playhouse ditty, or, above all, a Border-raid ballad; but names, dates, and the other technicalities of history escaped me in a most melancholy degree. The philosophy of history, a much more important subject, was also a sealed book at this period of my life; but I gradually assembled much of what was striking and picturesque in historical narrative; and when, in riper years, I attended more to the deduction of general principles, I was furnished with a powerful host of examples in illustration of them. I was, in short, like an ignorant gamester, who kept up a good hand until he knew how to play it.'[92]

During the same years Scott through his uncle Dr Daniel Rutherford made the acquaintance of ' a poetical preceptor [93] in the person of Dr Thomas Blacklock, a blind divine who had acquired something of a reputation by his poems, religious works, and translations. Scott went often to this kindly old man's house and was made free of his library. On Dr Blacklock's recommendation he ' became intimate with Ossian and Spenser '.[94] The Ossianic question, as we shall see,[95] was to occupy Scott not a little later on. But in the meantime, ' I was delighted with both, yet I think chiefly with the latter poet. The tawdry repetitions of the Ossianic phraseology disgusted me rather sooner than might have been expected from my age. But Spenser I could have read for ever. Too young to trouble myself about the allegory, I considered all the knights and ladies and dragons and giants in their outward and exoteric sense, and God only knows how delighted I was to find myself in such society. As I had always a wonderful facility in retaining in my memory whatever verses pleased me, the quantity of Spenser's stanzas which I could repeat was really marvellous.'[94]

Another similar ' valuable acquisition . . . made about this time ',[94] by which I take him to mean the summer of 1783 during his stay at Kelso, was Tasso's *Jerusalem Delivered* ' in the flat medium of Mr Hoole's translation '.[94]

And still another, indeed the one above all others for him at the time, was Bishop Percy's *Reliques of Ancient English Poetry*. The discovery by him, who was destined to be ' the last and greatest of the Border minstrels ',[96] of this landmark of the Romantic Revival was an epoch in his life, giving him something of reassurance and moral support, and awakening his more scholarly and antiquarian interest in ballads. ' As I had been from infancy devoted to legendary lore of this nature,' he says, ' and only reluctantly withdrew my attention from the scarcity of materials and the rudeness of those which I possessed, it may be imagined, but cannot be described, with what delight I

saw pieces of the same kind which had amused my childhood, and still continued in secret the Delilahs of my
imagination, considered as the subject of sober research,
grave commentary, and apt illustration, by an editor who
showed his poetical genius was capable of emulating the
best qualities of what his pious labour preserved. I remember
well the spot where I read these volumes for the first time.
It was beneath a huge platanus-tree, in the ruins of what
had been intended for an old-fashioned arbour [in his aunt's
garden at Kelso [97]]. The summer-day sped onward so fast,
that notwithstanding the sharp appetite of thirteen, I forgot
the hour of dinner, was sought for with anxiety, and was
still found entranced in my intellectual banquet. To read
and to remember was in this instance the same thing, and
henceforth I overwhelmed my schoolfellows, and all who
would hearken to me, with tragical recitations from the
ballads of Bishop Percy. The first time, too, I could scrape
a few shillings together, which were not common occurrences with me, I bought unto myself a copy of these
beloved volumes; nor do I believe I ever read a book half
so frequently, or with half the enthusiasm.'[98]

Less poetical and romantic reading at the same period
of his life was provided by the works of Richardson, Fanny
Burney, Henry Mackenzie, Fielding, Smollett, 'and some
others of our best novelists'.[99]

But his 'appetite for books was as ample and indis-
criminating as it was indefatigable '[100]; and over and above
all the already-named authors Scott had for 'random
perusal' [100] whatever other books he could borrow from
circulating or subscription libraries in Edinburgh or Kelso,[101]
or from such private collections as Dr Blacklock's which
has been previously mentioned [102] and Mrs Waldie's which
also deserves a word. She was an elderly Quaker lady,
always respectfully called Lady Waldie, whose son,[103]
Robert, was one of Scott's schoolfellows at Kelso and whose
house, household, and library supplied many hints for those
of Joshua Geddes in *Redgauntlet*.[104] In a note not very

necessary for the reader of the novel, Scott records with pleasure his particular indebtedness to her. He was solitary; he had few acquaintances and scarcely any companions; and 'books, which were at the time almost essential to my happiness', he says, 'were difficult to come by'. Mrs Waldie, then, allowed him 'to rummage at pleasure' in her small but well-selected library and to borrow what he wanted, provided that he also took away some Quaker tracts, without however having to promise to read them.[105]

Nor was he less avid of oral communication from his childhood onwards. I have already mentioned the balladry and anecdotes of his Scott grandmother, his aunt Jenny, and Auld Sandy Ormistoun. But there were others about Sandy-knowe to whose conversation the child Scott eagerly listened. He often heard, he says in the Introduction to *Guy Mannering*, stories of the Border gipsies, especially Jean Gordon,[106] and had himself seen Madge Gordon, her grand-daughter, 'a woman of more than female height, dressed in a long red cloak, who commenced acquaintance by giving me an apple'. Jean and Madge both provided suggestions for his Meg Merrilies, and several incidents, including first-hand reports by his grandfather and others, provided colour and detail in the gipsy episodes of the novel. Very different news of the larger world was brought to the isolated little community at Sandy-knowe by his uncle Thomas Scott on his weekly visits to his parents; and during the heat of the American war, little Walter waited anxiously to hear of Washington's defeat, 'as if I had had some deep and personal cause of antipathy to him'.[107]

But this co-existed with another partisanship which was to have a more lasting influence, 'a very strong prejudice in favour of the Stuart family, which I had originally im-bibed from the songs and tales of the Jacobites'.[108] The 'eventful year, still emphatically distinguished in Scotland as the FORTY-FIVE'[109] and all the circumstances leading up to it and all its romantic and tragic consequences provided a constant source of topic and anecdote for the rest of its century and beyond. And, as Scott observed in 1832, 'Most Scottish readers who can count the number of sixty years must recollect many respected acquaintances of their youth who, as the established phrase gently worded it, had been *out in the 'Forty-five,'*[110] and who in some cases had been *out* in 1715 and 1718 as well. Scott's own surmise was that the tragical stories of the barbarities at Carlisle and in the Highlands which so deeply confirmed his political sympathies and made him detest 'the name of Cumberland with more than infant hatred'[111] came to his precocious ears first from William Curle, husband of his aunt Barbara Scott. Curle had actually been present at the Carlisle executions. But, as several of Scott's own relations (not so distant by the Scottish estimate of kinship) had fallen at Culloden, stories of the '45 were no doubt as common subjects of talk at Sandy-knowe as they were anywhere.

It is not unlikely that Dr Alexander Duncan, the Minister of Smailholm already mentioned,[112] may have contributed some. At any rate he left in manuscript *A Journal of the Rebellion, 1745*, passages of which he read to Scott only a few days before his death in 1795,[113] but which has never been published.[114] Another very likely to have spoken in the little boy's presence of 'the remarkable epoch'[115] was John Home. He and his wife made much of Scott and his aunt at Bath.[116] Home had himself been actively engaged in the '45, on the Hanoverian side but with a divided sympathy which no one was better able to appreciate than Scott,[117] as he shows in his review of Henry Mackenzie's *Life and Works of the Author of 'Douglas'*: 'Under less strong influence of education and profession, which was indeed irresistible, it is possible he might have made a less happy option; for the feeling, the adventure, the romance, the poetry, all that was likely to interest the imagination of a youthful poet—all, in short, save the common sense, prudence, and sound reason of the national dispute—must be allowed to have been on the side of the Jacobites. Indeed, although mortally engaged against them, Mr Home could not, in the latter part of his life, refrain from tears when mentioning the gallantry and misfortunes of some of the unfortunate leaders in the Highland army; and we have ourselves seen his feelings and principles divide him strangely when he came to speak upon such topics.'[118] In 1779 Home settled in Edinburgh, where he was the object of general respect and veneration. He was an agreeable and ready talker; and though his memory was unreliable for recent events, it was strong and vigorous for those which had occupied his attention in his prime. Scott makes it quite clear that he listened to Home's reminiscences, whether at Bath or later in Edinburgh; and he describes, as if he had been present, a dinner at Home's house where the '45 ' called forth remarks and anecdotes without number '[119] from the veteran guests, some of whom remembered the turmoils of 1715 and 1718.

But there were many others from whom in his childhood, boyhood, and youth Scott picked up data about the '45; among them certainly Dr Alexander Carlyle who had been an active volunteer for the defence of Edinburgh against the Prince's army and had seen Sir John Cope routed at Prestonpans from his father's manse at Inveresk;[120] and, on the other side, Alexander Stewart of Invernahyle who had crossed swords with Rob Roy, had fought in the '15 and the '45, and had been forced, like the Baron of Bradwardine, to lie long hidden in a cave near his own house.[121] Scott describes Carlyle as ' a man of equal worth and humour [with John Home], and a particular intimate of the author of *Douglas* . . . whose character was as excellent as his conversation was amusing and instructive, and whose person and countenance, even at a very advanced age, were so lofty and commanding as to strike every artist with his resemblance to the Jupiter Tonans of the Pantheon '.[122] Alexander Stewart had been known to Scott as a client of his father, who was as diligent and impartial a ' doer '[123] for Tories [124] as for Whigs, long before he visited

Invernahyle on legal business and by invitation when an apprentice. '[This] man,' he told Mrs Hughes, 'was the delight of my childhood—he was often at our house, and I was never out of his sight and never weary of the anecdotes which he was pleased to tell one who, young as he was, had such real pleasure in listening to him.'[125] From such survivors, then, Scott heard with as much delight as Darsie Latimer 'the blawing, blazing stories which the Hieland gentlemen tell of those troublous times ',[126] and which, with the scenery and the manner of life he encountered on his travels, provided the background and not a few of the incidents in so many of his poems and novels. The fact is that practically all the elders of his grandfather's generation, whom he knew as friends or clients of his father or whom he met in casual encounters, were likely to have been his informants on every aspect of the '45, from a major incident to a chance remark.[127] He was speaking for himself when he made Darsie say: " Old ladies of family over their hyson, and grey-haired lairds over their punch, I had often heard utter a little harmless treason; while the former remembered having led down a dance with the Chevalier, and the latter recounted the feats they had performed at Preston, Clifton, and Falkirk."[128]

Scott may also have picked up other lore in the shape of literary *ana* from Dr Duncan, who could talk familiarly at firsthand of the Augustan wits surviving into the 1730s and 40s, having been chaplain in the household of the Earl of Marchmont who was the intimate of Bolingbroke and Chesterfield and the executor of Pope and the Duchess of Marlborough. Moreover, Dr Duncan was presented to Smailholm in 1743 by Grizel, Lady Murray of Stanhope, with the consent of her more famous mother, Lady Grizel Baillie, the Earl of Marchmont's grandaunt.[129]

During Scott's stay at Prestonpans for sea-bathing, in 1777 when he was in his eighth year or thereabouts, he encountered two elders to whose very different talk he attentively listened. The one was a half-pay Ensign, Dalgetty by name, who was always accorded the courtesy rank of Captain. It is possible that he provided more than his name for *A Legend of Montrose*, and that he was the prototype not only of the hero of the novel proper, but of Sergeant More McAlpin whose story is told in the original Introduction. For the veteran had been in all the German wars; and ' finding very few to listen to his tales of military feats, he formed a sort of alliance with me, and I used invariably to attend him for the pleasure of hearing these communications ',[130] until the intimacy was rather shaken by the boy's proving the better forecaster of the outcome of General Burgoyne's expedition in the American War. The other friend at Prestonpans was the already-mentioned George Constable, a retired lawyer and an antiquary, who supplied Scott with ' a great deal of curious information ',[131] in addition to Shakespearian matters.

But Scott was always ready to listen to the gossiprede of the older generation, however small the beer they chronicled; and from their conversation he picked up many an incident, character-sketch, pawky saying, and instance of quaint humour, which later fell happily into place in the novels and contributed both to their substance by way of plot and episode and to their confirming background and dialogue still more. Scott himself was born at the beginning of his country's transition from a lingering antiquity to an unromantic modernity; and not only in *Waverley; or 'Tis Sixty Years Since*, but in nearly all the novels set in Scotland (which means in all the best and most characteristic of the series) he contrasts what was with what is. And it was by the spoken and often casual reminiscences of his elders, even more than by books, that he recreated the past of the three or four generations before his own— not in respect of the history-book facts, but in respect of the unrecorded details of day-to-day existence and the ways in which real persons really behaved and spoke and felt. It is possible to name only some of his memorialists. His father, for instance, may not have been a very loquacious man; but he had a dry humour and liked a sly jest, often, I fancy, with a legal or professional flavour, such as Scott frequently introduces by the way. Old Mrs Scott, who was the more lively spouse and superior to her husband in talents and tastes, had keen powers of observation and a rich fund of anecdotes and was noted for her skill in telling a story well, not least in respect of the humorous. She was much addicted to family history, being a great genealogist like all Scottish ladies of gentle birth, and like them, or most of them, a Jacobite.[132]   Then there were such ladies of her acquaintance, kinswomen and others, as the evergreen Mrs Alison Cockburn; or Mrs Margaret Swinton, the narrator of the episode developed in *My Aunt Margaret's Mirror*; or Mrs Murray Keith, whom Scott disguised but slightly as Mrs Martha Bethune Baliol of the *Chronicles of the Canongate* [133] and who recognised so many of her anecdotes worked into the fabric of the Waverley Novels that the Great Unknown's identity could not be concealed from her. Or there was old John MacKinlay, ' an old servant of my father's, an excellent old Highlander, without a fault, unless a preference to mountain-dew over less potent liquors be accounted one ';[134] and, a little later, the venerable Mr Abercromby of Tullibody, grandfather of Scott's friend George Abercromby (Lord Abercromby), who supplied firsthand stories of Rob Roy, including an episode of cattle-lifting and ' protection ' which is used in *Waverley*.[135]

Finally, Scott traced some of the most striking passages in *The Pirate* [136] to the recollections of the talk of his eldest brother Robert, who had been present as a midshipman at most of Rodney's battles and had then passed into the East India Company's service. When in a good humour, which was by no means always, he regaled his brothers with many tales ' of bold adventure and narrow escapes '.[137] When in a bad humour, Robert ' gave us a practical taste of what was then man of war's discipline, and kicked and cuffed without mercy '.[138]

Such, then, was the ' great quantity of general informa-

tion, ill-arranged indeed and collected without system, yet
deeply impressed on my mind; readily assorted by my
power of connexion and memory, and gilded, if I may be
permitted to say so, by a vivid and active imagination ',[139]
which Scott took with him to the University in the autumn
of 1783, together with the less willingly acquired fruits of
his more regular schooling, which, it may be remarked,
did not include anything scientific or much of what is now
taught in the English classroom or any modern foreign
language except French. He likens his self-education to a
wading ' into the stream like a blind man into a ford, without the power of searching for my way, unless by groping
for it '.[139] It was an adventurous and generous initiation;
and he need never have repented, as he frequently did,
' that few ever read so much, and to so little purpose '.[139]
So far from his reading being to little purpose, he read with
delight and remembered with tenacity, as, I am afraid, very
few of even the most earnest school-leavers and university
students do. Scott's knowledge was not got up without
enthusiasm for an examination of a limited and prescribed
scope, and forgotten without regret sooner than it was
acquired.

NOTES ON REFERENCES

1   *Memoir*, I, 11.
2   *Memoir*, I, 8.
3   I, 25.
4   I, 36.
5   He is admirably characterised in the *Memoir* (I, 3), and
     presented in action with but little fictional disguise as
     Mr Saunders Fairford in *Redgauntlet*, as Mr Fairscribe in
     the introductory chapters of *Chronicles of the Canongate*,
     and also, though with more modification, as the elder
     Osbaldistone in *Rob Roy*. Cf. *infra*, 149, 154 note 20.
6   Lockhart, I, 22.
7   Lockhart, I, 165.
8   *Memoir*, I, 8.

9   Lockhart, I, 31-32. Owing to a confusion with Mrs Scott of Wauchope (*née* Rutherford), Mrs Walter Scott, ' who was an intimate friend of Allan Ramsay, Blacklock, and other poetical wits ', was said to have written ' verses, like them, in the vernacular language of Scotland. But this can be denied, upon the testimony of her own son ' (Chambers, 6).

10   *Memoir*, I, 8.

11   *Marmion*, Introduction to Canto Third.

12   *Memoir*, I, 8.

13   Mrs Scott's later letters show her becoming more and more serious and taking clerical counsel on points of doctrine (cf. Grierson, 8).

14   As early as 1776 the old man gave his grandson a four-volume edition of one of Scott's prime favourites, *Don Quixote*. His New-Year's-Day gift in 1778 was Andrew Tooke's *Classical Pantheon*; and in 1779 *The Student's Pocket Dictionary*.

15   She seems to have given her grand-nephew a Suetonius translated ' By Several Hands ' at an early but uncertain date. She also gave him Dryden's translation of Voiture's *Familiar and Courtly Letters* in 1788.

16   Lockhart mistakenly describes Mrs Cockburn as only ' distantly related to the poet's mother ' (I, 24).

17   *Marmion*, Introduction to Canto Third.

18   Lockhart, I, 24.

19   Allan, 9.

20   9.

21   *Letters*, I, 17 (30th September 1790). Captain Scott settled part of his estate on his nephew Walter (cf. Allan, 46).

22   Allan, 11.

23   *Memoir*, I, 6.

24   *Letters*, I, 4.

25   *Kenilworth*, Introduction.

26   *Memoir*, I, 6.

27   Cf. Allan, 9, 11.

28   Cf. *infra*, 139.

29   *Marmion*, Introduction to Canto Third.

30   Lockhart, I, 23.

31   The ballad, which runs to no less than forty-two stanzas

of eight lines each, is described by Scott as 'though evidently modern, . . . a most spirited and beautiful imitation' (*Introductory Remarks on Popular Poetry* in *Minstrelsy*, I, 25). Scott calls the authoress Mrs Halket of Wardlaw (ibid., I, 44). She was, in fact, Elizabeth, Lady Wardlaw (*née* Halket).

32   *Memoir*, I, 6.

33   *Marmion*, Introduction to Canto Third.

34   *Letters*, I, 4, note 1. At least one other instance of such effortless memorising of ballads is recorded: Scott recited for the amusement of a party sailing to the mouth of the Forth the eighty-eight stanzas of Hogg's *Gilman's Cleuch* and the seventeen of Southey's *Inchcape Rock*, having heard each only once from their respective authors; 'and he believed he recited them both without misplacing a word'. On the occasion when Hogg sang his ballad, Scott 'did not appear to be paying particular attention' (*Domestic Life and Private Manners of Sir Walter Scott*, ed by J. E. H. Thomson, 59).

35   Lockhart, I, 23.

36   *Redgauntlet*, Chapter VI.

37   *Memoir*, I, 5.

38   Lockhart, I, 24.

39   *Memoir*, I, 6.

40   *Memoir* I, 11.

41   A footnote in *The Monastery*, Answer by 'The Author of Waverley' to . . . Captain Clutterbuck, refers the reader to 'the History of Automathes', which I take to have been a children's book of the period. *Something New* by Richard Griffith, whose name does not appear on either of the recorded title-pages (1762, 1772), has a preface signed 'Automathes'.

42   *Memoir*, I, 6.

43   *Memoir*, I, 8.

44   Grierson, 12. Cf. *infra*, 119 note 3, 139.

45   41.

46   Gillies, 41.

47   Lockhart, I, 18.

48   *Memoir*, I, 8.

49   Chambers, 26.

50 Probably as translated by Mary Collyer, 1761, and frequently reprinted. Cf. *infra*, 250-51.

51 *Memoir*, I, 8.

52 Mrs Hughes calls *The Pilgrim's Progress* ' the darling of his childhood' (315).

53 Mrs Cockburn, 125.

54 Mrs Cockburn, 125.

55 Mrs Cockburn, 125.

56 Lockhart, I, 25. The concluding quotation is from *The Lay of the Last Minstrel*, Introduction.

57 Dickens, *The Pickwick Papers*, Chapter XX.

58 I, 24.

59 I, 7.

60 *Prose*, 805-6. Cf. *Drama*, 605, for a passage on the impression made by a first visit to a theatre on ' any rural friend of rough, but sound sense, and ardent feelings '.

61 *Memoir*, I, 10-11. Cf. *Letters*, X, 331 (to Mrs Hughes, 13th December 1827): ' How I regret the hours that I wasted when a boy in reading by fire light.'

62 Cf. *Chronicles of the Canongate*, Introduction; and *The Antiquary*, Advertisement.

63 *Memoir*, I, 7, note 1.

64 I.e. James Mitchell.

65 But cf. *supra*, 28-29.

66 Lockhart, I, 32.

67 Lockhart, I, 32.

68 He mentions two such manuscript books, one at least ' of poems . . . collected at an early period of Life ', in a letter of 17th February 1796 to George Constable (*Letters*, I, 43). Lockhart confuses the collected poems and ballads in manuscript with a collection of printed chapbooks about to be discussed (I, 34; cf. Lockhart's footnote in the 1833-34 *Poetical Works*, I, 227).

69 Irving speaks of Scott's taking down ballads from Mrs Irving's dictation. ' He used to get,' says Irving, ' all the versions of those ballads he could and chuse the best.'

70 *Letters*, XI, 342 (to John Strang, apparently May 1830).

71 They have at last been carefully catalogued in a card-index by Dr J. C. Corson, Honorary Librarian of the Abbotsford Library.

72   *Letters*, XI, 342 (to John Strang, apparently May 1830). Dr Corson notes that Scott's memory as to which of his chapbooks he acquired at this early age was occasionally at fault (*Sir Walter Scott's Boyhood Collection of Chapbooks in Abbotsford Library* in *The Bibliotheck*, III, 204).

73   I, 24.

74   *Redgauntlet*, Chapter XIII. Scott gives the booklet the plausible title of *Merry Thoughts for Merry Men; or, Mother Midnight's Miscellany for the Small Hours*.

75   ' Minister of the Gospel at Long-Govan, near Glasgow '.

76   Letter VIII.

77   Attributed to Dugald Graham, the Glasgow bellman.

78   *Romance*, 574.

79   His copy of Hamilton's abridgment, bought in 1785 and now in the Abbotsford Library, is not a chapbook.

80   ' By the famous Mr Allan Boyd, M.A.'

81   As ' Attested by me John Montague, M.A.'

82   Cf. *infra*, 65, 69.

83   ' By a Doctor of Divinity in the Church.'

84   Elspeth Simpson or Buchan, foundress of the Buchanite sect in or about 1783. It would seem, therefore, that the chapbook about her was not one of Scott's earlier purchases.

85   *Redgauntlet*, Letter IX. The two anti-Quaker tracts are quite genuine, but are not among Scott's early chapbooks. Cf. *Kenilworth*, Chapter XXII.

86   The last-named pamphlet may have had a local interest for the household at Sandy-knowe, being ' By Mr Archibald Deans, Minister of the Gospel at Bowden '.

87   Cf. *The Monastery*, Introductory Epistle, for the chapbook ' Sermons of Mr Peden'.

88   The title-page of Scott's copy is missing.

89   The *Elegy* is said to have been written ' by one Irving, a schoolmaster '. (*Letters from and to Charles Kirkpatrick Sharpe, Esq.*, I, 6.) In a Note to Letter XI of *Redgauntlet* Scott himself says that he had ' heard in my youth some such wild tale as that placed in the mouth of the blind fiddler ', and refers for the names of some of the less-known associates of Grierson to a tract, *The Judgment and Justice of God exemplified*, which is a kind of postscript to

John Howie of Lochgoin's *Account of the Lives of the most Eminent Scots Worthies.*

90   *Memoir*, I, 10.

91   *Memoir*, I, 10.

92   *Memoir*, I, 11.

93   *Memoir*, I, 11. Cf. *Letters*, I, 320 (to Anna Seward, ? September 1806): 'he was the worthiest and kindest of human beings, and particularly delighted in encouraging the pursuits & opening the minds of the young people by whom he was surrounded'.

94   *Memoir*, I, 11.

95   Cf. *infra*, 214-17.

96   Lockhart, I, 23.

97   Fondly described by Scott in his essay *On Landscape Gardening* in *Prose*, 776-77.

98   *Memoir*, I, 11. Cf. *Romance*, 560: 'This excellent person, to whose memory the lovers of our ancient lyre must always remain so deeply indebted.'

99   *Memoir*, I, 11.

100   *Memoir*, I, 11.

101   The many libraries of these types established in the eighteenth century, even in quite small towns, had remarkably well-stocked shelves, as any haunter of secondhand bookshops must know. The Kelso librarian, Elliot by name, was knowledgeable about books, particularly those of an antiquarian sort. Cf. *The Monastery*, Introductory Epistle, for Captain Clutterbuck's comment on 'the . . . circulating library' and 'the more rational subscription-collection'.

102   Cf. *supra*, 63.

103   So Lockhart (I, 33). But Allan has 'grandson' (47).

104   Especially Letter VII. Scott himself had Quaker ancestors: Walter Scott of Raeburn and his wife Isabella MacDougal, great-great-grandparents on the paternal side; and John Swinton of Swinton, great-great-great grandfather on the maternal (cf. *The Heart of Midlothian*, note to Prolegomenon).

105   Letter VII, note.

106   Scott senior remembered her (cf. *Guy Mannering*, Introduction).

107   *Memoir*, I, 5. Thomas Scott died in 1823 at the age of

ninety and in full possession of his faculties. 'It was a fine thing to hear him talk over the change of the country which he had witnessed' (*Memoir*, I, 5, note 3)—a change to which Scott often refers in the Waverley Novels (cf. *infra*, 69).

108   *Memoir*, I, 5. But perhaps this qualification should be quoted: 'Walter Scott was a Jacobite . . . in sentiment, but that sentiment [like others] was under the control of a directing and even rationalist outlook' (Grierson, 5).

109   *Home*, 828.

110   *Redgauntlet*, Introduction.

111   *Memoir*, I, 6. Scott severely criticised and condemned the toning-down or actual suppression of facts in this connection by John Home in his *History of the Rebellion in 1745*, out of deference to his dedicatee, George III, who was Cumberland's nephew (cf. *Home*, 842-43). Scott does not mention the Duke's present to Home of twenty guineas on the third night of the London presentation of *Douglas* (cf. Graham, 67).

112   Cf. *supra*, 52.

113   *Memoir*, I, 6. But Scott calls it 'a history of the Revolution', confusing it with Dr Duncan's published work on the Revolution of 1688.

114   Dr Duncan, who may have been the prototype of the Rev. Josiah Cargill in *St Ronan's Well*, published in 1790 *The History of the Revolution*, 1688. Two earlier works of his may have passed through Scott's hands at Sandy-knowe: *A Preventative against the Principles of Infidelity*, 1774, and *The Devout Communicant's Assistant*, 1777. A sermon on *The Evidence of the Resurrection of Jesus* was printed by the S.P.C.K. before whom it was delivered in 1788; and an account of the Parish of Smailholm was contributed to Sir John Sinclair's *Statistical Account of Scotland*, 1791-99.

115   *Home*, 835.

116   In what looks like a momentary lapse of memory, Scott said in one context, 'We ourselves only remember what a Scottish poet of eminence has called "Home's pale ghost just gliding from the stage"' (*Home*, 836).

117   They agreed also in their readings of the character of Prince Charles. Cf. *Waverley*, *Redgauntlet*, and *Home*, 843.

118   *Home*, 828-29. Scott speaks in very similar terms of Burns's propensity to Jacobitism which was dictated by feelings rather than principles; and as the passage is a reflex of his own attitude, I venture to quote it: ' Indeed, a youth of his warm imagination, and ardent patriotism, brought up in Scotland thirty years ago, could hardly escape this bias. The side of Charles Edward was the party, not surely of sound sense and sober reason, but of romantic gallantry and high achievement. The inadequacy of the means by which the Prince attempted to regain the crown, forfeited by his fathers, the strange and almost poetical adventures which he underwent, the Scottish martial character honoured in his victories, and degraded and crushed in his defeat, the tales of the veterans who had followed his adventurous standard, were all calculated to impress upon the mind of a poet a warm interest in the cause of the House of Stuart' (*Burns*, 850; cf. *Redgauntlet*, Introduction and Chapter XIX).

119   *Home*, 836.

120   Cf. *Home*, 831.

121   Cf. *Chronicles of the Canongate*, Introduction.

122   *Home*, 830, 834.

123   I.e. attorney.

124   Though Scott senior was as stout a whig as Saunders Fairford, Chambers quite erroneously describes him as ' a Jacobite, and employed mostly by that party' (5). Cf. *Redgauntlet*, Chapter I: Mr Fairford ' was an elder of the kirk, and, of course, zealous for King George and the government even to slaying, as he had showed by taking up arms in their cause. But then, as he had clients and connections of business among families of opposite political tenets, he was particularly cautious to use all the conventional phrases which the civility of the times had devised as an admissible mode of language betwixt the two parties'.

125   *Mrs Hughes*, 78. Her note to the effect that Stewart was the original of Pate-in-Peril in *Redgauntlet* is incorrect. Scott, who had seen the original in his youth, gives Pate-in-Peril's real name as either MacEwen or MacMillan (*Redgauntlet*, note to Chapter XI).

126 *Redgauntlet*, Letter IX.

127 Like the comment of an old Highland gentleman worked into a passage of dialogue: "A new Assembly Room! Umph—I mind quartering three hundred men in the old Assembly Room" (*Redgauntlet*, Chapter XI).

128 *Redgauntlet*, Chapter VIII.

129 Scott met about 1795 (and so outside the period with which I am dealing) the Earl of Marchmont's daughter, Lady Diana Scott. She likewise 'had conversed . . . with the brightest ornaments of the cycle of Queen Anne, and preserved rich stores of anecdote' (Lockhart, I, 69).

130 *Memoir*, I, 7.

131 Much later and probably during Scott's legal apprenticeship, Constable regularly dined at George Square on Sundays, and 'was authorized [by his host] to turn the conversation out of the austere and Calvinistic tone . . . upon subjects of history and auld langsyne. He remembered the '45 and told many excellent stories, all with a strong dash of a peculiar caustic humour' (*Memoir*, I, 7, note 1). But the oldest surviving servant of the Scott household recalled, probably with reference to an earlier and stricter phase, that only one gentleman, McIntosh by name, was occasionally admitted to sheep-head broth on a Sunday (cf. Allan, 17).

132 Cf. Chambers, 6-7 and Allan, 2-3.

133 Some traits of the character may have been suggested by Scott's mother.

134 *Guy Mannering*, Introduction.

135 Chapters XV-XIX.

136 But other hints were given later. William Clerk's midshipman brother James was startled when reading *The Pirate*, published in 1821, by 'a hundred traits of the table-talk' on board a lugger off Leith some thirty years before when Scott, in his early twenties, was one of the party (Lockhart, I, 41).

137 *Memoir*, I, 4.

138 *Memoir*, I, 4.

139 *Memoir*, I, 11. In a letter to George Crabbe he gives as his mental furniture when a youth: 'ghost stories, Border-riding ballads, scraps of old plays, and all the miscellaneous

stuff which a strong appetite for reading, with neither means nor discrimination for selection, had assembled in the head of a lad of eighteen' (*Letters*, III, 182, 21st October 1812).

CHAPTER IV

THE EDUCATIONAL INNOVATOR

Heaven, at whose pleasure we receive good and evil—and we are bound to receive both with thanks and gratitude—has afflicted you from infancy with a delicacy of constitution. With this misfortune there are often connected tastes and habits the most valuable any man can acquire, but which are indispensable to those who are liable, from indifferent health, to be occasionally confined to the solitude of their own apartment. The hours you now employ in reading are passed happily, and render you independent of the society of others, but will yet prove far more valuable to you in future life, since, if your studies are well directed, and earnestly pursued, there is nothing to prevent your rising to be at once an ornament and a benefit to society.

Tales of a Grandfather (*Third Series*),
Dedication to Master John Hugh Lockhart.

Beneath every King's reign Papa expects Sophia to write down neatly & in good spelling the following particulars.

Whether his reign was peaceful or warlike.

If warlike with whom he was at war & particularly whether with his own subjects or foreign nations. Also whether he was victorious in battle (generally) or defeated.

Whether any great alterations of government took place in his reign & what they were.

Whether he was a good man or a bad.

Whether the condition of his subjects was amended or became worse under his reign.

Letters, II, 462 (to Sophia Scott, ? 1810).

Charles is clever enough, but has alterations of indolence [of] which I am somewhat afraid, knowing from experience how fatal it is to the acquisition of knowledge even when associated with the power of working hard at particular times.

Letters, *VIII*, 421 (to Mrs Hughes, 11th November 1824).

THE sort of education that Scott tried to provide for his own children may to some extent be interpreted as a criticism of his own. But it should be remembered that he was not an educational theorist and still less a pedant. On the contrary, he would have preferred that (to adapt the words of Burke) ' a generous nature should be suffered to take its own way to perfection through a wise and salutary neglect '.[1] If he regretted the irregularity of his own education, it was more perhaps because he had himself not taken full advantage of his opportunities than because he had much faith in a highly systematised discipline. Such views as he expressed on education or as he implied are very plain and practical.

He sent his sons to the High School for the same curriculum as he had endured himself, having a horror of boarding schools (for boys or for girls), preferring to have his family about him, and ever ready to interrupt his own work and answer questions or tell a story or recite a ballad. As a result he was the companion of his children, partaking of ' all their little joys and sorrows, and [making] his kind informal instructions to blend . . . easily and playfully with the current of their own sayings and doings '.[2] Such a companionable relationship was very different from the genuine but rather overawed and formal affection Scott gave to his own father. He was quite prepared also to break into his sons' regular schooling and take them with him whenever he was resident in the country, himself becoming their tutor for the time being or else entrusting them to ' the happy " Dominie Thomson "[3] of the happy days of Abbotsford '.[4] He did not, however, like his father, fee a resident tutor for his boys when in Edinburgh; or send them, as he himself had been sent, to two schools at once.

His daughters were not even sent to a day-school, but were educated at home by a governess chosen ' with far greater regard to her kind good temper and excellent moral and religious principles, than to the measure of her attain-

ments in what are called fashionable accomplishments '.[5]
The amiable Miss Millar does not appear to have made a
fetish of grammar and spelling, to judge by the charming
letters her pupils continued to write to her. But under
her they acquired, to the complete satisfaction of their
parents, ' reading, writing, arithmetic, and the elementary
parts of music,[6] and of the French language . . . the elements
of drawing and the usual kinds of needlework '. Scott told
Miss Millar in the same letter that his wife and he ' had the
utmost reason to be satisfied, not only with your mode of
teaching and the instructions which you conveyed to our
children, but by your very ladylike and prudent conduct
. . . , a circumstance which is at least of as much importance
to the master and mistress of a family as the extent of
knowledge and the facility of communicating it.'[7]

As for what his children learned, both boys and girls,
in the schoolroom, ' It seemed,' says Lockhart, '. . . as if
he attached little importance to anything else, so [that] he
could perceive that the young curiosity was excited—the
intellect, by whatever springs of interest, set in motion.'[8]
And it was in regard to this kind of stimulus that Scott was
active and concerned, yet always tactfully and unobtrusively,
for he knew how little was given by schools and schoolmasters. It was just at the time when Mrs Trimmer, Mrs
Barbauld, Mary Wollstonecraft, and many others in the
wake of Rousseau's *Emile* were putting forth books for the
young calculated, where they did not disgust, to turn their
youthful readers into odiously knowledgeable prigs. Scott
' detested and despised the whole generation of . . .
children's books, in which the attempt is made to convey
accurate notions of scientific minutiae ';[9] and no doubt he
held in equal contempt the contemporary goody-goody
literature for the young. He would most heartily have
agreed, had he seen it, with Wordsworth's scathing attack
in Book V of *The Prelude* on the pragmatical and doctrinaire
stuff-and-nonsense and the monster of propriety and proficiency it was designed to engender.[10] And Scott would

as heartily have echoed Wordsworth's exclamation:

> 'Oh! give us once again the Wishing-Cap
> Of Fortunatus, and the invisible Coat
> Of Jack the Giant-killer, Robin Hood,
> And Sabra in the forest with St. George!
> The child, whose love is here, at least, doth reap
> One precious gain, that he forgets himself.'[11]

For he delighted in such books for the bairns (of all ages) as had circulated in his own youth—books ' which, addressing themselves chiefly to the imagination, obtain through it, as he believed, the best chance of stirring our graver faculties also'.[12]

Another of the new-fangled experiments which amused Scott, whose own education had been mostly in the hard way and usually against the grain, was the attempt to make education sweet and easy and to turn the schoolroom into the playroom. 'I am aware,' he says, 'I may be here reminded of the necessity of rendering instruction agreeable to youth, and of Tasso's infusion of honey into the medicine prepared for a child; but an age in which children are taught the driest doctrines by the insinuating method of instructive games has little reason to dread the consequence of study being rendered too serious or severe. The history of England is now reduced to a game at cards—the problems of mathematics to puzzles and riddles—and the doctrines of arithmetic may, we are assured, be sufficiently acquired by spending a few hours a week at a new and complicated edition of the Royal Game of the Goose. There wants but one step further, and the Creed and Ten Commandments may be taught in the same manner, without the necessity of the grave face, deliberate tone of recital, and devout attention hitherto exacted from the well-governed childhood of this realm.' But he adds, in the conviction that even the most elementary education is part of the preparation for life: 'It may, in the meantime, be subject of serious consideration whether those who are accustomed only to acquire instruction through the medium of amusement may not be brought to reject that which approaches under the aspect of study; whether those who learn history by the cards may not be led to prefer the means to the end; and whether, were we to teach religion in the way of sport, our pupils may not thereby be gradually induced to make sport of their religion.'[13]

There was, however, one contemporary preceptor of the young for whom Scott had a great though qualified admiration, Maria Edgeworth.[14] He read with delight and made his children read such stories as *Rosamond, The Purple Jar*, and *Simple Susan*. But he drew the line at *Harry and Lucy Concluded*, which was as Rousseau-ish as filial piety to the memory of Richard Lovell Edgeworth could make it. There 'is no great use', he writes to Joanna Baillie, 'in teaching children in general to roof houses [or] build bridges which after all a carpenter or a mason does a great deal better for 2s. 6d. a day . . . in the ordinary professions of the better informed orders I have always observed that a small taste for mechanics lands in encouraging a sort of trifling self-conceit founded on knowing that which is not worth being known by one who has other matters to employ his mind on and in short forms a trumpery gim-crack kind of a character who is a mechanic among gentlemen and most probably a gentleman among mechanics.'[15]

But of course Scott, the inexhaustible narrator with the marvellous memory for ballad and legend, supplied as much more from the best of the material he had so undiscriminatingly absorbed in his own youth. He tried to cultivate his children's memories by choosing for their recitation by heart such passages of popular verse as would be likely to appeal to them. And it is only right in this context to recall the delightful remark of Sophia Scott (Mrs Lockhart) when James Ballantyne asked her, shortly after the publication of *The Lady of the Lake*, if she, then aged ten or eleven, had read it: 'Oh, I have not read it; papa says there's nothing so bad for young people as reading bad poetry.'[16]

Scott also saw to it that his children were gradually made acquainted with the history of their own country, directing their attention to incidents and characters from it which illustrated the story he was telling; and in this way he probably largely anticipated for his children's ears what he later wrote for his grandchild in *Tales of a Grandfather*. He used the same methods ' of quickening curiosity as to the events of sacred history . . . and on [Sundays] inwove the simple pathos or sublime enthusiasm of Scripture, in whatever story he was telling, with the same picturesque richness as he did, in his week-day tales, the quaint Scotch of Pitscottie, or some rude romantic old rhyme from Barbour's *Bruce* or Blind Harry's *Wallace*',[17] Moreover, a frequent pastime for the family and their guests was reading aloud, Scott reserving Shakespeare to himself. Though done primarily for amusement, this reading had a cultural and educational value, even though some of it must have been above the children's heads.

But Scott was no believer in writing down or, it may be surmised, in speaking down to the supposed level of childish intelligence. 'Indeed,' he says, ' I rather suspect that children derive impulses of a powerful and important kind in learning things which they cannot entirely comprehend; and therefore, that to write *down* to children's understanding is a mistake: set them on the scent, and let them puzzle it out.'[18] Nearly twenty years later, when he had got the idea for *Tales of a Grandfather*, he recorded his conviction that children and the less literate readers hate books that write down to their capacity and prefer those composed for the fully literate. His would be a book that a child would understand and a man feel inclined to read. ' It will require, however,' he tells himself, ' a simplicity of stile not quite my own. The grand and interesting consists in ideas, not in words.'[19] He did in fact begin the *Tales* in a manner much simpler than his usual; but he soon discarded it on finding that a style considerably more elevated was actually more interesting to his grandson.

' There is no harm, but on the contrary there is benefit, in presenting a child with ideas somewhat beyond his easy and immediate comprehension. The difficulties thus offered, if not too great or too frequent, stimulate curiosity and encourage exertion.'[20]

There is another side to the question of the suitability for the young of some literature in its *ipsissima verba*, the question of bowdlerising. The boy Scott had apparently been allowed to read whatever he could lay his hands on; and no harm was thereby done. The man Scott took his literature with a healthy breadth, the bawdy being accepted as an occasional concomitant; and he was too much of a scholar not to give due respect to the text of any great author as it had come down. Accordingly, when in 1805 George Ellis recommended the omission from his edition of Dryden of ' whatever is in point of expression vulgar, whatever might have been written by any fool, whatever might be suppressed without exciting a moment's regret in the mind of any of his admirers ',[21] Scott was at first emphatic in his refusal to ' castrate John Dryden. I would as soon castrate my own father, as I believe Jupiter did of yore. What would you say to any man who would castrate Shakespeare, or Massinger, or Beaumont and Fletcher? '[22] He admits that ' it may be very proper to select correct passages for the use of boarding schools and colleges, being sensible no improper ideas can be suggested in these seminaries, unless they are intruded or smuggled under the beards and ruffs of our old dramatists '.[23] But he himself was preparing ' an edition of a man of genius's works for libraries and collections, and . . . I must give my author as I find him, and will not tear out the page, even to get rid of the blot, little as I like it '.[23] Swift, Pope, Prior and La Fontaine are all larded with indecency, sometimes of a very disgusting kind; yet they are to be seen ' upon all shelves and dressing-tables, and in all boudoirs '.[24] Manners, says Scott, are in fact corrupted, not by passages of humorous indelicacy, but by ' the sonnets which a prurient genius like

Master Little [25] sings *virginibus puerisque*—it is the sentimental slang, half lewd, half methodistic, that debauches the understanding, inflames the sleeping passions, and prepares the reader to give way as soon as the tempter appears '.[24]

Scott, however, was not very happy, even at the beginning of his undertaking, at the prospect of editing some of Dryden's comedies which are both stupid and gross; and he had to justify their inclusion on the score of considerable liveliness and humour in them and of the extraordinary pictures of the age which all the comedies present. When Scott had got as far in his editing as Dryden's translations of Lucretius, Ovid and Juvenal, he confessed to Ellis that ' After all, there are some passages . . . that will hardly bear reprinting, unless I would have the Bishop of London and the whole corps of Methodists about my ears. . . . They are not only double-entendres, but good plain single-entendres—not only broad, but long, and as coarse as the mainsail of a first-rate '.[26] Puzzled about what to do in the circumstances and strongly inclined to make some cuts, he referred the decision to Ellis, who made a volte-face (probably because for him the ancient classics were sacrosanct) and insisted that Scott must not omit the obnoxious passages.[27] And in the end Scott allowed himself to be persuaded.[28]

I do not think, however, that Scott's qualms in this special instance induced him to make any difference to the liberty his children enjoyed in their choice of books. No doubt he did put suitable literature into their hands. But they had the run of his well-stocked library, in which there was much that could be regarded as unsuitable. For he knew his children; he set them a good example; and he trusted Providence.

The fact of course is that Scott was more concerned to help his children to become men and women of the best type than to make them scholars. Nor did he set much store by most of what are called accomplishments. He once quoted to Mrs Hughes a stanza from one of his favourite ballads:[29]

> ' And I hae learnt my gay goss-hawk[30]
> Right weel to breast a steed,
> And I hae learnt my turtle duv
> As weel to write and read;'

to illustrate the simplicity in which he had tried to bring up his children and the active habits in which he had trained them.[31] He was no coddler of his children, boy or girl; and he would have been the last to discourage them from activities from which he had himself been to some extent debarred. But, as the stanza just quoted illustrates, there was one active accomplishment on which ' he fixed his heart hardly less than the ancient Persians of the Cyropaedia: like them, next to the love of truth, he held love of horsemanship for the prime point of education. . . . He taught [all his children] to think nothing of tumbles, and habituated them to his own reckless delight in perilous fords and flooded streams; and they all imbibed in great perfection his passion for horses—as well . . . as his deep reverence for the more important article of that Persian training. " Without courage," he said, " there cannot be truth; and without truth there can be no other virtue " '.[32]

As regards this primary virtue of truth-telling, I do not suppose that the young Scotts were uncommonly mendacious. But their father, with his penetrating awareness of human frailty, was under no sentimental delusion about the truthfulness of his own children or any others, as can be gathered from this frank passage in *Letters on Demonology and Witchcraft*: ' The melancholy truth that " the human heart is deceitful above all things, and desperately wicked ",[33] is by nothing proved so strongly as by the imperfect sense displayed by children of the sanctity of moral truth. . . . The child has no natural love of truth, as is experienced by all who have the least acquaintance with early youth. If they are charged with a fault while they can hardly speak, the first words they stammer forth are a falsehood to excuse it. Nor is this all: the temptation of attracting attention, the pleasure of enjoying importance, the desire to escape from an unpleasing task, or accomplish a holiday, will at any time overcome the sentiment of truth, so weak is it within them.'[34] We may conclude, then, that Scott took some trouble to teach the duty of truthfulness explicitly to his children and to enforce it gently and wisely. As for the other moral duties and also the courtesies and manners of good breeding, it would be more in character for him to trust in the main to the force of example, only occasionally dropping a word in season and from time to time directing their attention in their reading.

I have mentioned Scott's practice as regards Scriptural story-telling to his children. But his inculcation of religion went beyond the merely narrative, without becoming tiresomely didactic. As a boy and young man he had himself been accustomed to a religious discipline of the austerest kind, tempered, however, by the discreet concessions of Mrs Scott. His father's Presbyterianism and Sabbatarianism were those of the zealots in the Church of Scotland, whose leader, Dr John Erskine, was both one of his ministers at Greyfriars [35] and his confidential friend. His household had daily family worship (in addition to individual devotions) and graces before (if not also after) every meal, two protracted church services with an hour-long sermon in each on Sundays, and a catechizing on the Sunday evenings which included questions on the sermons heard, to say nothing of a strict prohibition of anything that could be called pleasure or recreation. Scott was repelled by ' the discipline of the Presbyterian Sabbath . . . severely strict, and I think injudiciously so . . . there was far too much tedium annexed to the duties of the day; and in the end it did none of us any good '.[36] And he waxed satirical at the depressing effect in his home of the whole week of services and sermons which were meant to be a preparation for the Communion: ' this being Sermon week . . . we are looking very religious

& very sour at home. However it is with *some folks selon les règles* that in proportion as they are pure themselves they are entitled to render uncomfortable those whom they consider as less perfect '.[37] He had, then, the most doleful memories of gloomy Sundays and fast days; and he reports with approval a friend's remarking that ' The chief reason for entering a Scottish Kirk is the pleasure of coming out again '.[38] Nevertheless Scott acquired a very thorough knowledge of the Bible and of the articles of Christianity. He held to them thereafter undeviatingly with a singular simplicity and sincerity, having, however, transferred his allegiance to the Anglican *via media*—or perhaps I should say ' most of his allegiance ', for he never broke entirely from the Church of Scotland. He never paraded his faith, and he disliked those who talked too much or unseasonably of religion. Hence his quaint advice to James Ballantyne ' of all things not to marry a very religious woman, for nothing can be a greater cause of unhappiness in a family '.[39] But his Christianity so suffuses his work that one who was not very far from the Kingdom of Heaven, Dean Stanley, declared his religion to be that of the Waverley Novels; and it was this faith that he mediated to his children with all his breadth and humanity and more by example than by precept.

After his own children had grown up, Scott got a chance to improve a scholastic curriculum in such a way as to set an example which every secondary school in the country has since followed. At the invitation of Henry Cockburn and Leonard Horner, who had conceived the idea of a new school for boys in Edinburgh, Scott joined them as one of the founders and original Directors of Edinburgh Academy, which was opened in October 1824. It is clear that what Cockburn and Horner originally wanted was simply a school with the same classical curriculum as the High School, but one in which the classical instruction would be better and carried further. Scott, however, weighed in with a revolutionary idea which Cockburn and Horner accepted. It was, to quote a letter of Scott's, the appointment of 'a separate master for English reading, orthography, geography, and history', who should give graded instruction to every class in the school. 'I am convinced,' he goes on to say, '. . . that by thus mixing the knowledge of the English language and Modern History with classical instruction the most useful impressions would be made on the youthful mind. We still carry the pedantry of former times a little too much into education, and boys are apt to think that learning Latin is the exclusive business of life and that all other acquisitions are of little consequence in comparison. Now though I am quite aware of the value of a classical education, yet I would not have it like Aaron's serpent swallow up all other attainments; and in my opinion, in order to form the *vir bonus*, domestic history and an acquaintance with our own language should be kept abreast of the acquisitions to be made in classical knowledge.'[40] I think that Scott himself drafted the Directors' prospectus, or at any rate the passage referring to the English master and his duty, which is now 'to give instruction in Reading, Elocution, and Modern History',[41] with a view to remedy a defect in the contemporary education of boys —the neglect of their native language and literature.

When Scott presided at the opening ceremony of the new Academy, he delivered an eloquent and highly characteristic speech. After giving a historical survey of education in Scotland, and explaining the motives and aims of the Directors, he suggested that, if 'they must lose some of the advantages of an ancient and venerable institution . . . the venerable Gothic temple, the long-sounding galleries, and turreted walls—where every association was favourable to learning,—they were also free from the prejudices peculiar to such seminaries,—the "rich windows that *exclude* the light, and passages that lead to nothing"'.[42] Then Scott went on to the curriculum for the new school, especially noticing the additions. Of course a thorough knowledge of Latin was to be imparted. Greek was to be begun earlier and carried farther than had hitherto been the practice in

Scottish schools. And writing, arithmetic, and mathematics were to be taught.[43] But it was on 'another class . . . which was not to be found in any other similar academy' that Scott expanded, 'a class for the study of English Literature. It has been justly remarked that the study of classics had sometimes led to the neglect of our own language. To avoid this error, a teacher . . . was to instruct the boys in the principles of English Composition, and to connect with this a knowledge of the history of their own country. He would have the youths taught to venerate the patriots and heroes of our own country, along with those of Greece and Rome; to know the histories of Wallace and Bruce, as well as those of Themistocles and of Caesar; and that the recollection of the fields of Flodden and Bannockburn should not be lost in those of Plataea and Marathon'.[42] In addition there would be prayers every morning and on Monday mornings a Scriptural lesson would be read by one of the boys.

NOTES ON REFERENCES

1   Cf. *Mr Burke's Speech on . . . Conciliation* in *Works* (1801), III, 46.
2   Lockhart, I, 64.
3   The Rev. George Thomson, who was the principal prototype of Dominie Sampson in *Guy Mannering* (cf. Mrs Hughes, 89, 299-300). Scott admired his ability and his character, but had to admit that 'there is an eccentricity about him that defies description' (*Journal*, I, 59; 28th December 1825). As has been noticed, James Ballantyne saw a considerable resemblance between Lancelot Whale and Dominie Sampson. And Gillies believed that a certain very learned 'law grinder', James Hogg, contributed something to the Dominie's portrait (49-50).
4   Lockhart, II, 760.
5   Lockhart, I, 165.
6   J. Frederick Pole long attended Scott's daughters as a teacher of the harp. Scott was deeply touched by Pole's offer in 1826 of £500 or £600. It was 'probably his all', said

Scott in his *Journal*. '. . . But I will involve no friend, either rich or poor. My own right hand shall do it—else will I be *done* in the slang language, and *undone* in common parlance.' (I, 76; 22nd January 1826).

7   *Letters*, V, 407-8 (8th July 1819).

8   I, 164.

9   Lockhart, I, 164.

10 V, 290-363 (1805-6 version).

11 *The Prelude*, V, 364-69 (1805-6 version).

12 Lockhart, I, 164. Charles Lamb had exactly the same objection to the works of Mrs Barbauld and Company which had 'banished all the old classics of the nursery . . . knowledge insignificant and vapid as Mrs Barbauld's books convey . . . must come to a child in the *shape* of *knowledge*; and his empty noddle must be turned with conceit of his own powers when he has learnt that a horse is an animal, and Billy is better than a horse, and such like; instead of that beautiful interest in wild tales, which made the child a man, while all the time he suspected himself to be no bigger than a child. . . . Think what you would have been now, if instead of being fed with tales and old wives' fables in childhood, you had been crammed with geography and natural history!' (*Lamb's Criticism*. Ed by E. M. W. Tillyard, 86).

13 *Waverley*, Chapter III.

14 In the *General Preface* Scott avows that his novel-writing was in part due to her example. 'Without being so presumptuous as to hope to emulate the rich humour, pathetic tenderness, and admirable tact' of Miss Edgeworth, he felt that something of the same kind as her Irish stories might be attempted for Scotland.

15 *Letters*, IX, 237-38 (12th October 1825).

16 Lockhart, I, 196.

17 Lockhart, I, 164-5.

18 *Memoir*, I, 7, note 1.

19 *Journal*, II, 55 (24th May 1827).

20 *Grandfather*, Preface.

21 To Scott, 26th October 1805 (*Letters*, I, 264, note 3).

22 *Letters*, I, 264-65 (to George Ellis, end of October or beginning of November 1805).

23   *Letters*, I, 265.

24   *Letters*, I, 265.

25   I.e. Thomas Moore, whose second publication was *The Poetical Works of the Late Thomas Little, Esq.*, 1801.

26   *Letters*, I, 284 (7th April 1806).

27   To Scott, 13th May 1806 (*Letters*, I, 284, note 1).

28   In the Introduction to Canto First of *Marmion* (begun in November 1806) he laments that Dryden for a ' niggard pay ' provided for ' a ribald King and Court . . . Licentious satire, song, and play '.

29   Cf. *The Abbot*, Note IX:—

> And you shall learn my gay goss-hawk
> > Right well to breast a steed;
> And so will I your turtle-dow,
> > As well to write and read.'

It does not in fact appear in the version in *Minstrelsy* (III, 187-98).

30   The name he affectionately applied to his son Walter (cf. *Letters*, VIII, 487; to John Richardson, 21st January 1825).

31   Mrs Hughes, 102.

32   Lockhart, I, 165.

33   *Jeremiah*, xvii, 9.

34   Letter VII.

35   The other, Principal William Robertson, was the leader of the Moderates in the Church.

36   *Memoir*, I, 8.

37   *Letters*, I, 38 (to Christian Rutherford, October or November 1794).

38   Grierson, 6.

39   Grierson, 5.

40   The letter appears to have been published for the first time in an article by D. C. Thomson on *Sir Walter and the Academy* in *The Scotsman*, 29th August 1952.

41   Ibid.

42   Lockhart, I, 526. The concluding quotation is from Thomas Gray's *Long Story*.

43   Apparently the High School in Scott's day had provided little or no instruction in these subjects; and Scott himself, as has been indicated (*supra*, 25, 26), had to go elsewhere for them.

CHAPTER V

FIRST UNIVERSITY PERIOD

[I]f my learning be flimsy and inaccurate, the reader must have some compassion even for an idle workman, who had so narrow a foundation to build upon. If, however, it should ever fall to the lot of youth to peruse these pages—let such a reader remember, that it is with the deepest regret that I recollect in my manhood the opportunities of learning which I neglected in my youth; that through every part of my literary career I have felt pinched and hampered by my own ignorance; and that I would at this moment give half the reputation I have had the good fortune to acquire, if by doing so, I could rest the remaining part upon a sound foundation of learning and science.

Memoir, I, 13.

THE number of students at the beginning of Scott's attendance at Edinburgh University, where he found himself again with his old High School intimates, was about a thousand, of whom nearly a half were in the Faculty of Arts. Owing to the average age at matriculation, at least in that Faculty, there must have been much less distinction between school and University than there is now (that is to say, particularly in respect of such classes as were academic continuations of scholastic ones); and such accounts of conditions as have come down indicate a scholastic, rather than an academic, discipline, and a scholastic relation between teachers and taught. It does not follow, however, that the standard was elementary. The curriculum for a degree required attendance during four regular sessions, and a course, which might be taken in any order, comprehending Latin, Greek, Rhetoric and Belles Lettres, Logic and Metaphysics, Moral Philosophy, Natural Philosophy, and Mathematics. It was customary, if not necessary, to attend some at least of these classes for two or more years. There were no regular written examinations, unless the class essays may be so regarded; proficiency appears to have been gauged by oral questioning and by the general observations of the professors. Candidates for a degree in Arts were examined by each professor at least a week before the Senatus meeting at which those who had satisfied the examiners could be recommended for graduation. In point of fact graduations were exceptional in the eighteenth century, not more than one or two per annum between 1750 and 1800.[1]

The name of 'Gaulterus Scott' (sic) appears for the first time in the Matriculation Album, under the date 1783 and among the 'Discipuli' of John Hill, Professor of Humanity. Unlike many of his fellow-students Scott figured in the class only for one session, perhaps giving attendance both in the Classis Tyronum or junior section for two hours a day and in the Classis Provectiorum or senior for one.[2] The authors read in both sections were pretty much the same and largely determined by the curriculum at the High

School, from which many of Hill's students came. In the advanced division of the class, however, greater proficiency was expected and two lectures a week were devoted to antiquities and other ancillary studies. Though Hill assumed considerable familiarity in his students with the Latin language and did not regularly teach the elements, he took the utmost pains in discriminating nice shades of meaning.[3] Apparently, however, he was too amiable to be a disciplinarian; and for all his sense of humour, his celebrity as a punster, and his general vivacity, he was not a very successful teacher of a large class of restive adolescents. Scott describes him as holding ' the reins of discipline very loosely, and though beloved by his students, for he was a good-natured man as well as a good scholar, he had not the art of exciting our attention as well as liking '.[4] His, then, in Scott's opinion was ' a dangerous character with whom to trust one who relished labour as little as I did '.[4] Scott's junior, Henry Cockburn, says of the class some ten years later that ' the mischief was that little Latin was acquired. The class was a constant scene of unchecked idleness and disrespectful mirth. Our time was worse than lost '.[5] So ' amid the riot of [Hill's] class ' [6] Scott acquired little and ' speedily lost much ' [6] that he had already gained under Adam and Whale. In his modest way he confided to his *Journal*: ' I know nothing of the Latin lingo ', when he was approached to review William Sotheby's polyglot Virgil.[7] And he regarded himself as ' no great judge ' when consulted ' about the propriety and possibility of retaining the northern pronunciation of the Latin in the new Edinburgh Academy '.[8] Nevertheless he left the University a very respectable Latinist, with no pretensions to accuracy, but with an ability to read a Latin author of any age so as to get the meaning without difficulty and to quote readily and by no means merely in tags and commonplaces. Phrases and longer passages in prose or in verse drop casually from his pen in his letters and *Journal*, in his novels and indeed everything he wrote, and always felicitously. Often enough

the quotation is adapted to the context; or Scott departs
from the original wording but retains the sense, very much
as the Academy boys who, when given the English by the
Rector, returned 'with singular dexterity the Latin [of
Virgil and Livy], not exactly as in the original, but often
by synonymes, which showed that the exercize referd to
the judgment, and did not depend on the memory'.[9]
Poetical quotations made by Scott are sometimes defective
metrically, not only because he had substituted one word
for another, but because 'Forty years ago, longs and shorts
were little attended to in Scottish education; and I have,
it appears, forgot the little I may then have learned'.[10]

Like his Edward Waverley, Scott 'would throw himself
with spirit upon any classical author . . . , make himself
master of the style so far as to understand the story, and,
if that pleased or interested him, he finished the volume.
But it was in vain to attempt fixing his attention on critical
distinctions of philology, upon the difference of idioms, the
beauty of felicitous expression, or the artificial combinations
of syntax. "I can read and understand a Latin author,"
said young Edward, with the self-confidence and rash
reasoning of fifteen, "and Scaliger or Bentley could not do
much more." '[11]

In later life Scott's favourite Latin poet (and historian)
was Buchanan. Of how many classical experts could it
be said that they had a favourite Latin author, or that they
had ever dipped into Buchanan? Other Latin poets for
whom Scott preserved or acquired a liking were the more
ancient but still notably post-classical Lucan and Claudian.[12]
As for Buchanan's place in his regard, it has to be taken
with such qualification as will be suggested by his remark
to Crabbe: 'To my Gothic ear, indeed, the *Stabat Mater*,
the *Dies Irae*, and some of the other hymns of the Catholic
Church, are more solemn and affecting than the fine classical
poetry of Buchanan'.[13]

As was the custom, Scott entered the Greek department
the same year as the Latin. He spent one session (1783-84)

in the Classis Tyronum and the next (1784-85) in the Classis Provectiorum, both of which met for two hours a day. Attendance at Greek for at least two sessions was necessary for graduation; and many students remained three, some four, and a few even six years. The reason for such prolonged sojourns was that, despite *The Book of Discipline's* scheme in 1560 for a four-years' course in Greek in Scottish grammar schools, Greek had never become a common or particularly well-taught school subject. Consequently few of their pupils went to the Universities with more than a smattering, if as much as that, however well read they were in Latin; and till late in the eighteenth century in Scotland only such philhellenists as James Burnett, Lord Monboddo had something like an adequate conception of the greatness of Greek culture. In actual fact, by teaching Greek at all, the schools were flouting authority and seventeenth-century regulations from at latest 1645 conferring a monopoly of the subject on the Universities, which with extraordinary shortsightedness did their best to retain this absurd privilege. As late as 1772 Principal Robertson, probably at the instigation of the retiring Professor Robert Hunter, protested against Adam's beginning to teach the rudiments of Greek to his senior pupils at the High School;[14] but the Town Council very properly declined to interfere.

The Professor of Greek in Scott's day was Andrew Dalzel, who had come to the Chair in 1772. His enthusiasm revived the subject, which had been sadly neglected in Edinburgh, particularly under his immediate predecessor; and he helped considerably in restoring the University's classical repute and in attracting students from England and abroad. 'Mr Dalzel,' said Alexander Monro *primus*,[15] 'had more to brag of than any man in the College, for Greek was going fast downhill till he revived it.'[16] By 1784 he could boast that he had 'about one hundred and eighty students attending me, which is the greatest Greek class ever was heard of since the foundation of our College'.[17] In the tyros' class he was forced to begin with the rudiments, in the teaching of which his 'patient industry . . . was perhaps never exceeded and his zeal the admiration of all'.[18] Cockburn, it is true, ten years after Scott's attendance, found him ineffective in the purely linguistic teaching of a hundred or more lads to many of whom the very alphabet was new.[19] But at any rate, his method at least was excellent for those who cared to profit; he knew moreover how to put that method down on paper; and his textbooks[20] were greatly admired and in use all over Britain.[21] It was, however, the general lectures twice a week to his senior class, on Greek history, antiquities, philosophy, art, and literature, with copious illustrations from the classics and modern poets, which won the highest praise. They were meant to serve as 'an introduction to the study of general literature; and . . . were well adapted to answer this end'.[22] They may be regarded, then, to some extent as carrying on the distinguished work of Hugh Blair, Professor of Rhetoric and Belles Lettres, who retired in 1784,[23] much better than Blair's successor in office, William Greenfield, whose class was never more than thinly attended.

To Cockburn it was 'a duty, and delightful, to record Dalzel's value as a general exciter of boys' minds. Dugald Stewart alone excepted, he did me more good than all the other instructors I had. Mild, affectionate, simple, an absolute enthusiast about learning . . .; with an innocence of soul and of manner which imparted an air of honest kindliness to whatever he said or did, and a slow, soft, formal voice,[24] he was a great favourite with all boys, and with all good men. Never was a voyager, out in quest of new islands, more delighted in finding one, than he was in discovering any good quality in any humble youth. . . . He could never make us actively laborious. But when we sat passive, and listened to him, he inspired us with a vague but sincere ambition of literature, and with delicious dreams of virtue and poetry. He must have been a hard boy whom these discourses, spoken by Dalzel's low, soft, artless voice did not melt'.[25]

Scott, unfortunately, proved himself a very 'hard boy' indeed. He admits that he 'might have made a better figure' than in Hill's Latin class, 'for Professor Dalzel maintained a great deal of authority, and was not only himself an admirable scholar, but was always deeply interested in the progress of his students'.[26] But Scott had somehow, probably by being only one and a half sessions in the Rector's class, missed the little Greek which most of his High School contemporaries had acquired. Apparently in a kind of stubborn self-defence, he declined to acquire it now, though languages came easily to him; 'and finding myself far inferior to all my fellow-students',[27] he says, 'I could hit upon no better mode of vindicating my equality than by professing my contempt for the language, and my resolution not to learn it. A youth who died early, himself an excellent Greek scholar, saw my negligence and folly with pain, instead of contempt. He came to call on me in George's Square, and pointed out in the strongest terms the silliness of the conduct I had adopted, told me I was distinguished by the name of the *Greek Blockhead*, and exhorted me to redeem my reputation while it was called to-day. My stubborn pride received this advice with sulky civility; the birth of my Mentor (whose name was Archibald, the son of an innkeeper) did not, as I thought in my folly, authorize him to intrude upon me his advice. He offered me his daily and nightly assistance, and pledged himself to bring me forward with the foremost of my class. I felt some twinges of conscience, but they were unable to prevail over my pride and self-conceit. The poor lad left me more in sorrow than in anger, nor did we ever meet again. All hopes of my progress in the Greek were now over.'[28] Moreover, whatever benefit Scott derived from Dalzel's general lectures, he went out of his way to assert in a class essay a preference for Ariosto to Homer, supporting 'this heresy by a profusion of bad reading and flimsy argument'.[28] The mild Dalzel for once was extremely angry, but 'at the same time he could not suppress his surprise at the quantity of out-of-the-way knowledge which I displayed. He pronounced upon me the severe sentence—that dunce I was, and dunce was to remain—which, however, my excellent friend lived to revoke over a bottle of Burgundy at our literary Club at Fortune's '.[29]

Perhaps Scott and Dalzel agreed also, though for different reasons, that Presbyterianism had not been an unmixed blessing in Scotland. In spite of his Clerkship to the General Assembly,[30] Dalzel was jealous of the happier state of Episcopal England in one respect at least, and, *teste* Sydney Smith, was heard to mutter on a dark night, ' If it had not been for that confounded Solemn League and Covenant, we would have made as good longs and shorts as they.'[31]

Scott's tincture of Greek, as it happened, very soon evaporated when he fell ill in the middle of his second session and was left to a self-education which did not include the classics. This illness should not be confused with the serious haemorrhage which nearly cost him his life in the following year and to which I shall have to refer later.[32] But it was sufficiently serious for him to be sent ' a second time to Kelso—where I again continued a long time reading what and how I pleased, and of course reading nothing but what afforded me immediate entertainment. The only thing ', he continues, ' which saved my mind from utter dissipation, was that turn for historical pursuit, which never abandoned me even at the idlest period. I had forsworn the Latin classics for no reason I know of, unless because they were akin to the Greek; but the occasional perusal of Buchanan's history, that of Matthew Paris, and other monkish chronicles, kept up a kind of familiarity with the language even in its rudest state. But I forgot the very letters of the Greek alphabet; a loss never to be repaired, considering what that language is, and who they were who employed it in their compositions.'[33]

Perhaps Scott never knew the Greek alphabet very well. As early as 1793 he wrote in a letter to an intimate friend,

Patrick Murray of Simprim, even so simple a tag as 'the real *To Kalon*', avoiding the Greek characters.[34]   On the other hand, in the 1813 Introduction to *The Bridal of Trier-main* he quotes two sentences in Greek characters.[35]   And in the *Essay on Chivalry* of 1818 he introduces 'ἱππόδαμος and 'Εκτορ into the text.[36]   It is possible that he was helped out on both occasions by a scholarly friend.[37]   Certainly in 1830 Lockhart had to insert for him ἀοιδός and ποιητής in the *Introductory Remarks on Popular Poetry* for the new edition of the *Border Minstrelsy*.[38]   It was probably also Lockhart who for the 1830 Introduction to *The Lady of the Lake* supplied a line and a half of the *Odyssey*; Scott himself having remembered an apt couplet from Pope's Homer.   When Scott visited Edinburgh Academy in 1827, he 'heard Greek, of which', he said, 'I am no otherwise a judge than that it was fluently read and explained.'[39]

This ignorance of one of the accepted corner-stones of a liberal education was the cause of deep regret to Scott— 'a loss never to be repaired, considering what that language is, and who they were who employed it in their composi- tions'.[40]   In his *Essay on the Drama* he speaks with awe of 'Greece—of that wonderful country, whose days of glory have left such a never-dying blaze of radiance behind them'.[41] Likewise in his speech at the opening of Edinburgh Academy in 1824 he spoke reverently of Greek as 'that beautiful language', 'the language of the fathers of history, and of a people whose martial achievements and noble deeds were the ornaments of their pages'.[42]   With a characteristic modesty he always regarded his own varied and self-chosen acquirements as no real compensation.   He was only 'half- educated' in his own opinion, 'almost wholly neglected or left to myself, stuffing my head with most nonsensical trash'.[43]   Throughout his literary career (he was writing in 1808; but he would have written in the same strain till the end of his days) he felt 'pinched and hampered' by his ignorance, and would have sacrificed half the reputation he had won if by so doing he might have based what remained on ' a sound foundation of learning and science '.[44]

But, if Scott was virtually ignorant of Greek as a language, he seems to have made himself tolerably familiar with its literature through translations, literary history, and the like. Perhaps as striking an illustration as any is his well-informed description of the Greek theatre and drama and his discussion, as acute as Dr Johnson's,[45] of the doctrine of the unities in respect of both ancient and modern dramaturgy.[46] But there is plenty of scattered evidence for Scott's acquaintance at secondhand with a considerable amount of Greek literature, some of it rather out-of-the-way. At some time or other, then, the Greek Blockhead had done his best to make up for his wilful neglect.

During the academic year 1784-85, the second of his sessions in the Greek department, Scott was also a member of the Classis Prima in Logic and Metaphysics; and in 1785-86 he entered his name for both the Classis Junior (i.e. Prima) and the Classis Provectior. But he himself does not state that he was two years in the department.[47] In consequence of this and through wrongly assuming that the illness which sent Scott to Kelso to convalesce in his second academic year was the same as the haemorrhage which nearly killed him in his third, Lockhart was led to suppose that Scott was not at the University at all in 1785-86.[48] The Professor of Logic and Metaphysics was John Bruce.[49] He was popular with his students and admired by them, perhaps because he had a clear head and was not too profound. But he had ambitions beyond the walls of a University, and the kind of talents which promised him a distinguished or at least a more lucrative career in affairs; and four years after Scott had ' sat under ' him, he resigned his Chair and moved to London where he held several important offices and was for six years a Member of Parliament.[50] His class was one in which Scott was ' rather more fortunate '.[51] He ' made some progress '[51] in the subject and was one of the students chosen to read an essay before Principal Robertson.[52] This success under Bruce and also

Scott's doing well in Dugald Stewart's Moral Philosophy rather controverts Lockhart's conviction that Scott would never have derived either pleasure or profit from ' a long course of Scotch metaphysics '.[53]

It would seem from Scott's attending at his father's instance, in 1784-85 or more probably in 1785-86, a class in mathematics, conducted by Dr Ebenezer MacFait in Merlin's Wynd,[54] that there may have been some intention of preparing him for the University class in the same subject under the joint Professors Adam Ferguson and John Playfair. MacFait, who died at an advanced age in 1786, ' had in his time been distinguished as a teacher ' of mathematics.[55] But he was also a physician of some note, a good Greek scholar, and a miscellaneous writer.[56] ' Age, however, and some domestic inconveniences had diminished his pupils, and lessened his authority amongst the few who remained.'[57] Nevertheless Scott entered on his mathematical studies ' with all the ardour of novelty '[58]; but he left off with what he regarded as only ' a very superficial smattering ',[58] though he believed he could have made better progress under different instruction and with ' the spur of emulation '.[58] The little that he picked up from MacFait included some knowledge of fortification,[59] which, as will be noted,[60] he later applied on a miniature scale to while away the tedium of convalescence.

NOTES ON REFERENCES

1   Except in 1778 when a batch of honorary degrees were conferred.

2   The list of students in the Matriculation Album is not divided into junior and senior. Another contemporary list of students gives Scott only in the junior section as paying half-a-crown (for Library purposes). But it is not now clear what convention governed the inclusion or the omission of a name in such cases.

3   He published a syllabus of his class-work, *Heads of Lectures for the Use of the Highest Class of Students in Humanity in the University of Edinburgh*, 1780; a laborious work on *The Synonymes of the Latin Language . . . with . . . Dissertations upon the Force of its Prepositions*, 1804; and a *Vocabulary*, intended as an Introduction to the Study of the Synonymes of the Latin Language, 1804. His *Account of the Life and Writings of Hugh Blair* was published posthumously in 1807.

4   *Memoir*, I, 12.

5   17.

6   *Memoir*, I, 12.

7   I, 256.

8   *Journal*, II, 12 (24th January 1827).

9   Ibid., II, 73 (9th July 1827).

10 *Letters*, VIII, 418 (to the Editor of *The Morning Post*, 12th November 1824). The following Latin classics at Abbotsford were in Scott's boyhood library (among, no doubt, others lost or given away): two copies of Juvenal and Persius (he dated one 19th May 1781 and the other 19th May 1784), and a 1601 Petronius Arbiter (given him by his uncle, Dr Daniel Rutherford). The following translations from Latin, acquired in boyhood, also survive at Abbotsford: Suetonius translated ' By Several Hands ' (given by Mrs Margaret Swinton), and *Terence's Comedies made English* by Laurence Echard, Sir Roger L'Estrange, etc.

11 *Waverley*, Chapter III.

12 On 29th May 1793 he bought himself a copy of Catullus, Tibullus, and Propertius.

13 *Letters*, III, 211 (to George Crabbe, about January 1813).

14 Greek had been taught there in the sixteenth century; but it apparently fell out of the curriculum and was reintroduced in 1614 by the Rector, John Ray, who died in 1630. Whether Greek continued to be taught is doubtful. There was certainly none at the High School when Henry Mackenzie was a pupil (1752-57).

15 Three Alexander Monros, grandfather, father, and son, held the Chair of Anatomy between 1720 and 1846.

16 Grant, II, 325.

17 Ibid., II, 325.

18 Bower, III, 137.

19   17.
20   Ἀνάλεκτα Ἑλληνικὰ Ἥσσονα, sive Collectanea Graeca
      Minora, 1785; Ἀνάλεκτα Ἑλληνικά Μείζονα, sive Collect-
      anea Graeca Majora, 1787; and Fragmenta Grammatices Graecae,
      left unfinished at Dalzel's death in 1806 but published the
      same year by James Moor in Elementa Linguae Graecae. These
      books were frequently reprinted, some of the editions being
      continental or American. A faint echo of Dalzel's Ἀνάλεκτα
      has been detected by its editor, J. G. Tait, in Scott's Journal
      (I, 8, 97, note 1).   Dalzel also published Description of the
      Plain of Troy, translated from the original [by Jean Baptiste
      Lechevalier] not yet published, 1791; and M. Chevalier's
      Tableau de la Plaine de Troye illustrated and confirmed, 1798.
      He wrote one or two other works of a biographical or
      genealogical kind and left unfinished A History of the Uni-
      versity of Edinburgh, which was edited with additions and
      published by David Laing in two volumes in 1862. The
      first volume contains a memoir of Dalzel by Cosmo Innes.
21   Dalzel indeed enjoyed a continental and American fame
      as well and corresponded with many scholars both at home
      and abroad.
22   Bower, III, 139.   After Dalzel's death, his son John pub-
      lished Substance of Lectures on the Ancient Greeks and on the
      Revival of Greek Learning in Europe, in two volumes in 1821.
23   He published his Lectures on Rhetoric and Belles Lettres in
      two volumes in 1783.
24   I hope that this voice did not suggest the name of Dugald
      Dalgetty's preceptor at Marischal College, Aberdeen—Pro-
      fessor Snufflegreek (A Legend of Montrose, Chapter XIII).
25   Cockburn, 17-18.
26   Memoir, I, 12.
27   He had felt the same sort of inferiority on first going to
      the High School (cf. supra, 16-17).
28   Memoir, I, 12.
29   Memoir, I, 12.   Fortune's Tontine Tavern was in Princes
      Street.
30   Says Cockburn 'this simple and worthy man' was 'long
      one of the curiosities of that strange place'; but, adds
      Cockburn, 'He was too innocent for it' (18).
31   Cockburn, 19.   But Graham attributes almost the same

remark to Dr Archibald Pitcairne (9).

32 Cf. *infra*, 106, 107, 136-39.

33 *Memoir*, I, 12.

34 *Letters*, I, 27 (13th September 1793). Cf. *Redgauntlet*,
Chapter XIV: ' Ay, I say the Jumping Jenny can run in
other wares as well as kegs. Put *sigma* and *tau* to *Ewart*,
and see how that will spell'; and *Kenilworth*, Chapter IX:
' [T]he erudite Diedrichus Buckershockius . . . dedicated
to me . . . his treatise on the letter *Tau*.' In a notebook
at Abbotsford begun by Scott in 1792 is a verse translation,
apparently by himself, of a ' Greek Ballad'; but he may
have got the substance secondhand.

35 *P.W.*, 586. The one sentence comes from Diogenes
Laertius; and the other from a *Homeri Vita* in Henri
Etienne's 1570 edition of Herodotus.

36 *Prose*, 525.

37 e.g. William Erskine (Lord Kinnedder), who suggested the
theme of *The Bridal* and who, through a mystification,
was half-supected of being the author; or George Cranstoun
(Lord Corehouse), who on account of his Greek had been
pronounced by Lord Monboddo ' the only *scholar in all
Scotland* (Paton, II, 438).

38 Lockhart, I, 36, and *Minstrelsy*, I, 4-5.

39 *Journal*, II, 73 (9th July 1827). Cf. *ibid.*, I, 97 (10th February
1826): ' it was always when I first opend my eyes that the
desired ideas thronged upon me. . . . There is a passage
about this sort of matutinal inspiration in the *Odyssey*,
which would make a handsome figure here if I could read
or write Greek. I will look into Pope for it who ten to
one will not tell me the real translation '.

40 *Memoir*, I, 12.

41 575.

42 Lockhart, II, 526.

43 *Journal*, I, 50 (18th December 1825).

44 *Memoir*, I, 13. In the context ' science' is used in the
now rather uncommon sense of merely ' knowledge '.

45 *The Rambler*, no. 156 and the Preface to Shakespeare.

46 *Drama*, 575-84, 593-601.

47 *Memoir*, I, 12. Chambers suggests that Scott may have
attended other classes without matriculating (25). But it

is very unlikely that he did or could have done so.

48   I, 35.

49   Scott gives ' Ethics ' as the subject of Bruce's class, mentioning ' Moral Philosophy ' a few lines later as the subject of Professor Dugald Stewart's class (*Memoir*, I, 12). Bruce published a syllabus of his lectures entitled *First Principles of Philosophy for the use of Students*, 1776; and *Elements of the Science of Ethics on the Principles of Natural Philosophy*, 1786.

50   In 1865 his daughter, Mrs Tyndall Bruce of Falkland, founded in his memory the Bruce of Grangehill and Falkland Scholarships, which are tenable at Edinburgh University.

51   *Memoir*, I, 12.

52   On 9th November 1827 Scott, as a member of the Royal Commission on the Scottish Universities, went to hear an essay read in one of the classrooms. But ' The lads . . . had so effectually taken possession . . . that, neither learning or law, neither Magistrates nor Magisters, neither visitors nor visited, could make way to the scene of action. So we grandees were obliged to adjourn the sederunt till Saturday the 17th ' (*Journal*, II, 130).

53   I, 36.

54   An Ebenezer McFait, musician, lived in Con's Close about the same time.

55   *Memoir*, I, 12.

56   His chief publications were:—*Remarks on the Life and Writings of Plato*, 1760; and *A New System of General Geography . . . With a View of the Solar System . . . with the . . . Natural History of the Earth*, 1780.

57   *Memoir*, I, 12.

58   *Memoir*, I, 12.

59   Mathematics and military architecture were taught in association by another versatile Edinburgh tutor, John Wright, mainly, it would appear, for young men going to India.

60   Cf. *infra*, 139.

CHAPTER VI

THE ROMANTIC AND ANTI-CLASSICAL

Alas! while he was thus permitted to read only for the gratification of his amusement, he foresaw not that he was losing for ever the opportunity of acquiring habits of firm and assiduous application, of gaining the art of controlling, directing, and concentrating the powers of his mind for earnest investigation—an art far more essential than even that intimate acquaintance with classical learning which is the primary object of study.

Waverley, *Chapter III.*

No, Captain, the funds, from which I have drawn my power of amusing the public, have been bought otherwise than by fortuitous adventure. I have buried myself in libraries, to extract from the nonsense of ancient days new nonsense of my own. I have turned over volumes, which, from the pot-hooks I was obliged to decipher, might have been the cabalistic manuscripts of Cornelius Agrippa . . . all the domestic inhabitants of the libraries were disturbed by the vehemence of my studies—

> *From my research the boldest spider fled,*
> *And moths, retreating, trembled as I read.*

The Monastery, *Answer by ' The Author of Waverley ',*
to . . . Captain Clutterbuck.

THE previous chapter brought us to the end of Scott's first academic period; and in this chapter I should like to make some general comments. He was at the University when there were no options for a degree curriculum, no modern language departments (Rhetoric and Belles Lettres hardly counting as one[1]), and (with the exception of Universal History) no medieval or antiquarian studies. The University gave its alumni what scholars considered to be the essentials of culture, and those who had other tastes had to satisfy themselves elsewhere. So it was with Scott, who had to educate himself in the subjects of his choice. The true explanation of his unimpressive academic record is that he was a man of the Romantic Revival, born into a world of neo-classic elders. He was not inclined, like Wordsworth, Coleridge, and Southey, to political rebelliousness in his youth; but he had received a double portion of the historical and medieval enthusiasm which was one of the symptoms of Romanticism, and not altogether creditable in the opinion of the orthodox. His familiarity with Latin had comparatively little to do with the ancient classics; Latin was a *sine qua non* in his antiquarianism, and he mastered it in order to devour Matthew Paris and the monkish chroniclers, Fordun, Buchanan and the Scottish annalists, rather than to savour Virgil. To the medieval and romantic he responded instinctively, to the classical scarcely at all.[2] When sick and old he visited Malta, he was so thrilled by the medieval remains of which he had read with boyish delight fifty years before in Vertot's *Knights of Malta* that he 'looked round earnestly, and said—" It will be hard if I cannot make something of this "'.[3] On the other hand, among the classical antiquities of Pozzuoli he replied to Sir William Gell's lecture ' that we might tell him anything, and he would believe it all, for many of his friends, and particularly Mr Morritt, had frequently tried to drive classical antiquities, as they were called, into his head, but they had always proved his " skull too thick "'.[4] And to Gell's dissertation on the Lake of Avernus he abstractedly remarked, but ' in a grave tone and with great emphasis ':[5]

> ' Up the craggy mountain, and down the mossy glen,
> We canna gang a-milking, for Charlie and his men.'[6]

It was something more than caprice or bravado that made Scott prefer Ariosto to Homer;[7] it was, as R. H. Hutton remarks,[8] a deep literary instinct.

Scott himself indeed realised what his true bent was and both avowed and excused it in the lines to William Erskine (later Lord Kinnedder) whose advice had been to follow in his poetry the acknowledged masters,

> ' Nor ramble on through brake and maze,
> With harpers rude of barbarous days.'

Thus Scott replies:

> ' But say, my Erskine, hast thou weigh'd
> That secret power by all obey'd,
> Which warps not less the passive mind,
> Its source conceal'd or undefin'd;
> Whether an impulse, that has birth
> Soon as the infant wakes on earth,
> One with our feelings and our powers,
> And rather part of us than ours;
> Or whether fitlier term'd the sway
> Of habit, form'd in early day?
> Howe'er deriv'd, its force confest
> Rules with despotic sway the breast,
> And drags us on by viewless chain,
> While taste and reason plead in vain. . . .
> For me, thus nurtur'd, dost thou ask,
> The classic poet's well-conn'd task?
> Nay, Erskine, nay; on the wild hill
> Let the wild heath-bell flourish still;
> Cherish the tulip, prune the vine,
> But freely let the woodbine twine,
> And leave untrimm'd the eglantine: . . .

> Though wild as cloud, as stream, as gale
> Flow forth, flow unrestrain'd, my Tale.'[9]

In the Introduction to Canto First of *Marmion* Scott had already addressed a less deprecating justification to a brother in the romantic faith, William Stewart Rose:[10]

> 'thou, my friend, can'st fitly tell,
> (For few have read romance so well,)
> How still the legendary lay
> O'er poet's bosom holds its sway;
> How on the ancient minstrel strain
> Time lays his palsied hand in vain;
> And how our hearts at doughty deeds,
> By warriors wrought in steely weeds,
> Still throb for fear and pity's sake.

Had not " The mightiest chiefs of British song ", Spenser, Milton, and Dryden, been drawn to the old romances?   So

> ' Warm'd by such names, well may we then,
> Though dwindled sons of little men,
> Essay to break a feeble lance
> In the fair fields of old romance.'

And in the Introduction to the last canto of *Marmion*, addressed to an orthodox classicist, Richard Heber,[11] Scott returns to a re-iteration of his romantic preferences, this time in a gently bantering way:

> ' Cease, then, my friend ! a moment cease,
> And leave these classic tomes in peace !
> Of Roman and of Grecian lore,
> Sure mortal brain can hold no more.
> These ancients, as Noll Bluff[12] might say,
> " Were pretty fellows in their day ";
> But time and tide o'er all prevail—
> On Christmas eve a Christmas tale[13]—
> Of wonder and of war.'

Then to Heber's imagined protest against the proposal:

> '"Profane!
> What! leave the lofty Latian strain,
> Her stately prose, her verse's charms,
> To hear the clash of rusty arms:
> In Fairy Land or Limbo lost,
> To jostle conjurer and ghost,
> Goblin and witch!"'

Scott replies that ghosts, omens, and the like are not unknown in the ancient classics themselves:

> 'Nay, Heber dear,
> Before you touch my charter, hear: . . .
> in realms of death
> Ulysses meets Alcides' *wraith*;
> Aeneas, upon Thracia's shore,
> The ghost of murder'd Polydore;
> For omens, we in Livy cross,
> At every turn, *locutus Bos*.
> As grave and duly speaks the ox,
> As if he told the price of stocks;
> Or held, in Rome republican,
> The place of common-councilman.'

Indeed:

> 'All nations have their omens drear,
> Their legends wild of woe and fear.'

'I was never a dunce,' said Scott, 'nor thought to be so, but an incorrigibly idle imp,[14] who was always longing to do something else than what was enjoined him.'[15] Bating the 'incorrigibly idle', there is Scott's University career in a nutshell; he did not long to do nothing, but to do something which, with a modest deference to the views of others, he thought unimportant. Even with respect to the regular academic studies in 'those admirable works of classical learning, on which such value is justly placed at the present time ',[16] he probably depreciated his own industry and underrated his own attainments. More than once he alludes to ' the same aversion to labour, or rather . . . the same determined indolence ' which he believed he shared with his brothers and his sister.[17] Perhaps a passage in the *Journal* expresses best his industrious perversity: ' never a being, from my infancy upwards, hated task-work as I hate it; and yet I have done a great deal in my day. It is not that I am idle in my nature neither. But propose to me to do one thing, and it is inconceivable the desire I have to do something else—not that it is more easy or more pleasant, but just because it is escaping from an imposed task. I cannot trace this love of contradiction to any distinct source, but [it] has haunted me all my life. I could almost suppose it was mechanical, and that the imposition of a piece of duty-labour operated on me like the mace of a bad billiard-player, which gives an impulse to the ball indeed, but sends it off at a tangent different from the course designed by the player '.[18] But the reason for Scott's self-depreciation as regards his University career was that he measured industry by diligence only in what his schoolmasters and professors taught, which was often but little to his taste. He never seemed to realise that the miscellaneous and undirected study which he voluntarily undertook shows a veritably colossal industry. Few men can ever have taken to their self-appointed tasks with more energy or continued at them with more perseverance; but as Scott's self-education was not against the grain, he never balanced it against the orthodox curriculum.

The goal of his incomparable energy was the variegated land of wonder and romance, ' the common taste of children, but in which I have remained a child even unto this day '[19], and in which he became the unrivalled authority. He discovered it in literature of many kinds, and in the history of many periods; not any literature, for he preferred something with a story in it, beginning with the frankly marvellous, but subsiding through all degrees of romantic lights and crosslights to the more realistic ingredients of the drama and the eighteenth-century novel; not any history, but that which recorded the more picturesque and dramatic, the more surprising and moving events of the past, especially of his native Scotland.

NOTES ON REFERENCES

1 The subject in itself might have been expected to attract Scott, though in fact he did not attend the class either in his first or in his second academic period. The Professor till 1784 was the celebrated Hugh Blair, than whom none of his colleagues had a higher reputation. He was one of the protagonists in the great Ossian controversy, in which Scott was to be keenly interested (cf. *infra*, 214-17). But the only reference to Blair in the *Memoir* is in an added footnote: 'though I have met Dr Blair at my father's and elsewhere, I never had the good fortune to attract his notice, to my knowledge' (I, 9, note 1). Lockhart never mentions Blair; nor does Scott in his *Journal*, though he recalls so many others of the same generation in its pages. As was mentioned before (cf. *supra*, 102), William Greenfield, who succeeded Blair and occupied the Chair till 1801, was very much less of a draw.

2 Among the poems sent to Jessie —— in 1787 was *An Anti-classical Ode, Written after beholding certain specimens of sculpture*, in which Scott made fun of the Venus and Vulcan story (cf. Cook, 36-37).

3 Lockhart, II, 739. At Naples Scott actually began and nearly finished a novel, *The Siege of Malta*, which is largely *verbatim* recalls from Vertot (cf. *supra*, 54; *et infra*, 139) and which has never been published. In 1942, to the disgust of all lovers of Scott, S. Fowler Wright published in two volumes what he called *The Siege of Malta. Founded on an unfinished romance by Sir Walter Scott.*

4 Lockhart, II, 741. In the *Journal* (I, 250, 19th October 1826) Scott objected to Southey's tendency in his *History of the*

Peninsular War ' to augment a work already too long by saying all that can be said of the history of ancient times appertaining to every place mentioned. What care we whether Iaen be the Aurigi Pringi or Onorigis of the ancient Spaniards or no—whether Saragossa be derived from Caeserea Augusta? Could he have proved it to be Numantium [*sc.* Numantia], there would have been a concatenation accordingly '.

5   Lockhart, II, 743.
6   Scott was quoting, with variants, one version of *Charlie is my Darling.* Cf. James Hogg, *The Jacobite Relics of Scotland,* II, 94.
7   Cf. *supra,* 103-4.
8   *Sir Walter Scott,* 20.
9   *Marmion,* Introduction to Canto Third.
10 Author of original poems on romantic themes and translator of Herberay des Essarts's *Amadis,* Boiardo's *Orlando Innamorato,* Ariosto's *Orlando Furioso,* etc.
11 Editor of Persius, Silius Italicus, and Claudian.
12 A character in Congreve's *Old Bachelor.*
13 The Introduction was written at Christmas, 1807.
14 Darsie Latimer also describes himself as ' incorrigibly idle ' (*Redgauntlet,* Letter I).
15 *Memoir,* I, 9. Cf. *Marmion,* Introduction to Canto Fourth:
           ' doing naught—and, to speak true,
           Not anxious to find aught to do '.
16 *Grandfather,* I, 311.
17 *Memoir,* I, 4. Scott senior, however, had ' indeed a turn for labour ' (ibid. I, 4).
18 I, 27. (1st December 1825).
19 *Memoir,* I, 8.

CHAPTER VII

FRENCH, ITALIAN, AND SPANISH

Blackford! on whose uncultur'd breast,
  Among the broom, and thorn, and whin,
A truant boy I sought the nest,
Or listed, as I lay at rest,
  While rose, on breezes thin,
The murmur of the city crowd,
And, from his steeple jangling loud,
  Saint Giles's mingling din.
Now, from the summit to the plain,
Waves all the hill with yellow grain;
  And o'er the landscape as I look,
Nought do I see unchang'd remain,
  Save the rude cliffs and chiming brook.
To me they make a heavy moan,
Of early friendships past and gone.
                    Marmion, *Canto Fourth.*

This slackness of rule might have been ruinous to a boy of slow understanding, who, feeling labour in the acquisition of knowledge, would have altogether neglected it, save for the command of a taskmaster; and it might have proved equally dangerous to a youth whose animal spirits were more powerful than his imagination or his feelings, and whom the irresistible influence of Alma would have engaged in field-sports from morning till night. But the character of Edward Waverley was remote from either of these. His powers of apprehension were so uncommonly quick as almost to resemble intuition.
                    Waverley, *Chapter III.*

FROM the imaginary world of others it was but a step for Scott to imagine a world of his own; and he soon attempted to imitate what he so greatly admired, but as the tale-teller rather than the bard. His closest friend at this time was John Irving. They were

> 'Just at the age 'twixt boy and youth,
> When thought is speech, and speech is truth';[1]

and their romantic friendship was even as that of medieval companions-in-arms or *fratres jurati*.[2] Both Scott and Irving have left affectionate records of their reading knight-errantry together and then striking out into continuations or imitations, 'in which the martial and the miraculous always predominated'.[3] These they rehearsed to each other as they walked to secluded coigns about Arthur's Seat and Salisbury Crags, or perhaps further afield.[4] 'Whole holidays', says Scott, 'were spent in this singular pastime, which continued for two or three years, and had, I believe, no small effect in directing the turn of my imagination to the chivalrous and romantic in poetry and prose.'[5] Scott 'read faster than I did', says Irving, 'and had . . . to wait . . . before turning the leaf. . . . [T]he Castle of Otranto, Spenser, Ariosto and Boiardo,[6] etc., were great favourites. . . . The number of books we read was very great. . . . [T]o my surprise Sir Walter . . . remembered most of what we read together, and could even repeat a whole page if there was any passage which struck him . . . and this even weeks or months afterwards'.[7] It was Scott who at length proposed the alternate spinning of such romances as the two boys could themselves invent. 'Sir Walter found no difficulty in doing this, and used to recite for half an hour or more at a time. . . . The stories . . . were . . . interminable, for we were unwilling to have any of our favourite knights killed, and we copied such tales as we had read in Italian being a continued succession of battles and enchantments.'[7]

From Tasso and 'the divine Ariosto'[8] in Hoole's transla-

tions Scott and his friend boldly plunged into the study of
Italian, in which language, as they had learned from one
of Hoole's notes, 'a fund of romantic lore'[9] was to be
found. At an Italian class[10] twice a week, on which Scott
spent some of his earnings as an engrosser of legal documents,[11] he rapidly acquired some proficiency and got as
his reward a firsthand 'intimacy with the works of Dante,
Boiardo, Pulci, and other eminent Italian authors'.[12] For
the satisfaction of the same romantic appetite Scott had
renewed and improved his knowledge of French before he
took up Italian, savouring the Comte de Tressan's reprints
of romances, the Marquis de Paulmy's *Bibliothèque Universelle
des Romans*, the *Bibliothèque Bleue*, and Le Sage's *Gil Blas*.[13]
About the same time or not much later he acquired also
enough of the 'noble and poetical' language of Spanish[14]
to read the *Guerras Civiles de Granada*, *Lazarillo de Tormes*,
and especially 'the inimitable romance' of *Don Quixote*.[15]

He might, therefore, regard his as a 'considerable facility
in acquiring languages',[16] despite his failure to retain any
Greek. Not that he attempted to acquire more than was
needful for his own purposes, 'of which a critical study of
any foreign language made at no time any part'.[17] He
read all the three modern languages mentioned with about
the same fluency, French perhaps rather more easily than
the other two;[18] but only once did Lockhart ever hear
him speak any, the language being French and the occasion
the visit to Abbotsford in 1830 of some members of the
exiled Charles X's suite, 'after the champagne had been
passing briskly round the table'. The comment of one
of the guests was: 'Comme il estropiait, entre deux vins,
le français du bon sire de Joinville.'[19] He himself admitted
that he spoke French 'as it comes, and [like] Doeg in
Absalom and Achitophel—

> dash on through thick and thin,
> Through sense and nonsense, never out or in.'[20]

There is no evidence of more than a reading knowledge of

Italian[21] and Spanish. His knowledge of several Teutonic languages and of Gaelic will be referred to later.[22]

NOTES ON REFERENCES

1   *Marmion*, Introduction to Canto Second.
2   Cf. *Chivalry*, 547-48: The knightly orders ' might, in part, be founded upon the union which knights were wont to enter into with each other as " companions-in-arms ", than which nothing was esteemed more sacred. The partners were united for weal and woe, and no crime was accounted more infamous than to desert or betray a companion-in-arms. They had the same friends and the same foes; and as it was the genius of chivalry to carry every virtuous and noble sentiment to the most fantastic extremity, the most extravagant proofs of fidelity to this engagement were often exacted or bestowed.'
3   *Memoir*, I, 13.
4   Irving says that the rambles extended to all the old castles within eight or ten miles of the city. Scott was particularly fond of Roslin; and frequently, Scott with his hand on Irving's shoulder and leaning on a stout stick, the two friends walked to Roslin before breakfast, fed there, and returned home by Lasswade before dinner. Scott regretted the destruction, for road metal, etc., of most of the seats they had sought out in Salisbury Crags, and was instrumental in stopping further blasting.

    Scott in the *Memoir* (I, 13) mentions these diversions immediately after what he read during his apprenticeship and in such a way as to make them coincide in time. But in the *General Preface* to the Waverley Novels he appears to place the ' childish mystery ' of himself and Irving in their schooldays. On the other hand, Irving dates it in the years when they were at the University, and says that it was after two years or more of reading romances together that Scott proposed the invention of others. Lockhart, who had Irving's letter before him, accepts the dating in it (I, 33), if ' dating ' it can be called. My conclusion is that these boyish amusements were probably begun at school and continued while they were at the University or for part of that time; but I think that both of the lads must have outgrown such boyish pleasures by the time they were W.S. apprentices.

5   *Memoir*, I, 13.

6   Scott used to read the *Orlandos* of Ariosto and Boiardo once every year.

7   15th May 1833.

8   *Romance*, 570. Cf. *Rob Roy*, Chapter VII: Ariosto ' this fascinating author.'

9   *Memoir*, I, 13.

10 Henry Mackenzie says that, when he was a lad, there was no Italian master in Edinburgh, but that in the 1820s ' every girl who plays on the pianoforte learns Italian, and Italian masters are to be found in every street' (*The Anecdotes and Egotisms of Henry Mackenzie*. Edited by H. W. Thompson, 66).

11 Cf. infra, 147-48.

12 *Memoir*, I, 13. The ' real Tasso and Ariosto' were apparently among the Italian authors read in his youth (Lockhart, I, 36). Curiously enough the only books borrowed by Scott from the University Library were Italian: Pulci's *Morgante Maggiore* in three volumes (23rd December 1791) and E. C. Davila's *Istoria delle Guerre Civili di Francia*, volume II (7th February 1792).

13 *Memoir*, I, 13, and Lockhart, I, 36.

14 *Romance*, 570.

15 *Chivalry*, 545. He had an unbounded admiration for ' the immortal work' of Cervantes (*Romance*, 570) to which he very frequently alludes, and was a constant reader, until disabled by illness, of the *Novelas Ejemplares*, which he thought ' had first inspired him with the ambition of excelling in fiction ' (Lockhart, II, 747).

16 *Memoir*, I, 8.

17 Lockhart, I, 36.

18 Charlotte Carpenter's postscript to her letter of 10th December 1797 is: ' *Étudiez-vous votre français?* Remember you are to teach me Italian in return, but shall I be but a stupid scholar' (Lockhart, I, 79). Scott was acquainted

in 1790 with a French tutor, Guildbert by name (cf. Grierson, 29).

19   Lockhart, I, 36. John Hughes similarly describes Scott in 1825 trying to entertain two French visitors by ' dashing freely at a language he does not much like, although I could see that the effort tried [? tired] him ' (Mrs Hughes, 236).

20   *Journal*, I, 262 (1st November 1826). He had already noted that his French was ' cursedly musty ' (I, 254, 22nd October 1826), that he only ' half understood ' a play at a Parisian theatre, and that he ' understood the langugage less well than I did ten or twelve years since ' (I, 259, 30th October 1826), that is, during his visit to the continent in 1815. In the same year he translated three French poems (*P.W.*, 727-28).

21   He ' could read Italian well once ', and regretted that he had not refreshed his knowledge so as to have spoken it when in Italy (*Journal*, III, 221, 18th March 1832). A ' scrap of a translation ' from Ariosto's *Orlando Furioso* appears in *Rob Roy*, Chapter XVI; and a single stanza from Boiardo's *Orlando Innamorato* in *Kenilworth*, Chapter XXXII, Note.

22   In the last year of his life he resolved to try Maltese! ' I scarce can follow their arabic. I must learn it, though, for the Death of Dragut [a famous corsair] would be a fine subject for a poem ' (*Journal*, III, 201, 24th November 1831).

CHAPTER VIII

VERSIFYING AND SKETCHING

I have been spoiling a vast quantity of good paper with my attempts at the poetical.
Letters, I, 3 to Jessie ——, 1787).

He asked himself in vain, why his eye could not judge of distance or space so well as those of his companions.
Waverley, *Chapter VII.*

SCOTT's reading in the foreign literature of romance seems to have induced him to try his hand again at versifying, which he had dropped since his schooldays.[1] The earliest may have been a poem on the most enterprising of the Norman adventurers in Sicily and Southern Italy, Robert Guiscard (c. 1015–85), and his love for a certain Matilda.[2] It is known to have existed only from a poem found among the papers of Scott's mother and entitled *Lines to Mr Walter Scott—on reading his poem of Guiscard and Matilda, inscribed to Miss Keith of Ravelston*.[3] They begin with sincere praise of what he had written:

> 'If such the accents of thy early youth
> When playful fancy holds the place of truth;
> If so divinely sweet thy numbers flow,
> And thy young heart melts with such tender woe;
> What praise, what admiration shall be thine,
> When sense mature with science shall combine
> To raise thy genius, and thy taste refine!'

And they go on with encouragement and lofty advice for the future. Lockhart thinks they must have been written when Scott was not more than fourteen or fifteen.[4] He was probably about the same age or only a year older when he produced a poem on the Conquest of Granada, described by someone to whom he had shown the manuscript as in four books of about four hundred lines each.[5] Scott is said to have destroyed this ambitious effort soon after finishing it.[6] It was presumably the fruit of his study of the *Guerras Civiles de Granada*, and, in Lockhart's opinion, may have been in the manner of William Julius Mickle's translation of Camoens's *Lusiads*.[7]

But Scott was busy on many other poems during his fifteenth and sixteenth years, of which Lockhart was ignorant. The evidence is in the 1787 letters to Jessie ——, with whom he fancied he had fallen in love at Kelso.[8] In the first of them he enclosed a sixteen-line song, which is addressed to her.[9] And in the third he tells how voluminous his versifying had been: 'I am glad that you have told me you like poetry, and . . . I am not less so at your liking my poor efforts in that way. However since this is the case I can afford you as much as you can find time to read,[10] for, for a long time past I have been spoiling a vast quantity of good paper with my attempts at the poetical. I have addressed the moon—that most be-rhimed of planets—so often I am ashamed to look her in the face. I have made odes to nightingales so numerous they might suffice for all that ever were hatched, and as for elegies, ballads, and sonnets and other small ware, truly I can assert their name is legion, for they are many. But,' he goes on, probably in reference to one or other of the two romantic poems mentioned above, 'besides these I have dared to attempt something of a more imposing character—an epic poem of hundreds upon hundreds of lines—a chronicle in verse of the wondrous doings of some famous knights whose names, even, I doubt much you have ever heard. Indeed the extent of my industry in this way is something marvellous.'[11]

Thereafter, till 1796, 'excepting the usual tribute to a mistress's eyebrow, which is the language of passion rather than poetry', Scott did not indulge 'the wish to couple so much as *love* and *dove*',[12] although he was 'most ready with *extempore* . . . rhymes [and] could almost have conversed in rhymes'.[13]

Scott's diligence in the pursuit of another voluntary endeavour, beginning probably about 1785 but having earlier anticipations, met with little success in spite of his fondness for it. This was sketching from nature.[14] As early at least as his schooldays at Kelso he could 'trace distinctly the awaking of that delightful feeling for the beauty of natural objects which has never since deserted me'.[15] Kelso with its noble river and its ancient Abbey offered just the union of natural beauty with the romantic relics of the past which most strongly appealed to Scott, such an association as 'gave to my admiration a sort of intense impression of reverence, which at times made my

heart feel too big for its bosom ';[16] and from the time of
his stay there in the summer of 1783 his delight in such
scenery became ' an insatiable passion, which . . . I would
willingly have gratified by travelling over half the globe '.[16]
This of course it was that made him eager to sketch. ' But
I could make no progress ', he says in his *Journal*, ' either
in painting or drawing. Nature denied me correctness of
eye and neatness of hand,[17] yet I was very desirous to be a
draughtsman at least and laboured harder to attain that
point than at any other in my recollection, to which I did
not make some approaches.'[18] His explanation of his failure
in the *Memoir* is longer but to very much the same effect ;[19]
and it is clear from it that Scott had studied both theory
and practice and that he had an ambition to be more than
merely a draughtsman. After

> ' gravely labouring to portray
> The blighted oak's fantastic spray '[20]

under two different art-masters,[21] ' I did learn myself to
take some vile views from Nature '.[22] One of the drawing-
masters was ' a little [Prussian] Jew animalcule—a smouch
called Burrell [23]—a clever sensible creature though ',[24] with
a wealth of stories of Frederick the Great's campaigns. The
other and later teacher was ' Blue-beard ' Walker,[25] who
was ugly enough ' to spean weans ' and very conceited
withal.[26] Somewhat later Scott sketched under the eye of
his friend William Clerk, who like all his family and
especially his father[27] had a natural gift of draughtsmanship
and who wondered at Scott's awkwardness ' as a New-
foundland dog would at a greyhound which showed fear
of the water '.[28] Perhaps the height of Scott's achievement
in this line was a sketch of Hermitage Castle, done ' in
my fashion . . . so accurately that with a few verbal instructions Clerk put it into regular form '.[28] H. W. (' Grecian ')
Williams made an improved copy from Clerk's drawing;
and finally from Williams's revision John Walker engraved
the frontispiece for the fine-paper copies of the first volume

of the *Minstrelsy of the Scottish Border* in 1802. I am afraid, however, that the original ' rough sketch ', done by Scott ' standing for that purpose for an hour or more up to his middle in the snow '[29] on the last of his ' raids ' into Liddesdale with Robert Shortreed, fell far short of a work of art. ' Nothing can be ruder than the performance, which I have now before me,' says Lockhart, '. . . Scott used to say, the oddest thing of all was, that the engraving, founded on the labour of three draughtsmen, one of whom could not draw a straight line, and the other two had never seen the place meant to be represented, was nevertheless pronounced by the natives of Liddesdale to give a very fair notion of the ruins of Hermitage.'[29] But if nature had denied Scott a draughtsman's eye and hand, yet, as he said, ' show me an old castle or a field of battle, and I was at home at once, filled it with combatants in their proper costume, and overwhelmed my hearers by the enthusiasm of my description '.[30] And the descriptions in the novels, whether of real or of imaginary scenes, show him to have had a sure sense of what constitutes the picturesque and the visually significant.

NOTES ON REFERENCES

1 Cf. *supra*, 21.
2 The names of his wives were (1) Alberada or Alberida and (2) Sikelgaita or Sicelgaeta.
3 Miss Keith was a daughter of Mrs Keith of Ravelston who was a sister of Scott's Swinton grandmother, Mrs Jean Rutherford (*née* Swinton).
4 Ibid., I, 34. In Lockhart's opinion, the writer was a woman and, probably, Scott's old admirer, Mrs Alison Cockburn. But the editor of her *Letters and Memoirs of her own Life*, T. Craig-Brown, believes Lockhart's attribution to be almost certainly wrong (xxiii).
5 Cf. Allan, 53.
6 Cf. Allan, 53.

7   I, 37.

8   None of the four letters is dated.

9   *Letters*, I, 1-2.

10 In 1932 Davidson Cook printed fourteen poems from the letters to Jessie in *New Love-Poems by Sir Walter Scott*, not all amorous.

11 *Letters*, I, 3-4.

12 *Intro. Note*, 650. The poems alluded to by Scott were written during and immediately after his courtship of Williamina Belsches.

13 Allan, 53.

14 A lady, who was herself an amateur artist, informed Allan that ' Scott's mother was no mean proficient in this elegant accomplishment' (44).

15 *Memoir*, I, 11.

16 *Memoir*, I, 12. Cf. *Letters*, I, 23-4 (to William Clerk, 30th September 1792): ' There are several lakes among the mountains above Hexham . . . surrounded by old towers and castles, in situations the most savagely romantic; what would I have given to have been able to take effect-pieces from some of them!' and ibid., IX, 164 (to Mrs Hughes, 2nd July 1825): ' It is really a charming quality to be able to steal a country's beauties in this way for the amusement of another.'

17 Cf. *Chronicles of the Canongate*, Introductory Chapter VI: (Chrystal Croftangry writes) ' nature has denied a pencil when she placed a pen in my hand '.

18 I, 118 (1st March 1826).

19 I, 15.

20 *Marmion*, Introduction to Canto Fourth.

21 John Irving was a fellow-pupil at one summer class; ' but although both fond of it, we found it took up so much time that we gave this up before we had made much progress '.

22 *Journal*, I, 119 (1st March 1826).

23 Perhaps connected with the firm of Burrel and Ferdinand, perfumers and hairdressers, 6 St Andrew Street.

24 *Journal*, I, 118 (1st March 1826).

25 There were two drawing-masters called George Walker, or one with two establishments—one in South Bridge and one opposite the Royal Exchange. A James Walker,

engraver, lived in Calton. Scott's singing-master, Alexander Campbell, sketched and painted in water-colours.

26 *Journal*, I, 118 (1st March 1826).

27 John Clerk of Eldin. He was an accomplished etcher and author of *An Essay on Naval Tactics, Systematical and Historical*, of which the first volume appeared in 1790 and the second in 1797. Nelson studied the *Essay* and applied its tactics at Trafalgar for the breaking of the French line. Rodney, who read the *Essay* in manuscript, wrote notes which were added to the 1827 edition. John Clerk's elder brother, Sir James, was noted for his artistic skill and for his picture collection at Penicuik House; and his elder son, John (Lord Eldin), drew, painted, and modelled.

28 *Journal*, I, 119 (1st March 1826).

29 Lockhart, I, 94.

30 *Memoir*, I, 15.

CHAPTER IX

THE STUDIOUS INVALID

He . . . became a strict Pythagorean in his diet, eating nothing but vegetables, and drinking only water or milk.
Life and Works of John Home *in* Prose, *838.*

I remember I used to think a slight illness was a luxurious thing. My pillow was then softened by the hand of affection, and all the little cares which were put in exercise to soothe the languor or pain were more flattering and pleasing than the consequences of the illness were disagreeable. It was a new sense to be watched and attended, and I used to think the Malade imaginaire gained something by his humour.
Journal, *I, 292 (16th December 1826).*

I fastened also, like a tiger, upon every collection of old songs or romances which chance threw in my way, or which my scrutiny was able to discover in the dusty shelves of James Sibbald's circulating library in Parliament Square.
Memoir, *I, 13.*

Scott's third session at the University, 1785-6, when he was attending for a second year the lectures of Professor John Bruce,[1] was interrupted by a very serious haemorrhage.[2] The illness, which, coming on the top of uncertain health, was so dangerous that Dr Daniel Rutherford regarded his nephew's recovery ' as little less than miraculous ',[3] appears to have begun late in 1785 or early in 1786 and to have been protracted by repeated relapses; and the time of convalescence, which was spent partly at Kelso, was so long that there can have been no return to the University that session. As we shall see,[4] Scott did not in fact return till the session of 1789-90.

As it happens, Scott and Lockhart are contradictory on the date and duration of this illness. I have already given my reasons for dating Scott's birth in 1770, not in the hitherto accepted 1771 ;[5] and to that redating I adhere. But in this paragraph I have to present statements as to ages and dates by Scott and Lockhart who both assumed that 1771 was the birth-year; and I request the reader, therefore, mentally to add one year to every age as given for Scott in the following passage. Scott, who admits to an inadvertent confounding of dates when speaking of ' this remote period ' of his life,[6] assigns the long illness due to a haemorrhage at one point of the *Memoir*[7] to the second year of his apprenticeship, which strictly would mean between March 1787 and March 1788, when he was between sixteen and seventeen; but at another point of the *Memoir* he speaks of ' the time of my illness at College ',[8] which he left when he was only fourteen and some months. Then in the *General Preface* of 1829 to the Waverley Novels, he states that the haemorrhage occurred when he was ' a growing youth, with the spirits, appetite, and impatience of fifteen ', which would put it, if ' fifteen ' is taken literally, between August 1786 and August 1787. And finally in the 1830 Introduction to *The Lay of the Last Minstrel*, he says that ' since my fourteenth or fifteenth year, my health, originally delicate, had become extremely robust '. His memory may have been at fault also about the duration of his indisposition, where he says in the *General Preface*: ' The lapse of nearly two years, during which I was left to the exercise of my own free will, was followed by a temporary residence in the country.'[9] I am inclined to think that without realising it Scott must have added together the shorter period of invalidism in session 1784-85 and the longer in session 1785-86. Lockhart refers to the *Memoir* and to the *General Preface* as if they said the same thing, and himself makes the confusion worse by saying that the illness ' interrupt[ed] for a considerable period [Scott's] attendance on the Latin and Greek classes '[10]—which would date the illness in session 1783-84, the only one in which Scott attended both Latin and Greek classes.[11]

The rigour of the prescribed regimen, when the illness was in its most dangerous stages, was of the strictest and most disagreeable kind and, one would have thought, more likely to kill than cure. But Scott's good nature and calm courage were important factors in his recovery. ' It was spring,' says Scott, who suffered greatly under the treatment but with a good grace, though his descriptions show how pardonable complaints would have been, ' and the weather raw and cold, yet I was confined to bed with a single blanket, and bled and blistered till I scarcely had a pulse left. I had all the appetite of a growing boy, but was prohibited any sustenance beyond what was absolutely necessary for the support of nature, and that in vegetables alone. Above all, with a considerable disposition to talk, I was not permitted to open my lips without one or two old ladies who watched my couch being ready at once to souse upon me, " imposing silence with a stilly sound ".'[12]

Even reading must at first have been out of the question in such circumstances. But when at last he could sit up and hold a book, he was, he tells us, ' abandoned to my own discretion, so far as reading (my almost sole amusement) was concerned, and . . . I abused the indulgence which left my time so much at my own disposal '.[13] Fortunately for him, thrown back ' on the kingdom of fiction, as it were by a species of fatality ',[13] he could draw on an unusually well-stocked circulating library of above thirty-thousand books, founded by Allan Ramsay[14] and run in Scott's day by James Sibbald[15] in Parliament Square, which contained ' many rare and curious works, seldom found in such a collection '.[16] Edinburgh Circulating Library, as it was called, was ' peculiarly rich in works of fiction . . . from the romances of chivalry, and the ponderous folios of Cyrus[17] and Cassandra,[18] down to the most approved works of modern times. I was plunged into this great ocean of reading without compass or pilot; and unless when someone had the charity to play at chess with me,[19] I was allowed to do nothing save read, from morning to night. I was, in kindness and pity, which was perhaps erroneous, how-ever natural, permitted to select my subjects of study at my own pleasure, upon the same principle that the humours of children are indulged to keep them out of mischief. As my taste and appetite were gratified in nothing else, I in-demnified myself by becoming a glutton of books. Accord-ingly, I believe I read almost all the old romances, old plays, and epic poetry in that formidable collection, and no doubt was unconsciously amassing materials for the task in which it has been my lot to be so much employed '.[20] But, as Scott says elsewhere, ' To the romances and poetry, which I chiefly delighted in, I had always added the study of history, especially as connected with military events. I was encouraged in this latter study by a tolerable acquaint-ance with geography,[21] and by the opportunities I had enjoyed while with Mr MacFait to learn the meaning of the more ordinary terms of fortification.'[22] Accordingly, when he was at last satiated in some degree with fiction, Scott turned ' to seek, in histories, memoirs, voyages and travels, and the like, events nearly as wonderful as those which were the work of imagination '.[23] He singles out two histories by name from what was no doubt a long list. ' I fought my way thus,' he says, ' through Vertot's

Knights of Malta[24]—a book which, as it hovered between history and romance, was exceedingly dear to me,'[25] and from which he was to remember for the rest of his life many pages word for word.[26] Along with it he mentions Robert Orme's 'interesting and beautiful' *History of the Military Transactions of the British Nation in Indostan*, on which he drew over forty years later for colour and atmosphere in *The Surgeon's Daughter*.

Other diversions, while Scott was still confined to his bed, were watching drilling and other sights in the Meadows through a complicated arrangement of mirrors, and working out campaigns with pebbles, shells and seeds,[27] a model fortress, and miniature artillery after the classic example of Uncle Toby, the copious plans and luminous explanations of Orme's *History* lending themselves well to the 'imitative amusement'[28] of reconstructing campaigns on his counterpane.[29]

As long as he was still bed-ridden, Scott had the companionship and moral support of his old ally, John Irving. Day after day Irving faithfully attended the invalid, relieving Mrs Scott and her daughter and playing chess for hours at windows open to the inclemency of an Edinburgh spring. And it was he, no doubt, who saw to it that 'The bed ... was piled with a constant succession of works of imagination, and sad realities were forgotten amidst the brilliant daydreams of genius drinking unwearied from the eternal fountains of Spenser and Shakespeare'.[30] After Scott was well enough to go to Kelso, where there was 'a good though old-fashioned library,[31] the omnivorous reading continued in a league with Captain Robert Scott, who entered eagerly into all his convalescing nephew's pursuits and was consulted on all his juvenile prose or verse.

Scott's enthusiastic but indiscriminate reading is pretty closely novelised, as he himself admits,[32] in his description of Edward Waverley's education, with such imaginary additions as the Great Unknown thought necessary to preserve his incognito. Waverley also 'was permitted, in a great measure, to learn as he pleased, what he pleased, and when he pleased. . . . With a desire of amusement . . . which better discipline might soon have converted into a thirst for knowledge, young Waverley drove through the sea of books like a vessel without a pilot or a rudder. . . . Edward . . . like the epicure who only deigned to take a single morsel from the sunny side of a peach, read no volume a moment after it ceased to excite his curiosity or interest'. He had, however, ' read, and stored in a memory of uncommon tenacity, much curious, though ill-arranged and miscellaneous information. In English literature he was master of Shakespeare and Milton, of our earlier dramatic authors, of many picturesque and interesting passages from our old historical chronicles, and was particularly well acquainted with Spenser, Drayton, and other poets who have exercised themselves on romantic fiction, of all themes the most fascinating to a youthful imagination, before the passions have roused themselves, and demand poetry of a more sentimental description. In this respect his acquaintance with Italian opened him yet a wider range. He had perused the numerous romantic poems which, from the days of Pulci, have been a favourite exercise of the wits of Italy, and had sought gratification in the numerous collections of *novelle*, which were brought forth by the genius of that elegant though luxurious nation in emulation of the "Decameron". In classical literature, Waverley had made the usual progress, and read the usual authors; and the French had afforded him an almost exhaustless collection of memoirs, scarcely more faithful than romances, and of romances so well written as hardly to be distinguished from memoirs. The splendid pages of Froissart,[33] with his heart-stirring and eye-dazzling descriptions of war and of tournaments, were among his chief favourites; and from those of Brantôme and De La Noue he learned to compare the wild and loose, yet superstitious character of the nobles of the League with the stern, rigid, and sometimes turbulent disposition of the Huguenot party. The Spanish had con-

tributed to his stock of chivalrous and romantic lore. The
earlier literature of the Northern nations did not escape the
study of one who read rather to awaken the imagination
than to benefit the understanding. And yet ', Scott charac-
teristically concludes, ' knowing much that is known but
to few, Edward Waverley might justly be considered as
ignorant, since he knew little of what adds dignity to man,
and qualifies him to support and adorn an elevated situation
in society '.[34]

NOTES ON REFERENCES

1   Scott does not indicate in the *Memoir* that he was in fact
a member of Bruce's classes for two sessions; and Lockhart
wrongly concludes that he was not at the University at all
in 1785-86 (cf. *supra*, 106).

2   Cf. *supra*, 104, 106.

3   Lockhart, I, 35.

4   Cf. *infra*, 184-86.

5   Cf. *supra*, 3-6.

6   *Memoir*, I, 13-14.

7   I, 14.

8   I, 16.

9   Cf. Allan, 43 : ' Sir Walter must have spoken from a very
vague recollection, for although unable to recover very
precise information respecting the dates of its commencement and termination, circumstances enable us to approxi-
mate very closely to them, and the result seems to confine
both the duration of his illness and of his residence in the
country considerably within the limits of the time he has
mentioned.'

10   I, 35.

11   Cf. *supra*, 98, 100-1. Allan, like Lockhart, was not aware of
Scott's being a member of Bruce's 1785-86 classes, at least
when the session started. His conclusion is that the illness
began early in session 1784-85 (40, 42). A little later and
less definitely he adds: ' the certainty of a near relative . . .
that he paid a long visit to the neighbourhood of Kelso

during his fourteenth or fifteenth year, is an additional circumstance for believing that it occurred at the time we have fixed upon. We assume, therefore, that his long confinement and his subsequent visit to the country occurred between the close of 1784 and some time in 1786' (44). Allan would like to interpret an inscription scratched on a window in George Square, 'Walter Scott—1785—ha, who art thou?—Begone', as expressing 'the impatience of a tardy convalescent' (45).

12 *Memoir*, I, 14. The quotation at the end is from John Home's *Douglas*. Another shorter description of the treatment is given in the *General Preface* to the Waverley Novels.

13 *General Preface*.

14 It is said to have been the oldest institution of its kind in Scotland.

15 He edited several periodicals and wrote on Scottish poetry and on religious subjects.

16 *Memoir*, I, 13. Scott had enjoyed the run of the place before he took ill, 'for the stores of old French and Italian books, which were little in demand' (ibid., I, 13). It was in this shop, which was a meeting-place for the Edinburgh literati, that Scott saw Burns for the first time (cf. *infra*, 160-62). He mentions also his seeing there the now-forgotten Andrew Macdonald, an Episcopal clergyman who like John Home became a dramatist (*Memoir*, I, 13). Scott is also said to have sought the acquaintance of James McCleish and bought or borrowed many a book from his shop opposite Greyfriars (cf. Allan, 25); and he was a frequent visitor, probably rather later, to the bookshop of the eccentric David Webster, enjoying there the colloquies between the proprietor and the still more eccentric 'Dr' John Brown (cf. Paton, II, 398-99).

17 *Artamène* or *Le Grand Cyrus* by Madeline de Scudéry, 1648. English translation by F. G., 1690.

18 *Cassandre* by Gautier de Costes de La Calprenède, 1642-45. English translation by George Digby, Earl of Bristol, 1652.

19 Scott soon dropped chess as 'a sad waste of brains' and of time which might be better spent in acquiring a new language (Lockhart, I, 35). The knightly pastime had been recommended as a relief from reading.

20 *General Preface.*
21 Scott had shown an interest in geography while at the High School (cf. *supra*, 62); and both Dr Adam and Dr MacFait published geographical books.
22 *Memoir*, I, 14.
23 *General Preface.*
24 René Aubert de Vertot D'Aubeuf, *Histoire des Chevaliers Hospitaliers de S. Jean de Jérusalem appelez depuis les Chevaliers de Rhodes, et aujourd'hui les Chevaliers de Malte*, 1726.
25 *Memoir*, I, 14.
26 Cf. *supra*, 54, 119, note 3.
27 Cf. *supra*, 51.
28 *Memoir*, I, 14.
29 According to Allan, one of Scott's diversions ' during the tedious hours of sickness [was] the scratching of flowers on paper ' (44).
30 Lockhart, I, 35.
31 *General Preface.*
32 *General Preface.*
33 Cf. *Chivalry in Prose*, 538: ' an inimitable artist '.
34 *Waverley*, Chapter III.

CHAPTER X

THE LAW APPRENTICE

He would have shuddered at Alan's acquiring the renown of a hero, and laughed with scorn at the equally barren laurels of literature. It was by the path of the law alone that he was desirous to see him rise to eminence; and the probabilities of success or disappointment were the thoughts of his father by day, and his dream by night.

Redgauntlet, Chapter I.

And what ill would the Scottish law do to him, though he had as much of it as either Stair or Bankton, sir? Is not the foundation of our municipal law the ancient code of the Roman Empire, devised at a time when it was so much renowned for its civil polity, sir, and wisdom? . . . Ars longa, vita brevis—were it not a sin to call the divine science of the law by the inferior name of art.

Redgauntlet, Letter II.

SCOTT not only made a good, if slow, recovery from his all-but-fatal illness, but also soon developed a breadth and depth of chest and began to acquire a robustness of health, great physical strength, and remarkable powers of endurance, such as could never have been expected from his earlier sickliness.[1] 'I had,' he says, 'since the improvement of my health, in defiance of this incapacitating circumstance,[2] distinguished myself by the endurance of toil on foot or horseback, having often walked thirty miles a day, and rode upwards of a hundred, without resting. In this manner I made many pleasant journeys through parts of the country then not very accessible, gaining more amusement and instruction than I have been able to acquire since I have travelled in a more commodious manner. I practised most silvan sports also, with some success, and with great delight.'[3]

But when he must still have been on the sick-list, his father on 31st March 1786 entered into a five-years' indenture of apprenticeship with him, which was duly presented by Scott senior to the officers of the Society of Writers to the Signet on 15th May.[4] As Scott was almost certainly not in any condition for office-work, and as indeed he was about to begin a long sojourn for his health at Kelso,[5] it looks as if his father may have had a therapeutic intention of raising his son's morale and giving him a forward look to a useful career. At any rate Scott was at the time psychologically depressed and afflicted ' with a nervousness which I never felt before or since. A disposition to start upon slight alarms—a want of decision in feeling and acting, which has not usually been my failing—an acute sensibility to trifling inconveniences—and an unnecessary apprehension of contingent misfortunes, rise to my memory '.[6]

But it had always been intended that Scott should become either an advocate or a Writer to the Signet, the life of a soldier, which he would himself have preferred, being out of the question because of his lameness.[7] He had been sent, he thought, to only a few University classes during his first period of attendance, none of them being of a professional character, because his father wanted him to concentrate on his legal studies. The decision to apprentice him left open the question of the branch of the law to be adopted later, since in Scott senior's opinion the technical knowledge and office-training of a solicitor would in any case be useful at least, if not essential, to an advocate. He probably knew that two at any rate of the most distinguished judges, Lord Kames and Lord Braxfield, had both qualified as solicitors before being called to the Bar;[8] and he would certainly be aware of the normal converse practice of intending advocates putting in six months or a year in a solicitor's office.

Scott may well have drawn on his own experience when he described the youth of Jonathan Oldbuck, with whom he shared a love of antiquities and ' a tinge of bibliomania':[9] ' He was . . . put apprentice to the profession of a writer, or attorney, in which he profited so far, that he made himself master of the whole forms of feudal investitures, and showed such pleasure in reconciling their incongruities, and tracing their origin, that his master had great hope he would one day be an able conveyancer. But he halted upon the threshold, and, though he acquired some knowledge of the origin and system of the law of his country, he could never be persuaded to apply it to lucrative and practical purposes.'[10]

Scott hated the confinement to an office,[11] the drudgery of book-keeping, and the mechanical work of copying amid ' the dry and barren wilderness of forms and conveyances ';[12] but he never rebelled against them. Nay, he contrived to turn his captivity to some profit, performing amazing feats of engrossing to earn pocket-money which was so sparingly doled out by his father and which in consequence was ' no trifling incentive to labour'.[13] He spent the money he made on books and old coins, the circulating library and the theatre, and partly, as has already been noticed,[14] on an Italian class. ' When actually at the oar,' he said, ' no man could pull it harder than I.'[15] On one occasion he transcribed a hundred and twenty folio sheets with no intervals for food or rest.[16] His handwriting in consequence acquired for good and all the marks of the professional engrosser; and along with the tireless ' pen of a ready writer ',[17] he picked up certain scribal tricks and flourishes [18] and a precise manner of folding and disposing of the written document.[19]

The state of Scott's mind at this time is faithfully delineated in passages in Letter II of *Redgauntlet*, in which Alan Fairford (as much an autobiographic sketch of Scott in his youth as Chrystal Croftangry in *Chronicles of the Canongate* is of Scott in his later years)[20] both mildly criticises and loyally accepts his father's strictness: ' my father considers every moment taken from the law as a step down hill; and I owe much to his anxiety on my account, although its effects are sometimes troublesome. . . . I wish my father would allow me a little more exercise of my free will, were it but that I might feel the pleasure of doing what would please him of my own accord. A little more spare time, and a little more money to enjoy it, would, besides, neither misbecome my age, nor my condition; and it is, I own, provoking to see so many in the same situation winging the air at freedom, while I sit here, caged up like a cobbler's linnet, to chant the same unvaried lesson from sunrise to sunset, not to mention the listening to so many lectures against idleness, as if I enjoyed or was making use of the means of amusement ! But then I cannot at heart blame either the motive or the object of this severity. For the motive, it is and can only be my father's anxious, devoted, and unremitting affection and zeal for my improvement, with a laudable sense of the honour of the profession to which he has trained me. . . . Then for the object of his solicitude. Do not laugh, or hold up your hands, my good Darsie; but upon my word I like the profession to which I am in the course of being educated, and am serious in prosecuting the preliminary studies. The law is my vocation—in an especial, and, I may say, in an hereditary way, my vocation '.

Scott as apprentice, then, was not an entirely useless member of his father's office-staff,

> ' A clerk, foredoomed his father's soul to cross,
> Who pens a stanza when he should engross.'

It is perhaps worth noting that he adapts these lines from Pope's *Epistle to Dr Arbuthnot* twice, once in the *Memoir* where he rejects their application to himself,[21] and once in *Rob Roy* where Francis Osbaldistone rejects them likewise.[22] It is more than likely that, as in *Redgauntlet*, the father-son relationship in this novel was suggested by passages between Scott senior and Scott junior, especially as Osbaldistone was the name of the chief clerk in the office.[23] So far from being an idle apprentice, Walter took pride and got pleasure in being useful. He was ambitious to excel, accepting the necessity of labour and resolute to please the father he loved and respected, whose highest hope for his able son was distinction in the law and that only.

Allan's statement, then, that Scott ' never acted regularly either as clerk or apprentice ' and that his apprenticeship was no more than ' nominal '[24] is quite contrary to the known facts; as is the allegation, made by more than one of the biographers of Scott before Lockhart, 'that in the ordinary indoor fagging of the chamber . . . he was always an unwilling, and rarely an efficient assistant'.[25] Quite apart from the evidence as to diligence in the *Memoir* and elsewhere, such conduct would have been entirely out of character in Scott who had a high filial respect for his father and who never shirked any duty in his life, especially if his dereliction would have cast the burden on someone else. That he had many a tough game of chess during office-hours with the clerk who was Allan's informant is very likely; and so is the rest of the story which tells how the chess-players ' were frequently interrupted by the inopportune entrance of the old gentleman; when pop, crash, down went chessboard and men into the desk, and the two delinquents assumed as grave and businesslike a deportment as their trepidation would admit of'.[26] There never was an office without occasional fooling or an apprentice who kept his nose to the grindstone all the time. Nay, Scott suspected that even the head of the firm ' was often engaged with Knox and Spottiswoode's folios, when, immured in his solitary room, he was supposed to be immersed in professional researches'.[27]

Moreover, Scott found, then or later, that strict application to his profession whetted rather than dulled his romantic appetite; and it drilled him in such methodical habits as ' few imaginative authors had ever before exemplified ' [28] —habits which became second nature, which regulated his life and his work without spoiling either, and without which he could not possibly have done all that he achieved. Scott was never heard in his mature life to regret his apprenticeship; and it was ever ' his favourite tenet, in contradiction of what he called the cant of sonneteers, that there is no necessary connexion between genius and an aversion or contempt for any of the common duties of life; he thought, on the contrary, that to spend some fair portion of every day in any matter-of-fact occupation is good for the higher faculties themselves in the upshot. In a word—he piqued himself on being *a man of business*; and did—with one sad and memorable exception—whatever the ordinary course of things threw in his way in exactly the business-like fashion which might have been expected from the son of a thorough-bred old Clerk of the Signet who had never deserted his father's profession'.[29]

However monotonous office-work might be, Scott lightened his drudgery by books of his own choosing and mingled with the text-books of conveyancing enough miscellaneous literature in poetry, romance, and chronicle to keep his imagination sweet. And he read it in his own way, often beginning in the middle or at the end of the volume, or skipping in ' a hop-step-and-jump-perusal ',[30] which, however, gave him more of the book so skimmed than a fellow-apprentice got by a more orthodox process. Here is the account of his reading which he gives for his apprenticeship: ' My desk usually contained a store of most miscellaneous volumes, especially works of fiction of every kind, which were my supreme delight. I might except novels, unless those of the better and higher class; for though I read many of them, yet it was with more selection than might have been expected. The whole Jemmy and Jenny Jessamy tribe I abhorred, and it required the art of Burney, or the feeling of Mackenzie, to fix my attention upon a domestic tale. But all that was adventurous and romantic I devoured without much discrimination, and I really believe I have read as much nonsense of this class as any man now living. Everything which touched on knight-errantry was particularly acceptable to me.' [31]

Of the books which Scott read at this time of his life one which particularly attracted him and of which he eagerly made himself master was Thomas Evans's *Old Ballads, Historical and Narrative*.[32] He was specially taken by poems in it by John Langhorne and William Julius Mickle. It was, as we shall see,[33] his ready citation of Langhorne's *Country Justice* which won Burns's approval at the house of Professor Adam Ferguson. Mickle's *Cumnor Hall* he was never tired of repeating to John Irving on moonlight walks in the Meadows; and it retained for him ' a peculiar species of enchantment '[34] till he wrote *Kenilworth* in 1820 and the Introduction thereto in 1831.[35]

Apart from his ever-ready escapes into literature, the chief compensations of his apprenticeship were the visits he paid during several years for business or pleasure (business probably, and pleasure certainly, entering into all of them) to Kelso and the Borders, which he knew well already, and to various parts of the Highlands, which were entirely new to him.[36] Scott senior had clients in the vicinity of Kelso; and Walter, in a letter to his mother on the happy fortnight he was spending there with ' some plan or other for every day ' for sport or for excursions afoot or on horseback, mentions that he had ' got two or three Clients, besides my Uncle, and am busy drawing tacks,[37]—not however of marriage. I am in a fair way of making money, if I stay here long '.[38] Scott says that he made his first acquaintance with the Highlands when he was ' not above fifteen years old ',[39] that is, in 1785-86. But Lockhart is probably right in thinking that it did not begin till the autumn of 1786 or of 1787,[40] that is, after his apprenticeship had begun. Whatever the year, he was enchanted with the beauty of the country, not least when he saw it ahead of him from the Wicks of Baiglie.[41] Among the clients of his father whom he visited on business were his old hero, Alexander Stewart of Invernahyle, apparently also Invernahyle's kinsman,[42] Duncan Stewart of Ardsheal and Appin, and no doubt other Highland lairds. We hear, too, of an episode which must have impressed Scott and which is not unlike several in the Highland novels. He, a mere lad, carried an eviction order against certain shilly-shallying tenants of Stewart of Ardsheal and Appin.[43] But as ' the king's writ did not pass quite current in the Braes of Balquhidder '[44] even as late as the 1780s, and as trouble was expected, Scott had an escort of six men of a Highland regiment under a sergeant, who ' was absolutely a Highland Sergeant Kite,[45] full of stories of Rob Roy and of himself, and a very good companion '.[46] 'And thus it happened, oddly enough,' says Scott, ' that the author first entered the romantic scenery of Loch Katrine, of which he may perhaps say he has somewhat extended the reputation, riding in all the dignity of danger, with a front and rear guard, and loaded arms.'[47] No doubt greatly to Scott's disappointment, the tenants had gone voluntarily and he and his supporters went and returned unmolested.

It is not known what other parts he may have visited north of the Highland Line in the days of his apprenticeship. But certainly he penetrated into districts not only strikingly beautiful in themselves, but abounding in legends, rich in ancient remains, and still affording glimpses of what Highland conditions were before the Disarming Act and the abolition of the heritable jurisdictions of the chiefs. His novel situation on such occasions was not so very dissimilar from Edward Waverley's at Glennaquoich; and, had the chance occurred to him as to others forty years before, he would have been 'a writer's ... apprentice who had given his indentures the slip, and taken the white cockade'.[48]

NOTES ON REFERENCES

1 He is said to have been able in his manhood to lift a blacksmith's anvil by the horn; and Chambers tells how, in a mood of mortification because he was debarred from being a soldier, he hung for upwards of an hour from his bedroom window, to prove that, if his legs were weak, his arms were not (23).

2 I.e. his lameness.

3 *The Lay of the Last Minstrel*, Introduction.

4 Scott vaguely dated his apprenticeship as beginning 'about 1785-6' (*Memoir*, I, 13).

5 Or was perhaps already there.

6 *Memoir*, I, 14.

7 Cf. John Gibson, *Reminiscences of Sir Walter Scott*, 5-6: 'his mother ... used to speak of his infirmity as a *blessing*, adding, that but for it he would have been a soldier, and would in all probability have fallen in battle'.

8 John Clerk (Lord Eldin) not only completed his W.S. apprenticeship, but practised for some years as an accountant, before going to the Bar at the age of twenty-eight in 1785 (cf. Paton, II, 438). Another Writer to the Signet, Archibald Fletcher, was forty-five when he became an advocate in 1790 (cf. ibid., II, 445).

9 Lockhart describes Scott's books as 'all in that complete state of repair which at a glance reveals a tinge of bibliomania' (I, 368). Cf. Gillies, 62: 'from earliest youth he shewed that passion for bibliography, which, in after life, was one of his distinguishing characteristics'.

10   *The Antiquary*, Chapter II.

11   Cf. *supra*, 25.

12   *Memoir*, I, 13.

13   *Memoir*, I, 13.

14   Cf. *supra*, 123.

15   *Memoir*, I, 13.

16   Darsie Latimer mentions 'the small characters in which my residence in Mr Fairford's house enabled me to excel, for the purpose of transferring as many scroll sheets as possible to a huge sheet of stamped paper' (*Redgauntlet*, Chapter IX).

17   *Psalms*, xlv. 1.

18   Cf. Lockhart, I, 39-40. Scott would sometimes mutter 'There goes the old shop again', when by force of habit he had concluded with a flourish of the pen.

19   Cf. Chambers, 29-30.

20   As already said (cf. *supra*, 71, note 5), Saunders Fairford is just as much a portrait of Scott's father. William Clerk, who is himself generally regarded as the prototype of Darsie Latimer, declared that nothing could be more exact, except for a few trifling circumstances (cf. Lockhart, I, 50). But Scott seems to me to have reproduced traits of his father also in the senior Osbaldistone in *Rob Roy*.

21   I, 13.

22   Chapter I.

23   Scott echoed the name again in Caleb Balderstone in *The Bride of Lammermoor*.

24   54.

25   Lockhart, I, 39.

26   55.

27   *Memoir*, I, 3.

28   Lockhart, I, 37. I feel sure that among other office-work Scott, like Alan Fairford, was 'sedulously trained' in the 'knowledge of accompts' (*Redgauntlet*, Chapter I). But Sir Herbert Grierson asserts that traits in Scott senior's character reappeared in the son, and that the former kept no books with the result that it took from 1799 to 1814 'to wind up the estate, and in more than one instance the losses had to be cut' (7).

29   Lockhart, I, 40.

30   *Memoir*, I, 13. Scott confesses to 'a strong fellow-feeling'
      with 'such as are addicted to the laudable practice of
      skipping' (*Redgauntlet*, Chapter I).
31   *Memoir*, I, 13.
32   The four-volumes edition at Abbotsford was not bought
      by Scott till 1792.
33   Cf. *infra*, 161-62.
34   *Kenilworth*, Introduction.
35   Among the items in English literature (in addition to some
      already mentioned) which have survived from his boyhood
      library and are now at Abbotsford are the following:
      John Arbuthnot, *Miscellaneous Works*; John Armstrong,
      The Art of Preserving Health; John Gay, *Poems on Several
      Occasions* and *Plays*; Sir John Hawkins, *Probationary Odes
      for the Laureateship* (signed in 1790); William Hayley, *The
      Triumphs of Temper* (bound in 1792); Lord Lyttelton,
      Works; William Mason, *Poems*; Thomas Parnell, *Poems on
      Several Occasions* (given to Scott by his mother who had
      owned it before her marriage); William Wilkie, *The
      Epigoniad*; and Edward Young, *Works*. Other works in
      English at Abbotsford which Scott collected (or may have
      collected) before his call to the Bar in 1792 include: the
      Earl of Anglesey, *Memoirs*; Sir David Dalrymple (Lord
      Hailes), *Annals of Scotland*; Robert Lindsay of Pitscottie,
      The History of Scotland; William Robertson, *The History
      of Scotland*; and Sir Philip Warwick, *Memoirs*. For this
      list, as for other information about Scott's early book-
      collecting, I am indebted to Dr J. C. Corson, but must
      take the blame for any errors or omissions in recording it.
36   Allan was informed by one of the office staff that Scott
      'was frequently absent on minor excursions' (55).
37   I.e. leases.
38   *Letters*, I, 9-10 (5th September 1788).
39   *The Fair Maid of Perth*, Chapter I.
40   I, 38. John Irving, however, believed (wrongly) that Scott
      'was little acquainted with the Highlands till he went . . .
      to visit his friend Mr [John James] Edmonstone at Newton',
      Perthshire in the 1790s.
41   Cf. *The Fair Maid of Perth*, Chapter I.
42   But not his brother-in-law, as both Lockhart (I, 39) and

Allan (57) say.

43   The MacLarens occupied the farm of Invernenty on a long lease at a very low rent. They had agreed to vacate it for £500 and then at some whim had changed their minds. The landlord was heavily in debt, ' chiefly to the author's family ' (*Rob Roy*, Introduction), and the creditors were likely to lose their money if the farm could not be offered for sale with free occupation. Allan states that ' The sum of £1000, being the whole or part of Mrs Scott's portion, had been lent upon a personal bond to Stewart of Appin, . . . and subsequently transformed into a burden on his estate in due form of law ' (57).

44   *Rob Roy*, Introduction.

45   A character in Farquhar's *Recruiting Officer*.

46   *Rob Roy*, Introduction.

47   Ibid.

48   *Home*, 831.

CHAPTER XI

SOCIAL AND FORENSIC AMBITIONS

There were men of literature in Edinburgh before she was renowned for romances, reviews, and magazines—

Vixerunt fortes ante Agamemnona;

and a single glance at the authors and men of science who dignified the last generation, will serve to show that, in those days, there were giants in the North . . . a phalanx, whose reputation was neither confined to their narrow, poor, and rugged native country, nor to England, and the British dominions, but known and respected wherever learning, philosophy, and science were honoured.

Life and Works of John Home in *Prose*, 827.

My progress in life during these two or three years had been gradually enlarging my acquaintance, and facilitating my entrance into good company. . . . It is not difficult for a youth with a real desire to please and to be pleased, to make his way into good society in Edinburgh—or indeed anywhere; and my family connexions, if they did not greatly further, had nothing to embarrass my progress. I was a gentleman, and so welcome anywhere, if so be I could behave myself, as Tony Lumpkin says, 'in a concatenation accordingly'.

Memoir, *I, 17.*

I have been readily received in the first circles in Britain. But there is a certain intuitive knowledge of the world, to which most well-educated Scotchmen are early trained, that prevents them from being much dazzled by this species of elevation. A man who to good nature adds the general rudiments of good breeding, provided he rest contented with a simple and unaffected manner of behaving and expressing himself, will never be ridiculous in the best society, and, so far as his talents and information permit, may be an agreeable part of the company.

Memoir, *I, 1, note 1.*

THOUGH Scott managed to interpolate not a little amusement in his apprenticeship, on the whole it was for him both an imprisonment of the body and a starving of the mind. His worthy father had a severely professional outlook and, having but a tepid regard for *belles lettres*, neither sought nor desired the society of the literary circles with which Edinburgh abounded. Scott himself had not come much into contact with them either,[1] his literary intromissions having been with the dead rather than the living; and his long hours on an office stool had largely cut him off from his old High School intimates,[2] and had given him for associates in his scanty leisure only his brother-apprentices and fellow-clerks who were more plodding than inspiring and as cool as his father towards polite letters. A remark he made in later life may well have echoed his own adolescent aware-ness of something lacking in the life he had to lead: ' I know nothing so essential to give the proper tone to a young mind as intercourse with the learned and the worthy '.[3]

But two extensions of his social horizon from his sixteenth or seventeenth year suggested to Scott the idea of abandoning the routine of conveyancing for the more attractive, if more precarious, chances of the Bar, ' which has ever . . . been regarded in Scotland as an honourable profession, and has produced many great men '.[3]

The first extension in point of time was his admission through the younger Adam Ferguson,[4] an old High School boy and a fellow law-apprentice, to the company of ' the most distinguished literati of the old time who still remained, with such young persons as were thought worthy to approach their circle, and listen to their conversation ',[5] The meeting-place was Sciennes Hill House, known to its *habitués* as Kamtschatka [6] because of its suburban isolation and the furry garments of its chilly owner (and despite its internal comforts), the home of the learned, versatile, and hospitable Professor Adam Ferguson, whose irascibility especially over the dusting and tidying-up of his study Scott may have recalled when characterising his Jonathan Oldbuck. He held frequent reunions there for dinner and conversation, particularly on Sundays. Scott was probably present on many such occasions. A specially notable one,[7] to which he had been brought by young Ferguson, occurred early in 1787 [8] when the chief guest was Burns, who had taken Edinburgh by storm from his arrival at the end of the previous November. Scott ardently desired to see ' the boast of Scotland ',[9] ' one of the most singular men by whose appearance our age has been distinguished '.[10] ' I . . . had sense and feeling enough,' he told Lockhart, ' to be much interested in his poetry and would have given the world to know him.' [11]

Among the company were John Home, who had himself been the poetic lion of the previous generation, and three celebrated fellow-professors of the host, Dugald Stewart, who had offered to bring Burns to the party,[12] Joseph Black,[13] and James Hutton. It appears that quite a number of others [14] were present, including several ladies.[15] ' Of course,' said Scott, ' we youngsters sate silent, looked, and listened.' [16] But how shrewdly the boy Scott observed the person, features, and bearing of ' this wonderful and self-taught genius ' [17] with his ' powerful but untamed mind ',[18] and how justly he evaluated Burns's conversation and opinions. He put his more deliberated judgement down in an 1809 review of R. H. Cromek's *Reliques of Robert Burns*, which is still one of the best critical essays on the subject.[19]

One passage in particular seems to me to be clearly the fruit of direct observation on the occasion in question: ' this ardent and irritable temperament had its periods, not merely of tranquillity, but of the most subduing tenderness. In the society of men of taste . . . he was eloquent, impressive, and instructing. But it was in female circles that his powers of expression displayed their utmost fascination. In such . . . his conversation lost all its harshness, and often became so energetic and impressive, as to dissolve the whole circle into tears. The traits of sensibility which, told of another,

DAVID HUME (Baron Hume), Professor of Scots Law

ALEXANDER FRASER TYTLER (Lord Woodhouselee),
Professor of Universal History

WALTER SCOTT, aged 26 to 27, in the uniform of the Royal Edinburgh
Light Dragoons

would sound like instances of gross affectation, were so native to the soul of this extraordinary man, and burst from him so involuntarily, that they not only obtained full credence as the genuine feelings of his own heart, but melted into unthought-of sympathy all who witnessed them. In such a mood they were often called forth by the slightest and most trifling occurrences, an ordinary engraving, the wild turn of a simple Scottish air, a line in an old ballad, were, like "the field mouse's nest" and "the upturned daisy", sufficient to excite the sympathetic feelings of Burns. And it was wonderful to see those, who, left to themselves, would have passed over such trivial circumstances without a moment's reflection, sob over the picture, when its outline had been filled up by the magic art of his eloquence'.[20]

What Scottish air was sung at Sciennes Hill House, or what ballad was quoted, we do not know. But the 'ordinary engraving' is known and still exists.[21] It is a fairly large print after a picture by H. W. Bunbury, 'representing a soldier lying dead on the snow, his dog sitting in misery on the one side, on the other his widow, with a child in her arms'.[22] The following six lines are printed below:

'Cold on Canadian hills, or Minden's plain,
Perhaps that parent mourn'd her soldier slain;
Bent o'er her babe, her eye dissolv'd in dew,
The big drops mingling with the milk he drew,
Gave the sad presage of his future years,
The child of misery, baptiz'd in tears!'

'Burns seemed much affected by the print,' said Scott, 'or rather the ideas which it suggested to his mind. He actually shed tears. He asked whose the lines were,[23] and it chanced that nobody but myself remembered that they occur in a half-forgotten poem of [John] Langhorne's, called by the unpromising title of *The Justice of the Peace*.[24] I whispered my information to a friend present, who mentioned it to Burns, who rewarded me with a look and a word, which, though of mere civility, I then received, and still recollect, with very great pleasure.'[25]

The second and perhaps more powerful influence in turning Scott's eyes towards the Bar was the renewal, probably in 1788,[26] after two or three years' lapse, of his intimacy with several old schoolfellows, whom he appears to have re-encountered in a literary-debating club and through whom he met other young men of the same class and outlook. His own statement is: 'I am particularly obliged to this sort of club for introducing me about my seventeenth year into the society which at one time I had entirely dropped; for, from the time of my illness at College, I had little or no intercourse with any of my class-companions, one or two[27] only excepted.'[28] The remission was not the fault of Scott who was remarkable for the length and strength of his affection for the friends of his youth. Lockhart, it should be added, though he dates the renewal of friendship in the winter of 1788, makes it coincide with Scott's entering the Civil Law Class at the University,[29] which did not in fact occur till the autumn of 1791.[30]

Till 1788, then, Scott had accepted as his lot the restricted way of life at George Square and his status as an apprentice who would in due course follow in his father's narrow track. The retired manner of life of his parents had not introduced him to a great many people beyond his own kith and kin or accustomed him much to social occasions. Hence the passage in one of Alan Fairford's letters to Darsie Latimer: 'my father, though a scrupulous observer of the rites of hospitality, seems to exercise them rather as a duty than as a pleasure; and indeed, but for a conscientious wish to feed the hungry and receive the stranger, his doors would open to guests much seldomer than is the case'.[31] The corresponding passage in the *Memoir* is: 'My father and mother, already advanced in life,[32] saw little society at home, excepting that of near relations, or upon particular occasions, so that I was left to form connexions in a great measure for myself.'[33] But in fact he had seen but little company of any kind outside his home up to 1788; and such con-

nexions as he had formed, apart from his friendship with
John Irving (which was somewhat in abeyance owing to
the lads being in different offices), were more casual than
of choice—that is to say, with his father's clerks and his
fellow-apprentices, from none of whom he got much in
the way of intellectual stimulus. Consequently Scott felt,
I think, but in fact felt quite wrongly, for he had naturally
the bearing and manners of a gentleman, that he was somewhat lacking in social dexterity. That is why he makes
Alan Fairford conscious of ' that native air of awkward
bashfulness of which I am told the law will soon free me ';[34]
and why Darsie Latimer admits that ' want of habitual
intercourse with the charmers of the other sex has rendered
me a sheepish cur, only one grain less awkward than thy-
self'.[35] There is a still more revealing passage following
the description of Edward Glendinning's diffidence in the
company of the voluble Sir Piercie Shafton: ' But, alas!
where is the man of modest merit, and real talent, who
has not suffered from being outshone in conversation and
outstripped in the race of life, by men of less reserve, and
of qualities more showy, though less substantial? and well
constituted must the mind be, that can yield up the prize
without envy to competitors more worthy than himself.'[36]

As we have seen, he had often been in poor health from
early childhood till his middle teens, and in consequence
left largely to his own devices, even when living with his
family at home and still more when he was a single child[37]
in the adult households at Sandyknowe and Kelso. Naturally
enough he had not only learned to tolerate solitude, but to
love it and, since, as he says in the *Journal*, ' The love of
solitude increases by indulgence ',[38] to prefer it.[39] Hence
his quaint reply when his uncle Robert Scott asked him if,
instead of lying reading on the carpet, he would not rather
be playing with the boys in George Square, ' No, Uncle,
you cannot think how ignorant those boys are—I am much
happier reading my books.'[40] In his adult life Scott certainly
appeared to be, and indeed was, an eminently sociable being.

'Few men,' he said, 'leading a quiet life, and without any strong or highly varied change of circumstances, have seen more variety of society than I—few have enjoyed it more, or been *bored*, as it is called, less by the company of tiresome people. I have rarely, if ever, found any one, out of whom I could not extract amusement or edification and were I obliged to account for hints afforded on such occasions I should [have to] make an ample deduction from my inventive powers.'[41] But this is only one side of Scott's character, and, as will be suggested, one deliberately cultivated by him. More than one passage of self-examination in the *Journal* shows his preference for a life withdrawn, not only in youth, but just as much when all the world was his friend and he the friend of all the world. On one occasion, speaking of ' the pleasure of being alone and uninterrupted ', he says, ' from the earliest time I can remember I preferd the pleasures of being alone to waiting for visitors, and have often taken a bannock and a bit of cheese to the wood or hill to avoid dining with company . . . if the question was eternal company without the power of retiring within yourself or solitary confinement for life, I should say, " Turnkey, Lock the cell ! " '[42] On another occasion, he makes a similar avowal: ' One is tempted to ask himself, knocking at the door of his own heart, Do you love this extreme loneliness? I can answer conscientiously, *I do*. The love of solitude was with me a passion of early youth when in my teens I used to fly from company to indulge visions and airy castles of my own—the disposal of ideal wealth, and the exercize of imaginary powers. This feeling prevailed even till I was eighteen, when love and ambition awaking with other passions threw me more into society, from which I have, however, at times withdrawn myself, and have been always glad to do so.'[43]

No two men of the Romantic Revival seem more unlike than Scott and Shelley. Yet Scott, though he never said so, drew himself as he was in boyhood and youth, to some extent at least, in a Shelleyan character, the sensitive and imaginative Wilfrid Wycliffe in *Rokeby*:

> 'still he turn'd impatient ear
> From Truth's intrusive voice severe.
> Gentle, indifferent, and subdued,
> In all but this, unmoved he view'd
> Each outward change of ill and good.
> But Wilfrid, docile, soft, and mild,
> Was Fancy's spoil'd and wayward child'.

Such a one is
> 'free
> From every stern reality,
> Till, to the Visionary, seem
> Her day-dreams truth, and truth a dream'.[44]

The memory remained vivid of his collisions with reality when as a timid and delicate child, acutely sensitive and imaginative, he was transferred from his happy and indulged seclusion in the country to the state of being odd-man-out in the bustling household at George Square and shortly after amid the unsympathetic rabble of the High School. As has been noticed,[45] he wisely adjusted himself to his uncongenial surroundings and began the process of acquiring a shell. And several times he alludes to the sorrows that await the addict of sensibility and imagination. The passage on this theme in *Rokeby* has, then, in addition to an overt reference to the fictional Wilfrid, a covert one to Scott himself:

> 'Woe to the youth whom Fancy gains,
> Winning from Reason's hand the reins!
> Pity and woe! for such a mind
> Is soft, contemplative, and kind;
> And woe to those who train such youth,
> And spare to press the rights of truth,
> The mind to strengthen and anneal
> While on the stithy glows the steel!

O teach him, while your lessons last,
To judge the present by the past;
Remind him of each wish pursued,
How rich it glow'd with promised good;
Remind him of each wish enjoy'd,
How soon his hopes possession cloy'd!
Tell him, we play unequal game
Whene'er we shoot by Fancy's aim;
And, ere he strip him for her race,
Show the conditions of the chase.
Two sisters by the goal are set,
Cold Disappointment and Regret;
One disenchants the winner's eyes
And strips of all its worth the prize,
While one augments its gaudy show
More to enhance the loser's woe.
The victor sees his fairy gold
Transform'd, when won, to drossy mold;
But still the vanquish'd mourns his loss,
And rues, as gold, that glittering dross.'[46]

But Scott in the poem sets beside the musing and retiring
Wilfrid the active and spirited Redmond O'Neale—beside
the youth he was not altogether proud of having been the
young man he was doing his best to become. It was the
gallant Redmond who impetuously led the pursuit of
Bertram:

'Instant to earth young Redmond sprung;
Instant on earth the harness rung
Of twenty men of Wycliffe's band,
Who waited not their lord's command.
Redmond his spurs from buskins drew,
His mantle from his shoulders threw,
His pistols in his belt he placed,
The greenwood gain'd, the footsteps traced,
Shouted like huntsman to his hounds,
"To cover, hark!" and in he bounds.'

And (a significant touch):

> ' With them was Wilfrid, stung with ire,
>   And envying Redmond's martial fire,
>   And emulous of fame.'[47]

A little later Scott describes his hero and in so doing consciously or unconsciously describes a young man such as his contemporaries saw in himself:

> ' 'Twas Redmond—by the azure eye;
>   'Twas Redmond—by the locks that fly
>   Disorder'd from his glowing cheek;
>   Mien, face, and form, young Redmond speak.
>   A form more active, light, and strong,
>   Ne'er shot the ranks of war along;
>   The modest, yet the manly mien,
>   Might grace the court of maiden queen;
>   A face more fair you well might find,
>   For Redmond's knew the sun and wind,
>   Nor boasted, from their tinge when free,
>   The charm of regularity;
>   But every feature had the power
>   To aid the expression of the hour:
>   Whether gay wit, and humour sly,
>   Danced laughing in his light-blue eye;
>   Or bended brow, and glance of fire,
>   And kindling cheek, spoke Erin's ire;
>   Or soft and sadden'd glances show
>   Her ready sympathy with woe;
>   Or in that wayward mood of mind,
>   When various feelings are combined,
>   When joy and sorrow mingle near,
>   And hope's bright wings are check'd by fear,
>   And rising doubts keep transport down,
>   And anger lends a short-lived frown;
>   In that strange mood which maids approve,
>   Even when they dare not call it love;

> With every change his features play'd,
> As aspens show the light and shade.[48]

It was William Erskine (who knew Scott only in his best days) who pronounced the lines above ' A face more fair . . . the expression of the hour ' to be ' an excellent portrait of the author himself'.[49]   But there are many descriptions of the vivacity and expressiveness of Scott in conversation and anecdote; and not the least revealing is one written down by Samuel Rogers after a meeting as late as 21st October 1831, two days before Scott left for Malta: ' The inimitable manner in which he told [a story of his schooldays]—the glance of the eye, the turn of the head, and the light that played over his faded features, as one by one the circumstances came back to him, accompanied by a thousand boyish feelings that had slept perhaps for years—there is no language, not even his own, could convey to you.'[50]

Confiding and open as he was, Scott early learned from fear of ridicule to keep to himself his most romantic ideals. He outgrew his invalidish timidity and sensibly put his sensibility on a leash. But he knew himself to be still the dreamer, whatever practical and matter-of-fact aspect he presented to the world, though it was only to his *Journal* that he confided the truth: ' My life, though not without its fits of waking and strong exertion, has been a sort of dream spent in

> " Chewing the cud of sweet and bitter fancy ".[51]

I have worn a wishing-cap the power of which has been to divert present griefs by a touch of the wand of imagination, and gild over the future prospect by prospects more fair than can ever be realized. Somewhere it is said that this castle-building—this wielding of the aërial trowel—is fatal to exertions in actual life. I cannot tell; I have not found it so—I cannot indeed say like Mad^e Genlis,[52] that in the imaginary scenes in which I have acted a part I ever prepared myself for anything which actually befell me. But I have certainly fashioned out much that made the present hour pass pleasantly away and much that has enabled me to contribute to the amusement of the public. Since I was five years old I cannot remember the time when I had not some ideal part to play for my own solitary amusement.'[53]

The boy Scott, it is true, had had one particular friend and confidant, John Irving. But it was one of those exclusive intimacies of boyhood in which the perfect number is only one more than one. Like Alan Fairford and Darsie Latimer, they ' were united by the closest bonds of intimacy; and the more so, that neither of them sought nor desired to admit any others into their society '.[54] But in the nature of things, two, however sympathetic, do not afford each other much variety of interchange. Irving clearly was the led rather than the leader in this innocent conspiracy, the hearer rather than the heard in its confabulations, whether when he tried to keep up with the quicker and readier Scott in romance-reading and romance-spinning, or when he gave a faithful attendance at the sick bed. It was, too, with Irving that Scott still in his boyhood began to go farther afield than the environs of Edinburgh, leaning on his companion and on a stout stick and roaming over the country—within a radius of eight or nine miles.

When at Kelso for a few weeks in his sixteenth year and away from Irving's society, Scott had chosen as a confidante (one cannot say ' fallen in love with ') a girl probably younger than himself and certainly of humbler origin, because the shy lad felt he could talk and write more readily to such an *ingénue*.[55] But for the most part Scott had been driven in on himself, his books, and the world of his own imagination.

But, he records in his *Journal*, ' As I grew from boyhood to manhood I saw this would not do; and that to gain a place in men's esteem I must mix and bustle with them.' And he adds, somewhat cryptically: ' Pride and an excitation of spirits supplied the real pleasure which others seem to feel in society, and certainly upon many occasions it was real.'[56]   However that sentence is to be interpreted, he deliberately set himself to be more of a participator in life than he had been, a young man with other young men, holding his place in a workaday world, developing a commonsense, humorous, and practical attitude to men and affairs, and not wearing his heart too much on his sleeve.   From his seventeenth or eighteenth year, then, his latent genius for friendship came to flower, and he began, as he says, ' to feel and take my ground in society.   A ready wit, a good deal of enthusiasm and a perception that soon ripened into tact and observation of character rendered me an acceptable companion to many young men whose acquisitions in philosophy and science were infinitely superior to anything I could boast '.[57]   He writes almost as if he had been admitted to the circle on specially easy terms. But he had gifts both of character and of mind which won from his friends their affection and admiration—his integrity, his high sense of honour, his complete lack of affectation, his unassuming and generous good-nature, his wise common-sense and judgement, his lively conversation, the range of his knowledge of books and of people, and his astonishing power of memory.

It was for Scott, however, not merely an entry into a congenial group of young men and a participation in their amusements.   In their company he ' came out ' into the wider society of Edinburgh and matured rapidly from a somewhat callow and retiring youth, in some ways not as old as his years, into a young man with a broad outlook on life and the capacity to play his part in it with ease and poise.   He began to dress himself with a new care;[58] he sought, rather than avoided, social occasions and the company of women, especially of young women; he made himself very agreeable at assemblies and the like; and he carried himself so well and had such a good presence, despite his disability, that one of Edinburgh's *grandes dames*, the

Countess of Sutherland,[59] described him as 'a comely creature'.[60]

Among the young men now his associates, all of good family, well-connected, and able, 'who sometimes plunged deeply into politics and metaphysics, and not unfrequently "daff'd the world aside, and bid it pass"',[61] were the following, according to Scott's own list: George Abercromby (Lord Abercromby); David Boyle (Lord President); William Clerk; the Honourable Thomas Douglas (Earl of Selkirk); John James Edmonstone of Newton; (Sir) Adam Ferguson; and John Irving. Others who were just as much of the circle, though Scott does not happen to mention them by name in the list of those 'with whom I chiefly lived at this period of my youth',[62] were: George Cranstoun (Lord Corehouse); Robert Davidson (Professor of Civil Law, Glasgow University); David Douglas (Lord Reston); James Fergusson (Clerk to the Court of Session); James Glassford of Dugalston (Sheriff of Dumbartonshire); Charles Kerr of Abbotrule; David Monypenny (Lord Pitmilly); (Sir) Patrick Murray of Ochtertyre; Patrick Murray of Simprim; and (Sir) William Rae (Lord Advocate).

The most important renewal of friendship was with the brilliant but indolent William Clerk, the original of Darsie Latimer in *Redgauntlet*,[63] who has already been mentioned in connection with Scott's attempts to sketch,[64] and who became his closest friend and ally in his young manhood, as the less volatile and stimulating John Irving had been in his boyhood.[65] Scott described Clerk in 1808, admiringly but not very hopefully, as 'a man of the most acute intellects and powerful apprehension . . . who, should he ever shake loose the fetters of indolence by which he has been hitherto trammelled, cannot fail to be distinguished in the highest degree'.[66] Seventeen years later he had to describe the able idler in very much the same terms: 'I have . . . never met a man of greater powers or more complete information on all desirable subjects . . . Clerk will, I am afraid, leave the world little more than the report of his fame. He is too indolent to finish any considerable work.'[67]

With Clerk and the rest, Scott's way of life became more ranging as well as more sociable. The scope of his expeditions, afoot or, as often as he and his friends could manage it, on horseback in which exercise he always delighted, was greatly widened.[68] 'My principal object in these excursions,' he tells us, 'was the pleasure of seeing romantic scenery, or what afforded me at least equal pleasure, the places which had been distinguished by remarkable historical events.'[69] It was the age when many besides Dr Syntax toured in search of the picturesque; and Scott's love of it was understood and met a general approval: 'but', he rather surprisingly adds, 'I often found it difficult to procure sympathy with the interest I felt in the latter.[70] Yet to me, the wandering over the field of Bannockburn was the source of more exquisite pleasure than gazing upon the celebrated landscape from the battlements of Stirling Castle'.[71]

> 'Yet, Albin, yet the praise be thine,
>   Thy scenes and glory to combine!
>   Thou bid'st him, who by Roslin strays,
>   List to the deeds of other days;
>   'Mid Cartland's Crags thou show'st the cave,
>   The refuge of thy champion brave;
>   Giving each rock its storied tale,
>   Pouring a lay for every dale,
>   Knitting, as with a moral band,
>   Thy native legends with thy land,
>   To lend each scene the interest high
>   Which genius beams from Beauty's eye.'[72]

When on foot Scott the 'lamiter'[73] could tramp at a steady three miles an hour from five in the morning till eight in the evening, covering often twenty or thirty miles in a day and not feeling at all fatigued at the end of it.[74] His expeditions frequently extended over more than one day and sometimes for the greater part of a week without previous warning at home and indeed without any such intention on his setting-out. 'Wood, water, wilderness itself,' he said, ' had an inexpressible charm for me, and I had a dreamy way of going much farther than I intended, so that unconsciously my return was protracted and my parents had sometimes serious cause of uneasiness.'[75] Scott was rather pleased than mortified by his father's declaring that he was ' born to be a strolling pedlar ', and thought, like the good Shakespearian he was, of Autolycus's *Jog on, jog on the footpath way*.[76] As for the domestic alarms, they were somewhat allayed after old Mr Scott's dry remark, in Mr Saunders Fairford's vein, that Walter was pretty sure to find his bread buttered on both sides wherever he went.[77] On one occasion, however, the tired company with not a sixpence between them and nearly thirty miles to go were reduced to eating hips and haws and canvassing cottage-doors. Like Sisera they asked for water and like Jael the goodwives gave them milk. It was on Scott's return from this expedition that his wish for George Primrose's musical gift provoked his father's celebrated sarcasm: " I greatly doubt, sir, you were born for nae better than a gangrel scrape-gut."[78] Such informal activities were the equivalent in Scott's time of the more organised athletics and team games of today. From the latter, or some of them, he would necessarily have been excluded; but he was a tall man of his hands and able to use them—' the first to begin a row, and the last to end it '[79]—and, as in his schooldays, took more pride in his feats of personal agility and prowess than in his mental gifts:

> ' High privilege of youthful time,
> Worth all the pleasures of our prime.'[80]

Most of Scott's new set were destined for the Bar and had adopted the budding advocate's disdain for the mere law agent—a tincture of prejudice not confined to the Scottish *noblesse de la robe*. Moreover they were cultivators of general literature on a broad front in ambitious preparation for the highest rewards of forensic eloquence. Their more liberal culture and the moral support in it they received from their families probably contrasted rather sharply with the situation in George Square and the less encouragement that Scott's literary interests obtained there, however well-intentioned Scott senior was according to his lights. It is not surprising, then, that Scott the son soon wanted to enter the 'highly honourable profession '[81] of an advocate.

But it is not the case that there were no other motives actuating Scott, as several of his biographers state or imply.[82] On the contrary, Scott had many motives, as is clear from the following passage in the *Memoir*: 'Amidst these studies, and in this society, the time of my apprenticeship elapsed; and in 1790, or thereabouts, it became necessary that I should seriously consider to which department of the law I was to attach myself. My father behaved with the most parental kindness. He offered, if I preferred his own profession, immediately to take me into partnership with him, which . . . afforded me an immediate prospect of a handsome independence. But he did not disguise his wish that I should relinquish this situation to my younger brother, and embrace the more ambitious profession of the Bar. I felt little hesitation in making my choice—for I was never very fond of money; and in no other particular do the professions admit of a comparison. Besides, I knew and felt the inconveniences attached to that of a writer; and I thought . . . many of them were " ingenio non subeunda meo ".[83] The appearance of personal dependence which that profession requires was disagreeable to me; the sort of connexion between the client and the attorney seemed to render the latter more subservient than was quite agreeable to my nature; and, besides, I had seen many sad examples . . . that the utmost exertions, and the best meant services, do not secure the *man of business* . . . from great loss, and most ungracious treatment on the part of his employers. The Bar, though I was conscious of my deficiencies as a public speaker, was the line of ambition and liberty; it was that also for which most of my contemporary friends were destined. And, lastly, although I would willingly have relieved my father of the labours of his business, yet I saw plainly we could not have agreed on some particulars, if we had attempted to conduct it together; and that I should disappoint his expectations if I did not turn to the Bar. So to that object my studies were directed with great ardour and perseverance during the years 1789, 1790, 1791, 1792.'[84]

One or two comments on this passage are required. To begin with, Scott is a little vague about the date of the decision. It can in fact be assigned almost certainly to the first half of 1789. But at that time he had not resumed his attendance at the University, although the opening phrase of the passage, ' Amidst these studies,' implies that he had.[85] Nor had his five-years' apprenticeship elapsed: the termination of it, if it had ever run out, would have been in March 1791. The offer, therefore, of an ' immediate partnership ' must be understood as meaning to begin as soon as possible after Scott had qualified as a Writer to the Signet and indeed after his twenty-first birthday in August 1791. Again, the decision to go to the Bar was taken with the full approval of Scott senior who had probably precipitated and had certainly anticipated it, his offer of a partnership not being an attempt at dissuasion.

NOTES ON REFERENCES

1   The only exceptions were: his uncle, Dr Daniel Ruther-ford, who had literary as well as scientific interests; John Home, whom he had known in his childhood at Bath and at whose house near Edinburgh he was later a frequent visitor; and Dr Thomas Blacklock, who had advised him in literary matters during his schooldays.

2   Even John Irving, who, though also a W.S. apprentice, was in a different office.

3   *Grandfather*, I, 209; cf. ibid, I, 321.

4   Knighted in 1822.

5   *Home*, 838.

6   The Tower of Glendearg in *The Monastery* is called 'the very Kamtschatka of the Halidome' (Chapter XV).

7   Commemorated in the well-known picture by C. M. Hardie.

8   In narrating the episode Scott said he 'was a lad of fifteen in 1786-7 when [Burns] came first to Edinburgh' (Lockhart, I, 37), but does not date it more precisely. Nor does Lockhart in his biography of Scott. But in his *Life of Robert Burns* he gives 1786 (ed. Ernest Rhys, 80).

9   *Memoir*, I, 13.

10 *Burns*, 848. Cf. *supra*, 142 note 16 for Scott's first glimpse of Burns in Sibbald's bookshop.

11 I, 37.

12 Stewart had come back to Edinburgh at the beginning of November with a copy of the Kilmarnock Burns. This he showed to Henry Mackenzie who wrote a generous review of it for *The Lounger*, no. 97.

13 Brother-in-law of Professor Adam Ferguson.

14 E.g. Dr Daniel Rutherford; Henry Mackenzie; Dr Thomas Blacklock; and Dr Edmund Cartwright, whose *Armine and Elvira* had brought him an ephemeral celebrity as a poet.

15 One of the ladies was Joan Keir, who supplied Lockhart with several anecdotes of Scott's youth, but would not let her name be attached to them. She was the earliest and most intimate friend of Scott's sister Anne, a grand-niece of Alexander Keith of Ravelston, and by her marriage mother of W. E. Aytoun.

16 Lockhart, I, 37.

17 *Burns*, 852.

18 Ibid., 849.

19 *Prose*, 847-52.

20 *Burns*, 849-50.

21 In the Museum of the Chambers Institution, Peebles.

22 Lockhart, I, 37.

23 Langhorne's name is given as the poet, but in small print.

24 The correct title is in fact *The Country Justice*. In substance and mood it anticipates the work of Scott's favourite, Crabbe.

25 Lockhart, I, 38. Sir Adam Ferguson's account adds a few

details: 'Burns seemed at first little inclined to mingle easily in the company; he went round the room looking at the pictures on the walls. The print described by Scott arrested his attention; he read aloud the lines underneath, but before he reached the end his voice faltered, and his eyes filled with tears. A little after, he turned with much interest to the company, pointed to the picture, and with some eagerness asked if any one could tell him who had written those affecting lines. The philosophers were silent; no one knew: but, after a decent interval, the pale lame boy near by said in a negligent manner: "They're written by one Langhorne." An explanation of the place where they occur followed, and Burns fixed a look of half-serious interest on the youth, while he said: "You'll be a man yet, sir."' (*The Life and Works of Robert Burns*. Ed. Robert Chambers. Revised William Wallace, II, 82-83.)

26 He had become the second-eldest member of his family by the death of his brother Robert on 7th June 1787.

27 I.e. John Irving, Adam Ferguson, and James Ramsay. For the last-named, cf. *Letters*, I, 13 (3rd September 1790, to William Clerk).

28 *Memoir*, I, 16.

29 I, 40.

30 Cf. *infra*, 184, 187.

31 *Redgauntlet*, Letter V.

32 Walter Scott senior was born in 1729, and was therefore nearly sixty at the time of which Scott junior is speaking. Mrs Scott was a few years younger than her husband.

33 I, 17.

34 *Redgauntlet*, Letter VIII.

35 *Redgauntlet*, Letter XII.

36 *The Monastery*, Chapter XIV.

37 Allan, however, avers that 'There were two more of the old man's grand-children inmates of the house when Walter arrived, both of whom were younger than the stranger. One of them still remembers him as kind and attentive to them—as "a famous play-fellow". He used to limp about, leaning on his little crutch, with the lesser imps trotting after him' (10).

38 I, 104 (14th February 1826).

39   Cf. *supra*, 25.
40   Grierson, 13, note 1.
41   *Journal*, I, 58 (27th December 1825).
42   I, 58 (27th December 1825).
43   *Journal*, I, 143 (28th March 1826). The passage continues more in relation to his middle and later life as follows: ' I have risen from a feast satiated, and unless it be one or two persons of very strong intellect, or whose spirits and good-humour amuse me, I wish neither to see the high, the low, nor the middling class of society. This is a feeling without the least tinge of misanthropy, which I always consider as a kind of blasphemy of a shocking description. If God bears with the very worst of us, we may surely endure each other. If thrown into society, I always have, and always will endeavour to bring pleasure with me, at least to shew willingness to please. But for all this " I had rather live alone ", and I wish my appointment [i.e. as Clerk of Session] so convenient otherwise did not require my going to Edinburgh. But this must be, and in my little lodging I will be lonely enough.'
44   Canto First.
45   Cf. *supra*, 11-12.
46   Canto First.
47   Canto Second.
48   Canto Third.
49   *Letters*, I, lxvi.
50   Lockhart, I, 26.
51   *As You Like It*, IV, iii (for ' cud' read ' food').
52   Madame de Genlis.
53   I, 58-59 (27th December 1825). Cf. *Waverley*, Chapter V: ' So far was Edward Waverley from expecting general sympathy with his own feelings, or concluding that the present state of things was calculated to exhibit the reality of those visions in which he loved to indulge, that he dreaded nothing more than the detection of such sentiments as were dictated by his musings. He neither had nor wished to have a confidant, with whom to communicate his reveries; and so sensible was he of the ridicule attached to them that, had he been to choose between any punishment short of ignominy, and the necessity of giving a

cold and composed account of the ideal world in which he lived the better part of his days, I think he would not have hesitated to prefer the former infliction.'

54 *Redgauntlet*, Chapter I.

55 Cf. *Letters*, I, 1-8.

56 I, 58 (27th December 1825).

57 *Memoir*, I, 16.

58 Partly, it would appear, as a result of William Clerk's raillery.

59 In the *Journal* he describes a letter from her as ' kind and friendly after the wont of Banzu-Mohr-ar-chat' (I, 42; 13th December 1825). He was having a shot at her Gaelic title, ' Banamhorar-Chat ' (= the Great Lady of the Cat). After Scott's death and the creation of the Dukedom, she was known as the Duchess-Countess.

60 Lockhart, I, 44.

61 *Memoir*, I, 16. The quotation within the quotation is from *I Henry IV*, IV, i.

62 *Memoir*, I, 16.

63 Lockhart had ' no sort of doubt that William Clerk was, in the main, Darsie Latimer ' (I, 44). But he found many coincidences between *Redgauntlet* and the letters of a young man whom Scott had befriended and advised in sundry scrapes (cf. ibid., I, 43-44). His name, which Lockhart omits, was Charles Kerr of Abbotrule. According to Sir Herbert Grierson, it was he, not Clerk, who sat for Darsie (cf. *Letters*, I, lvii).

64 Cf. *supra*, 130-31. Scott became friendly also with an older brother, John Clerk (Lord Eldin), and a younger, James Clerk, R.N.

65 Clerk and Irving were nearly related.

66 *Memoir*, I, 17.

67 *Journal*, I, 2 (20th November 1825). Cf. *Letters on Demonology and Witchcraft*, Letter X: William Clerk, ' one of the most accurate, intelligent, and acute persons whom I have known in the course of my life '. Lockhart reports Scott's retort, ' I think William Clerk well worth you all put together,' made when his fellow-clerks showed resentment at his finding such new friends as " Clerk and some more of these dons that look down on the like of us "

(I, 43). The only offices which Clerk ever held were those of Advocate-Depute and Chief Clerk of the Jury Court (for civil actions).

68 Several excursions by sea were made when William Clerk's midshipman brother James was stationed at Leith.

69 *Memoir*, I, 15.

70 He received encouragement, however, in his antiquarian studies from John Clerk of Eldin. John Clerk was one of the prototypes of Jonathan Oldbuck, the other being George Constable (cf. *supra*, 57).

71 *Memoir*, I, 15.

72 *Rokeby*, Canto Second.

73 As Midshipman James Clerk called him. Scott often alluded in conversation to the fact that two of his ancestors were lame, John the Lamiter (Scott of Sinton) and William Boltfoot (Scott of Harden). 'But, if the scholarship of John the Lamiter [who had been at Glasgow University] furnished his descendant with many a mirthful allusion, a far greater favourite was the memory of William the Boltfoot . . . one of the "prowest knights" of the whole genealogy—a fearless horseman and expert spearsman, renowned and dreaded.' (Lockhart (abr.), I, 3, note 1.)

74 Cf. *Memoir*, I, 14-15 and Lockhart, I, 43-4 for accounts of such excursions; and *Letters*, I, 18-20, for a description to William Clerk on 26th August 1791 of Scott's first visit to Flodden.

75 *Memoir*, I, 14.

76 Ibid.

77 Lockhart, I, 42.

78 Lockhart, I, 42. Cf. *Letters*, I, 38 (to Christian Rutherford, October or November 1794): 'I want the assistance of your eloquence to convince my honoured father that nature did not mean me for a vagabond or *travelling Merchant* when she honoured me with the wandering propensity, lately so conspicuously displayed'; and *Redgauntlet*, Letter II: 'scouring the country like a landlouper, going he knows not where, to see he knows not what'.

79 Said by the admiring Midshipman James Clerk in introducing Scott to a company (Lockhart, I, 41).

80 *Rokeby*, Canto Fifth.

81 *Grandfather*, I, 321.
82 E.g. Lockhart, I, 40; Grierson, 16, 18-19.
83 This phrase from Milton's first *Elegy* is a good example of
    Scott's ready quotation from by no means hackneyed texts.
    He does not himself give the reference, nor does Lockhart.
    In *Drama*, 615, he adapts the phrase to the context as ' haud
    subeundo ingenio suo '.
84 *Memoir*, I, 16-17.
85 He began his second academic period in the autumn of
    1789, not, however, entering a Law class till the following
    session. Of course Scott presumably studied law textbooks
    through his apprenticeship; and it is possible that he did
    so under a tutor or ' grinder '. An odd but able advocate,
    John Wright, taught Roman and Scots Law extra-murally.

CHAPTER XII

SECOND UNIVERSITY PERIOD

Deprived of the personal patronage enjoyed by most of his contemporaries, who assumed the gown under the protection of their aristocratic alliances and descents, he early saw that he should have that to achieve for himself which fell to them as a right of birth.
                                        Redgauntlet, Chapter X.

But he need not be afraid that a lad of your steadiness will be influenced by such a reed shaken by the winds as I am. You will go on doubting with Dirleton, and resolving those doubts with Stewart, until the cramp speech has been spoken more solito *from the corner of the bench, and with covered head; until you have sworn to defend the liberties and privileges of the College of Justice; until the black gown is hung on your shoulders, and you are free as any of the Faculty to sue or defend.*
                                        Redgauntlet, Letter I.

SCOTT resumed his attendance at the University in the session 1789-90 in the Class of Moral Philosophy, not, as Lockhart states, in 1788-89 in the Class of Civil Law.[1] The fame of Professor Dugald Stewart, ' whose striking and impressive eloquence riveted the attention even of the most volatile student ',[2] was then at its height. He had a fine presence, a superb command of words and periods, and a natural grace of delivery and gesture. Though not a very original or profound thinker,[3] he was a brilliant exponent of Thomas Reid's commonsense philosophy with some of David Hartley's associationism,[4] which his oratory made irresistibly attractive to young men of promise, flocking to his large classes from every quarter of Britain and from overseas, and listening spellbound to every word. ' To me his lectures were like the opening of the heavens,' says Cockburn. ' I felt that I had a soul. His noble views, unfolded in glorious sentences, elevated me into a higher world. . . . They changed my whole nature.'[5] The more strictly philosophical side of Stewart's teaching probably made little appeal to Scott who found ' much of water-painting in all metaphysics, which consist rather of words than ideas '.[6] But in fact Stewart ' dealt as little as possible in metaphysics, avoided details, and shrunk . . . from all polemical matter. Invisible distinctions, vain contentions, factious theories, philosophical sectarianism, had no attractions for him; and their absence left him free for those moral themes on which he could soar without perplexing his hearers, or wasting himself, by useless and painful subtleties '.[7] Stewart, who was a man of many talents and interests,[8] really made Moral Philosophy a course in *litterae humaniores* and was himself the ideal Professor of Things in General. Something of the range of topics discussed in his course may even be deduced from one of Scott's class essays, ' On the Manners and Customs of the Northern Nations ', though the subject appears not to have been a prescribed one. Stewart is reported to have said of it: ' The author of this paper shows much knowledge of his subject, and a great taste for such

researches.'[9] The author indeed could probably speak on
the subject with a good deal more of authority than the
Professor himself. He had already presented to the Literary
Society in 1789 what was no doubt substantially the same
essay, ' On the Origin of the Feudal System '.[10] And he
delivered it[11] as his first essay for the Speculative Society,
in 1791.[12] Before the end of the University session Scott
had become a frequent visitor at the house of Professor
Stewart, with whom he remained on the most friendly
terms till Stewart's death in 1828.

Another acquaintance begun in the Moral Philosophy
classroom was with a modest and industrious young man,
considerably older than Scott himself and obviously very
poor. It was only after the two had become intimate and
companions in walking excursions that Scott discovered
his friend's father to be a venerable Blue-gown or King's
Bedesman. Scott describes him in the Advertisement to
The Antiquary as a ' thin wasted form . . . who stood by
the Potter-row port . . . and, without speaking a syllable,
gently inclined his head and offered his hat, but with the
least possible degree of urgency '. Not only did Scott visit
the Bedesman's cottage at St Leonard's, dining there plainly
and solidly on an excellent gigot of mutton and potatoes
with whisky as good to wash them down, but he was
instrumental in doing something towards the fulfilment of
the old man's ambition: " Please God, I may live to see
my bairn wag his head in a pulpit yet."[13] Scott acquainted
his mother with the whole story and his own wish to help
his poor friend to a tutorship in some gentleman's family.
Thereupon Mrs Scott, discreetly concealing the situation
from her husband (who would have been scandalised more
by the gigot than by the whisky), satisfied herself as to the
young man's character, and through Dr John Erskine of
Greyfriars had him placed as a tutor in the North of Scotland.

It seems to have been during the same session of 1789-90
that Scott attended the lectures of Professor Alexander Fraser
Tytler on Universal History.[14] Tytler, as the son of the

lawyer-historian, William Tytler, had been nurtured in antiquarian studies and trained for the Bar.[15] He was a man of wide literary interests, as his miscellaneous works show.[16] His appointment in 1780 to the History Chair was highly congenial, and he entered with enthusiasm on the duties of it, reviving a taste in the University for historical studies which had been sadly neglected despite the fame of the Scottish school of historians.[17] But one may be permitted to doubt whether Scott, who could 'hash history with anybody, be he who he will',[18] derived much inspiration from Tytler's jejune, methodised, and generalised history.

The two classes of Moral Philosophy and Universal History which Scott attended in the first session of his second University sojourn, like the classes he took in the first spell, were meant to broaden his outlook before his professional studies began.[19] As for the latter, he says, 'Let me do justice to the only years of my life in which I applied to learning with stern, steady, undeviating industry.'[20] The unassuming Scott really believed this in spite of the abundant proofs to the contrary.[21] The learning to which he refers was Scots Law in the academic sessions 1790-91 and 1791-92 and Civil Law in 1790-91. He says in reference to this period, 'The severe studies necessary to render me fit for my profession occupied the greater part of my time; and the society of my friends and companions who were about to enter life along with me filled up the interval, with the usual amusements of young men.[22] I was in a situation which rendered serious labour indispensable; for, neither possessing, on the one hand, any of those peculiar advantages which are supposed to favour a hasty advance in the profession of the law, nor being, on the other hand, exposed to unusual obstacles to interrupt my progress, I might reasonably expect to succeed according to the greater or less degree of trouble which I should take to qualify myself as a pleader.'[23] He certainly laboured with exemplary diligence; either in the little parlour in George Square in which he was enfeoffed at this time and of which he took

' the exclusive possession . . . with all the feelings of novelty and liberty ';[24] or at William Clerk's home at the west end of Princes Street, to which, when Clerk's resolution proved unequal to coming every other day to George Square, Scott trudged to rouse his indolent friend with great punctuality before seven every morning but Sunday during the two summers either of 1790 and 1791 or of 1791 and 1792. In the course of them, says Scott, ' we went by way of question and answer through the whole of Heineccius's Analysis of the Institutes and Pandects, as well as through the smaller copy of Erskine's Institutes of the Law of Scotland '.[25]

His application to Civil Law, however conscientious,[26] was very distasteful. Though the University course in it, which Scott attended only for the one session in 1791-92, was not obligatory for prospective advocates or Writers to the Signet, an accurate and extensive knowledge of the Justinian code had always been regarded as an indispensable qualification for a sound Scottish lawyer; and those who did not acquire it at Leyden or elsewhere abroad sought it in the commentators rather than at the University. Professor Robert Dick, who had very few pupils, does not seem to have lectured regularly every session or very effectively at any time. I can discover little about him, except that he followed the lead of his learned brother in Glasgow of lecturing in English,[27] and that in Scott's day his Chair ' might . . . be considered as in *abeyance*, since the person by whom it was occupied had never been fit for the situation, and was then almost in a state of dotage '.[28] Dick applied for an assistant in 1792; and the same year his successor as Professor, John Wilde,[29] was appointed. Scott speaks feelingly in his letters of the dullness of the civilians; ' peace be with them ', he writes to William Clerk, ' and may the dust lie light upon their heads: they deserve this prayer in return for those sweet slumbers which their benign influence infuses into their readers '.[30] The date of the letter is 3rd September 1790; and the two summers during which he and Clerk worked in conjunction were likely to have been

those of 1790 and 1791.[31]   But Scott had been studying
Civil and also Scots Law on his own at least three years
before, during his apprenticeship.[32]   The evidence is a lively
piece entitled *Law versus Love*, which was among the poems
sent to the coy Jessie at Kelso.   As it is not readily procurable,
I quote it in full:

> ' Away with parchments, warrants, bills—
>   Come fairies, brownies, knights, and giants:
> Avaunt all stupid books of Law,
>   Shakespeare and Spenser are my clients.
>
> Heineccius to your shelf return
>   With brother Erskine's dryer labours,[33]
> For I have to supply your place—
>   Romance and Love, those pleasant neighbours.
>
> Heav'n keep your slumbers undisturbed,
>   You weary, dreary, dull civilians !
> Love's are the only Institutes;
>   His Pandects are the laws of millions.
>
> Glad as I 'scape from thy dull rule,
>   A fresher air seems breaking o'er me;
> There tow'rs a castle strong and high,
>   Here blooms a fair pleasaunce before me.
>
> A lady's bower mine eye invites,
>   My feet gang there in willing duty;
> I enter, and amid its flow'rs
>   I find a flow'r of matchless beauty.
>
> There sits my peerless queen enthroned;
>   And whilst in haste my joy I'm proving,
> I'm roused by Tom[34] who sharply cries,
>   "Hey, Wattie, man !   Ye're unco loving ! "
>
> The inky boards again transform
>   To Mother Nature's verdant bosom;
> The inkstands turn to goodly trees
>   And all the pens begin to blossom.

Our shabby cloth and corduroy
  Now change to richest silk and satin;
And nought but fairy music sounds
  'Stead of broad Scotch or musty Latin.

But greater changes still ensue
  (I fear that I'm *non compos mentis*):
I spy a horrid Saracen
  In ev'ry yawning gouk[35] apprentice.

These paynims vile I fierce assault,
  Till stopped by cry of snoring dolour;
I find by Allan's[36] bloody pate
  I've cracked his noddle with the ruler.[37]

Whatever the romantic apprentice may have said about
it, Scott did not speak in the same bored strain of his addic-
tion to Scots Law when he came to study it seriously. It
had indeed for him something of the attraction of a country
in romance. He found it rich in vestiges of Scottish history
and custom; it was both a monument of his country's past
and a precious reliquary of the lives out of which it had
arisen; and it was to supply him later with suggestions for
many a complicated plot and ingenious *dénouement* and for
many a passage of manners-painting and characterisation.
The Professor of Scots Law was David Hume, nephew of
the philosopher; he was ' a man as virtuous and amiable
as conspicuous for masculine vigour of intellect and variety
of knowledge ',[38] and from 1811 till 1822 was Scott's
colleague as one of the Clerks of Session. Though a very
able and distinguished lawyer and a brilliant expositor, he
gave strict injunctions that none of his lectures should be
published after his death.[39] Many manuscript copies, however, were in circulation, and his academic opinions were,
and probably still are, frequently quoted by the Bench and
the Bar. Scott, after taking full notes in the Class which
he attended for the two sessions of 1790-91 and 1791-92,
actually twice transcribed the lectures in full, presenting the

second copy bound in volumes to his father, who was delighted by this proof of his son's assiduity in the law and by the 'very pleasant reading for leisure hours'[40] which it afforded. Besides this tacit tribute to Hume, Scott gives high praise in his *Memoir* to the learned 'architect' of the Law of Scotland who could so lucidly and fascinatingly explain that complex legal structure: ' I can never sufficiently admire the penetration and clearness of conception which were necessary to the arrangement of the fabric of law, formed originally under the strictest influence of feudal principles, and innovated, altered, and broken in upon by the changes of time, of habits, and of manners, until it resembles some ancient castle, partly entire, partly ruinous, partly dilapidated, patched and altered during the succession of ages by a thousand additions, yet still exhibiting, with the marks of antiquity, symptoms of the skill and wisdom of its founders, and capable of being analyzed and made the subject of a methodical plan by an architect who can understand the various styles of the different ages in which it was subjected to alteration. Such an architect has Mr Hume been to the law of Scotland, neither wandering into fanciful and abstruse disquisitions, which are the more proper subject of the antiquary, nor satisfied with presenting to his pupils a dry and undigested detail of the laws in their present state, but combining the past state of our legal enactments with the present, and tracing clearly and judiciously the changes which took place, and the causes which led to them.'[41]

Scott did not attend the Class of Public Law, the only other one at that time in the Faculty; perhaps because he had had enough of legal abstractions in his study of the *jus civile* without going on to more in the *jus gentium*, or because public international law was of little practical use to an advocate practising in the Scottish Courts.

NOTES ON REFERENCES

1 I, 40. Lockhart wrongly dates Scott's membership of the Moral Philosophy Class in ' the winter of 1790-91 ' (I, 47). Cf. *infra*, 187-89, for Scott's Civil Law Class in 1791-92. I have not attempted to point out more than a few of the inaccurate statements made by Scott's earlier biographers (which later ones have repeated) as to his classes in either his first or his second University period.

2 *Memoir*, I, 12. Scott gives the impression inadvertently that he went straight from Bruce's Logic and Metaphysics to Stewart's Moral Philosophy.

3 His chief works in philosophy were: *Elements of the Philosophy of the Human Mind*, 1792-1827; *Outlines of Moral Philosophy*, 1793, etc.; *Philosophical Essays*, 1810; *A General View of the Progress of Metaphysical, Ethical, and Political Philosophy since the Revival of Letters*, 1815-21; and *The Philosophy of the Active and Moral Powers*, 1828. He also published biographies of Adam Smith, William Robertson, and Thomas Reid. His collected works were edited by Sir William Hamilton and published in eleven volumes in 1854-58.

4 Scott told Crabbe that the ' association of ideas ' was ' the universal pick-lock of all metaphysical difficulties . . . when I studied moral philosophy ' (*Letters*, III, 211, about January 1813).

5 24.

6 *Journal*, II, 263 (14th June 1828).

7 Cockburn, 22. Cf. Grant, II, 341: Stewart's bias was towards ' the topics lying between mental science on the one hand and jurisprudence on the other '.

8 He had professed Mathematics and Natural Philosophy before his translation to the Moral Philosophy Chair. He was Joint-Professor of Mathematics at the age of 19 and sole Professor at 24.

9 Lockhart, I, 47.

10 He gave a summary of it in a letter to his uncle Captain Robert Scott, mentioning the Literary Society, but not the Moral Philosophy Class (*Letters*, I, 17; 30th September 1790).

11   The ' same opinions more at length ', according to Lockhart (I, 47).

12   Cf. *infra*, 213-14.

13   Lockhart, I, 48. Cf. *Guy Mannering*, Chapter II, where the fond wish for their ' bairn ' is attributed to the parents of Dominie Sampson.

14   Unfortunately the list of Tytler's students was not entered in the register. But Scott's name does not appear in the lists for 1788-89, 1790-91, and 1791-92.

15   He was raised to the Bench as Lord Woodhouselee in 1802.

16   Essays in *The Mirror*, 1779-80, and *The Lounger*, 1785-87; the first *History of the Society* in *Transactions of the Royal Society of Edinburgh*, Vol. I, 1788 (Tytler was one of the original Fellows); critical-biographical studies of Henry Home (Lord Kames), Allan Ramsay, Petrarch, and others; an edition of Phineas Fletcher's *Piscatory Eclogues*, etc., 1771; *Essay on the Principles of Translation*, 1791, etc.

17   Tytler published a syllabus of his lectures in 1783, *Plan and Outline of a Course of Lectures on Universal History, Ancient and Modern, delivered in the University of Edinburgh*. It was much enlarged in his *Elements of General History, Ancient and Modern*, 1801, which has been described as ' useful and interesting information, conveyed in an agreeable manner, and remarkable both for perspicuity of style and methodical arrangement ' (Bower, III, 236).

18   *Journal*, II, 171. In a letter to Mrs Hughes Scott calls himself ' a professed pedlar in antiquarian [matters] ' (*Letters*, VIII, 366, 13th September 1824).

19   Perhaps for the same reason he acquired in 1789 the just-published fifth edition of Adam Smith's *Wealth of Nations*. In the same year his aunt Mrs Russell gave him another book of a mind-opening kind, Burke's *Sublime and Beautiful*.

20   *Memoir*, I, 17. Cf. Lockhart, I, 50: ' that course of legal study . . . on which he dwells in his *Memoir* with more satisfaction than on any other passage in his early life '.

21   We hardly need Irving's declaration that ' Sir Walter when a young man always shewed the greatest diligence and zeal in every thing in which he engaged '.

22   Lockhart's suggestion that Scott's ' unfortunate passion [for Williamina Belsches] had a powerful influence in nerving

[his] mind for the sedulous diligence with which he pursued his proper legal studies ' (I, 45) seems to me to show surprisingly little knowledge of human nature. University students who fall deeply in love invariably neglect their studies. In any case Scott's love for Miss Belsches did not begin, I feel sure, until at least the summer and more probably the autumn of 1792, by which time his sedulous legal studies were behind him. I also think that Scott, who had a marked autobiographical tendency, as his prefaces and introductions show, broke off his formal autobiography, the Ashestiel *Memoir*, at the early summer of 1792, just because he was approaching a subject which his natural delicacy and romantic chivalry shrank from publishing. He had said nothing about his much more transient attachment in 1787 to Jessie —— at Kelso. *A fortiori* he felt it impossible to tell his grand passion to the world, whatever soft echoes of it he allowed to sound in his poems and novels. For the earlier episode, cf. *Letters*, I, 1-8; Grierson, 17-18; and Davidson Cook, *New Love-Poems by Sir Walter Scott*; and for the later episode, cf. Lockhart, I, 44-45; Grierson, 28-45; and Sir C. N. Johnston (Lord Sands), *Sir Walter Scott's Congé* (1931 ed.). Lockhart does not give Miss Belsches's name in his extended biography; in his abridgement he wrongly calls her ' Margaret, daughter of Sir John and Lady Jane Stuart Belches of Invermay ' (I, 63-4). Sir John did not assume the addition of ' Stuart ' till 1798.

23 *General Preface.*

24 *Memoir*, I, 17. Cf. *Redgauntlet*, Letter II: ' I ... slunk ... into my own den, where I began to mumble certain half-gnawed and not half-digested doctrines of our municipal code '; and Lockhart, I, 49, for a description of the parlour and its contents, the germ of the library and museum at Abbotsford.

25 *Memoir*, I, 17. Boswell and Charles Hay (later Lord Newton) pursued very similar studies, but after their call to the Bar: ' Mr Charles Hay and I this day resumed our study of Erskine's Institutes where we left off last vacation. I went to his house then. He agreed to come to mine now ' (*Boswell's Journal*, 18th August 1774).

26   How conscientious may be realised from his careful timing of his reading as recorded in his copy of Heineccius's *Elementa Juris Civilis*, vol. I. He aimed at finishing it in 56 days at 16 pages a day, and did in fact finish it in less by exceeding his prescription most days (even though he took an occasional day off).

27   Cf. Graham, II, 189: 'Even in the middle of the [eighteenth] century Edinburgh professors of philosophy, law, and divinity persisted in their lumbering Latin . . . till finally they acquired enough good sense and moral courage to discourse in the vernacular, in all chairs, except the conservative divinity.'

28   *Memoir*, I, 17.

29   Cf. *infra*, 208, 232, note 57.

30   *Letters*, I, 14. Cf. ibid., I, 11 (6th August 1790); and *Lives of the Novelists* (*Prose*, 346): 'some of Harley's feelings were taken from those of the author himself [Henry Mackenzie] when, at his first entrance on the dry and barbarous study of the municipal law, he was looking back, like Blackstone, on the land of the Muses, which he was condemned to leave behind him.'

31   Scott acquired three Civil Law textbooks in 1789: a *Corpus Juris Civilis*; Johann Gottlieb Heineccius's *Elementa Juris Civilis*; and his *Recitationes in Elementa Juris Civilis*.

32   But Chambers is mistaken in stating that Scott attended the Civil Law Class while still an apprentice, 'that being the most approved method [i.e. through a legal apprenticeship] by which a barrister could acquire a technical knowledge of his profession, though it has never been uniformly practised' (29).

33   John Erskine, *The Principles of the Law of Scotland*, 1754; and *An Institute of the Law of Scotland*, 1773. He was the father of the Rev. Dr John Erskine.

34   His younger brother.

35   *Daft, foolish* from *gouk* or *gowk* = *cuckoo*.

36   An unidentified apprentice of Scott senior.

37   Cook, 32-34.

38   Lockhart, I, 141.

39   He published, however, a work of great learning and research, *Commentaries on the Law of Scotland respecting the*

Description and Punishment of Crimes, in 1797, and left a volume of *Decisions of the Court of Session*, 1781-1822 for posthumous publication (1839). *Baron David Hume's Lectures*, 1786-1822, edited and annotated by G. C. H. Paton, were published in six volumes, 1939-58; and the same editor published *A Supplement to Baron Hume's Lectures*, 1958.

40   Lockhart, I, 50.
41   *Memoir*, I, 17.

CHAPTER XIII

CLUBS AND SOCIETIES

When the necessity of daily labour is removed, and the call of social duty fulfilled, that of moderate and timely amusement claims its place, as a want inherent in our nature.

Essay on the Drama in Prose, 616.

To Noble House, sir! and what had you to do at Noble House, sir? Do you remember you are studying law, sir?— that your Scots Law trials are coming on, sir?—that every moment of your time just now is worth hours at another time? —and have you leisure to go to Noble House, sir?—and to throw your books behind you for so many hours? Had it been a turn in the Meadows, or even a game at golf—but Noble House, sir!

Redgauntlet, Letter II.

In my better days I had stories to tell. . . . My pains were then of the heart, and had something flattering in their character; if in the head, it was from the blow of a bludgeon, gallantly received and well paid back.

Journal, I, 293-4 (18th December 1826)

INTO the more sedentary amusements of his contemporaries, from which, I suppose, the present Students' Union and other student organisations derive, Scott threw himself with zest during his second academic spell. He then began, he says, 'to make some amends for the irregularity of my education'[1] by joining successively several societies for debating and essay-writing. And he was also a member of brotherhoods of a more purely social, not to say convivial, character. For Edinburgh was a city of clubs and societies, some staid bodies for serious philosophical and literary discussion or for promoting improvements in science, agriculture, and industry, some more sociable and less sedate, and some, as readers of *Guy Mannering* will recall,[2] jovial and anything but strait-laced; and the young men were as clubbable as their parents and elders.

I quote, without accepting it *au pied de la lettre*, Scott's own modest opinion of the part he played in the literary societies of which he was a member: 'In the business of these societies . . . I cannot boast of having made any great figure. I never was a good speaker unless upon some subject which strongly animated my feelings; and, as I was totally unaccustomed to composition, as well as the art of generalizing my ideas upon any subject, my literary essays were but very poor work. I never attempted them unless when compelled to do so by the regulations of the society, and then I was like the Lord of Castle Rackrent, who was obliged to cut down a tree to get a few faggots to boil the kettle; for the quantity of ponderous and miscellaneous knowledge, which I really possessed on many subjects, was not easily condensed, or brought to bear upon the object I wished particularly to become master of. Yet there occurred opportunities when this odd lumber of my brain, especially that which was connected with the recondite parts of history, did me, as Hamlet says " yeoman's service ".[3] My memory of events was like one of the large, old-fashioned stone-cannons of the Turks—very difficult to load well and discharge, but making a powerful effect when by good chance any object did come within range of its shot. Such fortunate opportunities of exploding with effect maintained my literary character among my companions, with whom I soon met with great indulgence and regard.'[4] That Scott did not generally shine in debate can readily be understood; but there were, no doubt, many occasions in which his feelings were engaged on one side or the other and in which he spoke with the eloquence of conviction. If his essays were indeed ' poor work ' (and Professor Dugald Stewart did not think the one he read contemptible),[5] they probably showed as much art of composition and generalisation as did those of any other member. Scott's mastery in these respects was not all learned later, but had developed naturally from the gift of story-telling which had been his from his boyhood at the High School. He felt himself to be embarrassed by his own abundant information; but even he realised that he possessed what others had not, but greatly enjoyed, when he brought forth treasures new and old in his essays or in his contributions to debates.

Besides joining one existing sodality to be mentioned later, Scott was a co-founder some time in 1789 of at least two others: the Literary Society which he attended during the year of its foundation and the year following, and in which he was known as Duns Scotus in honour of his multifarious knowledge; and an inner, entirely sociable circle of the Literary, known as the Club, in which he was called Colonel Grogg, apparently because of his grogram breeches.[6] The Literary Society, in which Scott frequently spoke, met every Friday evening in a Masonic lodge in Carrubber's Close; and it was the custom of Scott and his cronies who formed the Club to adjourn to an oyster tavern in Covenant Close. In the next room ' the Doctors' Club used to meet, of which Sir A[dam] Ferguson's father [Professor Adam Ferguson], Dr Hutton, Dr Black, Mr J. Clerk of Eldin . . ., etc., were members. . . . It is likely this led to our going to the same tavern, where I believe we used to disturb the Doctors' Club . . . by our noise and singing '.[7] The Club, which is said to have originated in a ride to Penicuik House, the home of William Clerk's uncle, consisted at the outset of nineteen members and apparently added none later.[8]

Scott was also a member, possibly as a founder, of the Teviotdale, another and modester social brotherhood which supped together once a month. The young members, of whom James Ballantyne was one, probably all hailed from Kelso or Roxburghshire or at least, as in Scott's case, had some connection therewith. Many student societies since have had such a territorial link. Though he was as boon a companion as any in the Club,[9] Scott was the most moderate drinker in the Teviotdale (which he regularly attended), no doubt, as Lockhart suggests, because ' the club consisted chiefly of persons . . . somewhat inferior to Scott in birth and station '.[10] At the same time he was accorded a ' remarkable ascendancy ', says Ballantyne ,' which appeared to arise from their involuntary and unconscious submission to the same firmness of understanding, and gentle exercise of it, which produced the same effects throughout his after life. Where there was always a good deal of drinking, there was of course now and then a good deal of quarrelling. But three words from Walter Scott never failed to put all such propensities to quietness '.[11]

Of Scott's clubs in his student days only the Speculative Society still survives—survives indeed with a much greater vitality than it displayed during his active membership. After a quarter of a century of existence, in which the Society had had its ups and downs, there came eight lean sessions from 1789-90 to 1796-97 after eight fat ones. Only forty-three new members were added to the roll in the lean years, and the numbers in attendance at the meetings not infrequently fell below the quorum.[12] Nevertheless there were very able young men among the few, and the Society's business continued to be conducted with as much attention and decorum as if the house had been full, and, as Gillies who knew the Society from 1808 says, ' with far more adherence to dignified formality than that of the British senate '.[13]

The first historian of the Society attributes the decline almost entirely to the political situation; the French Revolution and its consequences having in his opinion brought all speculation into discredit, and causing even the weekly meetings of a few young men for the consideration of an essay by one of themselves and a debate on a second topic to be regarded with little favour. He argues from the suggestions made for the revivifying of the Society, or rather from the second of the three.[14]

On 2nd December 1794 Scott had moved and Francis Jeffrey had seconded a motion, which was carried unanimously, to the effect ' that a general meeting be called to consider the present declining state of the Society and the means which ought to be adopted for its support '.[15] To indicate the importance of the occasion the Society directed the general meeting to be summoned for 9th December by a letter above the signatures of Scott as Secretary and all the five Presidents. The general meeting, however, came to no firm decision except to pass a motion at the instance of two senior members for the nomination by the President of an *ad hoc* committee, as had been done in the earlier depression of 1777. The Committee named was unusually large and included the Principal of the University,[16] all the Professors who were members of the Society, William Creech who was the prime mover in the foundation of the Society in 1764,[17] six other senior members only one of whom was still on the active list, and Scott.[18] Whether Creech attended and gave the committee the benefit of his advice is doubtful; but clearly he was in a critical mood, for on 13th January 1795 Scott had to inform the Society ' that Mr Creech in his accounts as given in for this year had for the first time charged interest to the amount of £10, 10s. on the arrear due to him.'[19]

The report of the committee, dated 12th December 1794

and read to the Society by Scott on 16th December, recommended three not very remarkable measures ' to restore the society to its former flourishing and respectable situation ': (1) That by a circular letter the honorary and extraordinary members should be asked to attend meetings as often as possible and to bring the Society favourably to the attention of suitable ' young gentlemen of their acquaintance '; (2) ' That the Society at the present juncture should be cautious in admitting as subjects of discussion or debate the political topics of the day '; and (3) That the Secretary should have a correct list of all the members ' inserted as formerly in the almanacs of this place '. Scott was appointed one of a committee of five to draw up the circular letter; and on 13th January 1795 he reported that it had been sent out and also that the city almanacs were too far advanced towards publication for the list of members to be inserted.

The second of the above recommendations was apparently a dead letter from the outset. In spite of what the Society's historian says,[20] political topics were not rare before and they were not any rarer thereafter. The recommendation must have been futile in any case, for ' the political topics of the day ' can be easily brought into the discussion of any subject under the sun. And so far from the French Revolution bringing speculation into discredit, it was the topic of topics for young and old alike. The young men of Edinburgh had as much to say about it as had Southey and Coleridge and their sets at Oxford and Cambridge, if only a few chose to come to the forum of the Speculative Society to say it. It was not till the French Revolution lost the *couleur de rose* which it had at first in the eyes of most people in this country,[21] not till it began to pour out blood at home and show its aggressive claws abroad, and not till Britain found itself compelled to go to war with France, that clubs and societies, spirited as their debates sometimes had been before, began to think like the committee of the Speculative Society that they were in danger of being disrupted altogether by the fiercer political antagonisms that recent events had fanned into flame. We can be sure that Scott himself was all for the avoidance, if possible, of discord and acrimony. For, while he delighted in the exchange of ideas, he was one of the least disputatious of men and one of the most persuasive of harmonisers. 'As it was next to impossible to inveigle Sir Walter into a colloquial dispute,' said R. P. Gillies who knew him well, ' it became also scarce practicable for others to carry on an angry controversy in his presence. Some ridiculous anecdote, or bizarre mode of stating the question at issue, generally succeeded in making the antagonists both laugh and abandon their hostility.'[22] Even such notoriously thorny disputants as the quarrelsome John Pinkerton, the irritable Joseph Ritson, and the half-mad H. W. Weber succumbed to a charm that had been as potent when Scott was young as in his maturity. It is said that Henry Mac-kenzie was one of the few people with whom Scott ever engaged in anything remotely like an argument; and the word is too strong, for the two friends differed ' only from a wish for mutual instruction and entertainment, not from the pugnacious obstinacy of a narrow mind bent on assert-ing its own dogmas, or proving its own fancied superiority'.[23]

As for the temporary decline of the Speculative Society, the simple fact is that all such bodies suffer from debility from time to time; and the primary cause is always to be found internally, not externally. It is quite clear from other evidence, to be given later, that the Speculative Society's finances had got into a tangle, from which Scott helped to extricate them; and it seems likely that the members had been remiss in recommending the Society to their friends.

The following members of Scott's band of intimates had already been admitted to the Speculative Society before him: George Abercromby,[24] David Douglas,[25] the Honour-able Thomas Douglas,[26] James Fergusson,[27] James Glassford of Dugalston,[28] David Monypenny,[29] and William Rae.[30] Two others came in after Scott: David Boyle[31] and Patrick

Murray of Simprim. But neither John Irving nor William Clerk[32] ever joined—rather surprisingly in the case of Clerk, who ' piqued himself on his talents for conversation '[33] and as a young man ' had strongly the Edinburgh *pruritus disputandi* ',[34] so much so, according to Irving who may have been a little jealous of his place in Scott's friendship, that he delighted in prolonging an argument and would sometimes insist on debating the same question for several days on end.

The legal element was strong in the Society then, as it has always been; many of the members were young advocates not yet overwhelmed with briefs or, like Scott himself at his admission, aspirants to the Bar; and not a few of the rest were or were to become Writers to the Signet. The weekly meetings from November to April or early May were held on Tuesdays in a Hall which, with an anteroom, the Society had been permitted to build within the University precincts.[35] Outsiders were not permitted to attend any meetings, even when themselves candidates for admission.[36]

On 14th December 1790, in accordance with the accepted procedure, a petition from ' Mr Walter Scott, attested and presented by Mr Irving[37] and Mr Thos Douglas ' and another from ' Mr George Greenlaw[38] attested and presented by Mr Monypenny and Mr J. Fergusson, Praying to be admitted members of the Society were read to the meeting '. It was ordered that the petitioners should be balloted for at the next meeting, which was on 21st December. They were duly elected and admitted, Scott's formal introduction to the President and Society in session being probably effected by his seconder owing to his proposer's absence from the meeting.[39] From then on for fully five sessions Scott hardly ever missed a meeting,[40] and served on nearly every committee.

It was on 18th January 1791 that Scott spoke in debate for the first time.[41] And on the same evening he was elected Librarian[42] to fill the vacancy caused by the resignation of Alexander Irving and Gilbert Hutchison[43] who had held office jointly for the three preceding sessions. It was probably rather the scarcity of eligible members of some standing than an immediate recognition of Scott's suitability which led to his early election to office; and Lockhart is, I think, mistaken in attributing it to 'the early reliance placed on his careful habits of business, the fruit of his chamber education '.[44] As Librarian, Scott had to supervise the borrowing of books and their return, to report once a year to a committee on the state of the Library, and to carry out instructions as to new acquisitions. It would seem that each of the joint Librarians who preceded him in office had expected the other to do the work. At any rate Scott found a number of books missing, and difficult to retrace and recover, and a considerable sum for fines unpaid. But he was methodical by nature and in nothing more than in respect for books, with what indeed has been called a touch of bibliomania; and it is certain that long before he demitted office he got the Library into perfect order.

Shortly after his appointment as Librarian, Scott was twice called, on 8th March and 12th April 1791, to supply the place *pro tempore* of the regular Secretary, John Weir by name,[45] who was absent. His first absence was due, according to the letter he submitted, to his father's recent death. But the second was obviously an evasion of embarrassment. For on the night in question the committee appointed to examine his books gave in its report which ended thus: 'The committee are sorry to add that from the absence of the Secretary at their meeting, and from the inaccurate way in which his books are kept, they could not enter so minutely into the state of the funds as they otherwise would have done.' As the meeting was the last of the 1790-91 session, the same committee[46] was directed to remain in being and pursue the matter during the long vacation.[47] It was after their second unfavourable and more detailed report on 26th November 1791 that, on the motion of David Monypenny and James Oswald,[48] Scott was appointed Secretary, in which capacity he had to serve likewise as Treasurer.[49]

Unlike his predecessor the new Secretary kept the minutes and other records with scrupulous care and many an arbitrary spelling.[50]   As Treasurer he had to collect (if he could) all sums due to the Society by way of entry-money, subscriptions, and fines, to pay out wages, to pay for coals, candles, new books, newspaper advertisements, and the registration of bills, and to report to a committee annually on the Society's finances.   His accounting duties were of course complicated by the situation which Weir's negligence had created, especially Weir's failure to collect arrears due to the Society, his uncertainty about how much the Society itself owed and, apparently, his easy-going but not dishonest confounding of his own and the Society's monies; and it was probably Scott's experience as Secretary-Treasurer, rather than his training in accounts in his father's office, which initiated him into the mysteries of protested bills and promissory notes with which unhappily his own affairs later were to make him only too familiar.   The already-mentioned summer committee did a good deal to clear the situation up before he took over, getting a series of diminishing bills from Weir as he paid instalments of his indebtedness and at the same time lodging £50 in the Royal Bank as part of the Society's contribution to the building of the present Old College.[51]   In this way Weir's debt to the Society was reduced from £65, 1s. 8d. to £20, 4s. 6d.   For this sum, or rather for the revised figure of £20, 5s. 2d., Weir on 5th November 1791 gave a promissory note payable on demand.   But Scott had more trouble over this residue than over all the rest.   Weir was very evasive; and in spite of many applications, most of which seem to have been ignored, and in spite of the protesting of the bill and the registration of the protest ' before expiry of six months, so as to preserve the right of doing summary diligence upon the bill ', it was not till 26th November 1793 that Scott could report that Weir had at last paid up and received in exchange ' the documents of the debt'. Meanwhile Scott had to manage the rest of the financial affairs of the Society. But at first, through no fault of his own, both sides of his ledger were in question, with a considerable proportion of the assets in arrears difficult or impossible to recover and with an uncertain amount of debts outstanding. Gradually he ascertained the total of the debts, paid the most pressing creditors of the Society as well as the running expenses, and got in such new monies as were due and some at least of the old arrears. The report of the last committee to examine his books and vouchers was read on 8th December 1795 and gave the deficit as only £11, 5s. 3d. The Tuesday before ' Mr Walter Scott intimated to the meeting, that owing to his other avocations it was now out of his power to retain any longer the offices of Secretary and Librarian, and accordingly gave in his resignation, which the Society accepted. Mr Greenshields[52] then moved and was seconded by Mr Waugh [53] that the thanks of the Society be returned to Mr Scott for the attention he had paid to their interest, and the able manner in which he had discharged the duty of these offices, which was unanimously agreed to, and done by the President[54] in their name '. On the proposal of Scott himself the Society appointed Waugh as his successor in both of the vacated offices. And Waugh reaped the fruit of Scott's husbandry; for the first committee on the new Secretary-Librarian's management[55] in a report read on 22nd November 1796 found a credit balance of £4, 7s. 4d. with a small sum lying out in arrears. The Society had emerged from its depression, largely through the active care and devotion of Scott; and the committee just mentioned ended its report on an optimistic note: ' From a view of all these circumstances and the prospect there is of a considerable accession of members they are encouraged to hope that the Society will soon rise to the same celebrity that ever at any time distinguished it.'

Three other episodes during Scott's tenure of the Secretaryship were a little out of the ordinary. The first to some extent involved the Speculative Society with the Revolutionary government in France. A Frenchman, M. Terray,[56] had been admitted to the Society on 25th January 1791, a month and a few days after Scott himself, and had been granted non-residing privileges on 15th November following. It is not known where he went and he never seems to have returned. But on 19th February 1793 when the situation in France was indeed critical (Louis XVI had been guillotined on 21st January), Alexander Manners told a meeting of the Society 'that the life and fortune of a non-resident member . . . Mr Terray depended upon his being able to establish by documents from this country that he was in Edinburgh for the purpose of prosecuting his studies only—and that otherwise he would be included under the edict lately passed by the French government against emigrants'. The meeting appointed Manners, Professor John Wilde,[57] and Scott as a committee to draw up a certificate under the Society's seal and ' otherwise authenticated in the most ample manner '. Subscribed by several Presidents, the Secretary, and a number of other members, the document, which may have been in French but was probably in Latin, was delivered to Manners to forward to Terray's friends in France. It is perhaps still extant in the French archives.

The second episode was such a one as Scott must have enjoyed. He had to report on 3rd April 1793 that the Society's officer and door-keeper, Alexander Fraser, had left Edinburgh for a time and that several applications for the temporary vacancy had been made to him. Empowered to make an appointment, he announced a week later that he had chosen Mungo Watson. Fraser was an Edinburgh worthy with no small conceit of himself, whose chief occupation was clerking of a sort.[58] But Mungo Watson was a professional concierge and even better known. His spruce, brisk, consequential figure was recorded to the life by John Kay in one of his etchings. He was the beadle of Lady Yester's Church, the hall-keeper of the Society in

Scotland for Propagating Christian Knowledge,[59] and one of the door-keepers during the sittings of the General Assembly. In these capacities he exacted, when he could, tribute from strangers for admission to a seat, not being averse to pickings and profit however petty.[60] His ushering gave him unrivalled opportunities of hearing (and divining) what had just happened or was about to happen in what he called the religious world; and this ecclesiastical gossip he disseminated to a large circle of elderly female admirers, making a regular charge for his visits. He appears also to have raised his voice in prayer and exhortation on some of these occasions.[61] Hence the motto Kay put at the foot of Mungo's portrait, 'Prayers at all prices.' 'The gravity of his manners,' says Paton, 'was well calculated to make an impression on the ignorant or the weak. . . . There was a peculiar degree of solemnity about his features. The ponderous weight of his nether jaw gave a hollow tone, not only to his words, but even when closing on the tea and toast, a dram, or a glass of wine, it was excellently adapted to produce the effect—*solemn.*'[62] One can imagine Scott's delight in interviewing this own brother of Andrew Fairservice, Thomas Trumbull, Johnie Mortsheugh, and Douce Davie Deans.

The third episode concerns the relation of the Speculative Society with the Historical Society of Trinity College, Dublin. The latter was of exactly the same age, having been founded by Edmund Burke in 1764; and it had entered into a fraternal reciprocity with the Speculative Society in 1783. There was a considerable interchange for twenty-three years thereafter,[63] but with more coming from Dublin to Edinburgh than going the other way. On 10th March 1795 Dr Toumy[64] and Mr Magrath were duly admitted to a meeting of the Speculative Society and presented a letter from their own Society together with a pamphlet entitled *Transactions between the Historical Society and Board of Trinity College.* There had been a dispute between the Historical Society and the College authorities; and the

Society had moved out from its College quarters to others nearby. Or the greater part of the Society had done so, for there seems to have been a sufficient minority for the College Board to set it up with the old name in the old meeting-place, but under the regulations over which the quarrel had arisen. The letter which Toumy and Magrath carried was couched in a style of high-flown cordiality and lofty indignation. The Historical Society, assured of the Speculative Society's congeniality, 'almost anticipate' its approbation and consider it 'almost needless to urge the necessity of independence'. 'Among the many sacrifices demanded of the Historical Society their invaluable alliance with the Speculative was evidently, although silently, involved. But it should be a powerful motive indeed which could at *any time* induce the Historical Society to forgo the benefits of that amicable tie which they so highly estimate, and they conceive such conduct on their part would be a peculiar violation at *this time* when the weight of obligation is so much against them.'

The immediate action of the Speculative Society was to set up a committee of no less than thirteen, of which Alexander Manners was the chairman and Scott a member, to draw up a suitable reply and submit it on 17th March 1795. It was approved on submission and after being attested by the Society's seal and the subscription of the Secretary and one of the Presidents was entrusted to Magrath to forward to Dublin, Scott at the same time writing a separate letter to the Auditor of the Historical Society to request him to read to it the formal communication.

The Speculative Society's letter, though submitted by a committee, is likely to have been in the main the Secretary's composition; and as it has never been published, I give it now in the original spelling as an addition to Scott's letters in print:

' To the Historical Society of Dublin.

GENTLEMEN—The Speculative Society of Edinburgh conceive themselves highly indebted to you for your friendly communication of the 21rst Jan.^r 1795 which they have ordered to be inserted in their records. They do not fail to meet and return with equal warmth the obliging expressions of esteem and regard which that Letter contains nor to take the most sincere concern in whatever regards the Interest of an Institution, their amicable connection with which they so highly value. As this connection is founded upon the basis of their common Literary pursuits the Speculative Society conceive that it subsists independant of the private internal Regulations by which each Institution is governed and ought not therefore to be affected by such changes in these Regulations which either may find it convenient or proper to adopt. As therefore they do not conceive that the original Compact of 1783 is in any degree affected by the circumstances announced by the Historical Society they beg leave to assure you that they consider it as subsisting in its original force and will be happy to receive with all the usual priviledges such Members of the Historical Society bringing with them proper certificates as may favour them with their attendance during their residence in the city of Edinburgh. We have the honour to subscribe ourselves &c.'

Scott was never one of the five Presidents; and he never applied for extraordinary membership, as is customary after attendance for three sessions, the reading of three essays, the performance of all casual duties, and the payment of any arrears. But he was one of the most popular members. When the Society raised George Husband Baird to honorary membership[65] and gave him a complimentary dinner on 10th December 1793 on his appointment as Principal of the University in succession to William Robertson, it was Scott who was called to the chair for the second half of the proceedings ' by the unanimous acclaim of the sturdier convivialists. . . . He *hirpled*[66] towards it . . . in his usual

quiet way, and only remarked before he sat down, that
he was not the first man who had been called upon to fill
a place of which he was not worthy.[67] The unintentional
blow struck home, and was received with bursts of
laughter '.[68] He was himself elevated to the select band of
honorary members on 28th January 1794.[69]

I have already quoted from the *Memoir* a passage in
which Scott speaks of the part he played generally in his
societies.[70] There follows a paragraph which refers, I think,
though not directly, to his membership of the Speculative
Society: ' I cannot applaud in all respects the way in which
our days were spent. There was too much idleness, and
sometimes too much conviviality;[71] but our hearts were
warm, our minds honourably bent on knowledge and literary
distinction; and if I, certainly the least informed of the
party, may be permitted to bear witness, we were not without the fair and creditable means of attaining the distinction
to which we aspired. In this society I was naturally led
to correct my former useless course of reading; for—feeling
myself greatly inferior to my companions in metaphysical
philosophy and other branches of regular study—I laboured,
not without some success, to acquire at least such a portion
of knowledge as might enable me to maintain my rank in
conversation. In this I succeeded pretty well; but unfortunately then, as often since through my life, I incurred the
deserved ridicule of my friends from the superficial nature
of my acquisitions, which being, in the mercantile phrase,
got up for society, very often proved flimsy in the texture;
and thus the gifts of an uncommonly retentive memory
and acute powers of perception were sometimes detrimental
to their possessor, by encouraging him to a presumptuous
reliance upon them.'[72]

Small as were the numbers in attendance at the meetings,[73]
the essays of the various members were of a high order;
the debates, as has been said,[74] were conducted with great
decorum; and Scott himself took the keenest interest in
all the business of the Society, not least in the complexities

of its ' private business ', in which participants (especially if they were office-bearers) required readiness, ingenuity, and a thorough familiarity with the Society's laws and conventions.

In his essays for it, Scott avoided (to use his own phrase) ' metaphysical philosophy and other branches of regular study '[75] in which he considered himself to be deficient, and displayed instead his romantic and antiquarian predilections. His essays number four, which is more than all save one or two of his fellow-members contributed.

The first was on ' The Origin of the Feudal System ',[76] read on 26th November 1791.[77] He had already presented what was no doubt substantially the same essay to the Literary Society in 1789. He sent ' the scroll copy ' of it to his uncle Robert Scott on 30th September 1790. 'As you are kind enough,' he says, ' to interest yourself in my style and manner of writing, I thought you might like better to see it in its original state, than one on the polishing of which more time had been bestowed. You will see that the intention and attempt of the essay is principally to controvert two propositions laid down by the writers on the subject: 1st, That the system was invented by the Lombards; and, 2dly, that its foundation depended on the King's being acknowledged the sole lord of all the lands in the country, which he afterwards distributed to be held by military tenures. I have endeavoured to assign it a more general origin, and to prove that it proceeds upon principles common to all nations when placed in a certain situation. I am afraid the matter will but poorly reward the trouble you will find in reading some parts. I hope, however, you will make out enough to enable you to favour me with your sentiments upon its faults.'[78] Under the fresh title ' On the Manners and Customs of the Northern Nations ' the essay was revised and submitted, as has already been noticed,[79] as classwork to Professor Dugald Stewart in the academic session of 1790-91. According to Lockhart,[80] the version for the Speculative Society expounded the same view but at greater length. Parts of the final version or at least the principal theses in it may well survive in the *Essays on Chivalry* and *on Romance* and in the fourth series of *Tales of a Grandfather. Being Stories taken from the History of France*; for Scott never changed his opinions on the circumstantial development of feudalism and was delighted to find in 1831 a confirming oriental parallel in Colonel James Tod's *Annals and Antiquities of Rajast'han*, which was published two years before.

His second essay, delivered on 14th February 1792, was on ' The Authenticity of the Poems of Ossian '. And either as a sequel continuing the argument or as a repeat of the original with a greater or less revision, he read as his fourth essay ' The Authenticity of Ossian's Poems ' on 3rd April 1793. The submission of the same topic twice is indicative of course of Scott's own interest in it,[81] and probably also of the interest of his fellow-members,[82] for it was scarcely possible to be indifferent on what he calls ' the great national question of Ossian '.[83] His old friend John Home had been the first person to encourage James Macpherson to publish translations from the Gaelic;[84] and Principal William Robertson and at least three of the Edinburgh professors in Scott's day, Hugh Blair, James Gregory, and Adam Ferguson,[85] not to mention such legal sifters of evidence as Lords Kames and Monboddo, were among the many in Scotland who maintained the genuineness of what in due course appeared. Protagonists on the other side came forward almost as soon as Macpherson's first ' translations ' were published, notably Dr Johnson and, after a first profession of enthusiastic faith, his bugbear, David Hume. But the dispute was not soon settled; nor was it even likely to be when Scott wrote his essays in the seventeen-nineties. What his mature conclusions were we know. They may be compendiously summarised in two couplets from *Absalom and Achitophel*:

' Some truth there was, but dashed and brewed with lies
To please the fools and puzzle all the wise:

Succeeding times did equal folly call
Believing nothing or believing all.'

He quotes the second couplet himself in the 1831 *Introductory
Note* to *Glenfinlas*, which was 'supposed to be a translation
from the Gaelic' but, unlike Macpherson's, in stanza and
rhyme.[86] He adds that, whatever may be thought as to
the authenticity, he had never heard of competent Gaelic
scholars disputing the similarity in spirit and diction between
Macpherson's translations and pieces of genuine antiquity.
What he calls 'with the utmost sincerity my creed on the
great national question of Ossian . . . formed after much
deliberation & enquiry' he expounds in a long letter to
Anna Seward.[87] It had taken shape, I think, in the main
after his essays for the Speculative Society. In that interval
had appeared three important contributions to the controversy. Two of these were by a fellow-advocate and
fellow-member of the Speculative Society, Malcolm Laing:
an appendix to his *History of Scotland* (1800) and *Poems of
Ossian, with Notes and Illustrations* (1805). The third item
was the *Report of the Committee of the Highland Society of
Scotland appointed to enquire into the Nature and Authenticity
of the Poems of Ossian* (1805).[88] Scott reviewed Laing's *Ossian*
and the Highland Society's *Report* in the *Edinburgh Review*
for July 1805, tempering Laing's more-than-scepticism with
a little of the Highland Society's will-to-believe[89] and
inability to go very far in that direction. 'As for the great
dispute,' he tells Anna Seward, 'I should be no Scottish
man if I had not very attentively considered it at some
period of my studies & indeed I have gone some length in
my researches for I have beside me some twenty or thirty
of the unquestioned originals of Ossians poems.[90] After
making every allowance for the disadvantages of a literal
translation & the possible debasement which those *now*
collected[91] may have suffered in the great & violent change
which the Highlands have undergone since the researches
of Macpherson I am compelled to admit that incalculably

the greater part of the English Ossian must be ascribed to Macpherson himself and his whole introductions notes &c &c is an absolute tissue of forgeries.'[92] On the other hand, Scott as a boy had enthusiastically learned whole duans of Macpherson by heart, on being lent Dr Blacklock's copy.[93] Though the rhapsodical prose came to pall on him, he remained deeply interested. And I am inclined to think that his essays for the Speculative Society were, as the similar titles suggest, assertions of the authenticity, or at least a qualified acceptance, of what Macpherson offered.

It is worth while asking: How familiar was Scott himself with Gaelic, either at the time or later? I am afraid that the mere fact of his tackling a Gaelic subject is not enough to prove his knowledge of the language. In the eighteenth and earlier nineteenth centuries ignorance of Gaelic appeared to be no reason for declining to offer an opinion on 'the questionable authenticity of Ossian'.[94] James Macpherson himself was by no means a proficient. On the other hand Scott, as has been said,[95] had something of a flair for languages. If he acquired Italian and Spanish in order to extend his reading in romance, it is not unreasonable to assume that he would make as great an effort or a greater to acquire one of the languages of his own country —the speech of the Highland clans in whose culture, customs, and picturesque history he was so deeply and sympathetically interested. I am sure that, as soon as Scott made contact with the Highlands as an apprentice, if not earlier, he tried to pick up as much Gaelic as he could. He certainly sought the advice of Gaelic-speaking friends[96] about various matters connected with the Highlands; and at one time or another he seems to have read nearly every book that illustrated 'The ancient manners, the habits and customs of the aboriginal race by whom the Highlands of Scotland were inhabited'.[97] The non-existence in his day of manuals of the Gaelic-without-groans type and indeed of more formal grammars must have made the task of the beginner the more difficult, if he was unable to live for a considerable time in a Gaelic-speaking family or community. This Scott never did, though from boyhood on he made many excursions into the Gaelic area, and sooner or later learned that 'the seat of the Celtic Muse is in the midst of the secret and solitary hill, and her voice in the murmur of the mountain stream. He who woos her must love the barren rock more than the fertile valley, and the solitude of the desert better than the festivity of the hall '.[98] It was apparently to his Highland visits that Scott himself 'somewhere attributes the occurrence of so much " bad Gaelic " (so he is pleased to term it) in his Novels '.[99] But all the same my guess is that Scott, who knew the Authorised Version almost by heart,[100] got a good deal of his Gaelic by working his way through the Gaelic Bible, with the occasional help of a dictionary.[101]

It is true that in 1810 Scott, recalling a meeting 'many years ago' with a mad woman in Glencoe, says 'As she spoke no English, I no Gaelic, we could have no communication '.[102] But his inability to speak Gaelic does not preclude an ability to read it more or less easily. And four years earlier in the already-quoted letter to Anna Seward he speaks of Gaelic poems in terms that he could hardly have used if he was in fact acquainted with them only in translation or if he was giving no more than a secondhand opinion.[103] The same is true of a passage in the *Letters on Demonology and Witchcraft* in which after noticing the frequent mention in Macpherson's 'paraphrases' of Fingal's sword, called 'the Son of the dark brown Luno, from the name of the armourer who forged it ', he adds 'but the Irish ballad, which gives a spirited account of the debate between the champion and the armourer is nowhere introduced '.[104]

Scott tried for the first time to catch something of the spirit of Gaelic poetry, though without having any specific lyric in mind, in 'a certain doleful ditty adapted to a curious Gaelic air literally picked up' from Highland reapers.[105] The poem, *Where shall the lover rest*, has a Gaelic phrase in the refrain and is introduced thus in the third canto of *Marmion*:

> 'A mellow voice Fitz-Eustace had;
> The air he chose was wild and sad;
> Such have I heard, in Scottish land,
> Rise from the busy harvest band,
> When falls before the mountaineer,
> On Lowland plains, the ripen'd ear.
> Now one shrill voice the notes prolong,
> Now a wild chorus swells the song:
> Oft have I listen'd, and stood still,
> As it came soften'd up the hill,
> And deem'd it the lament of men
> Who languish'd for their native glen;
> And thought how sad would be such sound
> On Susquehanna's swampy ground,
> Kentucky's wood-encumber'd brake,
> Or wild Ontario's boundless lake,
> Where heart-sick exiles, in the strain,
> Recall'd fair Scotland's hills again.'[106]

But Scott had already decided to write, as he told Miss Seward, ' a Highland poem, somewhat in the style of the *Lay*; giving as far as I can a real picture of what that enthusiastic race actually were before the destruction of their patriarchal government. It is true that I have not quite the same facilities as in describing border manners where I am as they say more at home. But to balance my comparative deficiency in knowledge of Celtic manners you are to consider that I have from my youth delighted in all the Highland traditions which I could pick up from the old Jacobites who used to frequent my father's house '.[107] The poem, which ultimately appeared in 1810 after great labour and long delay, was *The Lady of the Lake*. The poem itself and still more its elaborate notes prove Scott's familiarity with Highland conditions, scenery, and history—the kind of familiarity which must have involved a considerable linguistic knowledge. Moreover in Canto Second he introduces an imitation of a *jorram* or rowing song, with a Gaelic refrain, and in Canto Third an imitation of a *coronach* or lament, with a prose note giving a literal translation of the Gaelic one Scott was partly indebted to. *The Lord of the Isles*, which followed five years later in 1815, makes very much of Highland material, though without any inset imitations of Gaelic poetry.

However, Scott had by this time begun his career as a novelist. And his knowledge of Gaeldom, including its language and poetry, is obvious in such novels as are set partly or wholly north of the Highland Line, especially *Waverley*, *Rob Roy*, *A Legend of Montrose*, and *The Fair Maid of Perth*. In them many Gaelic words and phrases occur; and in *Waverley* Chapters XXI and XXII are largely about Highland minstrelsy. Between 1814 and 1822 Scott wrote about a dozen poems, some for inclusion in his novels and the rest independently, which should be noticed in this connection. Some are translations of actual Gaelic poems;[108] and the rest are imitations or echoes.[109]

Whereas Scott's knowledge of French, Spanish, Italian, and even German (the modern language which he studied the most systematically) tended to decay, his knowledge of Gaelic probably improved steadily. I do not mean that he ever became a Gaelic scholar or even a fairly ready speaker of Gaelic. But he must have accumulated a considerable vocabulary; and if he perhaps never mastered the complexities of the grammar and the finer shades of the idiom, he seems to have been able to get the gist of a passage. So as late as 1829 he hoped ' to knock the marrow out of the bone ' of a ' curious Irish MS.' in his possession, with the help of the young Gaelic scholar, Mackintosh Mackay;[110] and he expressed the cautiously discriminating opinion that ' some ' of the poetry of Rob Donn ' seems pretty ' as Mackintosh Mackay explained it.[111]

From 1820 Scott was an enthusiastic member of the

Celtic Society which existed to foster the Gaelic language, to maintain traditional Highland manners and customs, and to encourage education in remote districts of the North. He regularly presided at the annual festivals (on which occasions he would have to air his Gaelic) and also in 1822 during George IV's visit to Edinburgh acted as Adjutant-General of the Society's corps and presented it with a set of colours. On all those occasions Scott duly wore the tartan[112]—but in the shape of trews. He records in his *Journal* the presentation by a deputation of the Celtic Society, soon after the news of his bankruptcy, of ' the most splendid broadsword I ever saw; a beautiful piece of art, and a most noble weapon. . . . This was very kind of my friends the Celts, by whom I have had so many merry meetings '.[113]

To return after a long digression to Scott and the Speculative Society: His third essay, which discussed ' The Origin of the Scandinavian Mythology ', was delivered on 11th December 1792 to a house so ' uncommonly thin ' that it was decided at the outset to admit at once four candidates of whom Jeffrey was one by suspending the law requiring petitions to lie on the table for a week before being put to the ballot, and after the essay to adjourn without a debate. There has survived at Abbotsford a notebook begun by Scott in 1792 which contains an item running to seven closely written quarto pages and headed as follows: '*Vegtams Kvitha*,[114] or The Descent of Odin, with the Latin of Tho⁵· Bartholine,[115] and the English poetical version of Mr Gray:[116] with some account of the death of Balder both as narrated in the Edda and as handed down to us by Northern historians—*Auctore* Gualt°· Scott.'[117] The Norse original, the Latin paraphrase, and the English translation of the Latin are transcribed in full in parallel columns; and then comes a long but unfinished ' Historical account of The death of Balder ',[118] for which Scott may have consulted some of the authorities in addition to Bartholine mentioned in Mason's Gray[119] and other authorities as well.[120] It is difficult to believe that Scott presented this

recondite and undigested matter as an essay, to be listened
to by an audience of young men who, one may assume,
were anything but familiar with the language and culture
of the Vikings. It is more likely that what is in the notebook is merely a gathering of material in preparation for
the essay. Scott may well have recalled it and used ideas
or passages from it when he had occasion later to refer to
Scandinavian antiquities, especially in *Rokeby*, the *Abstract of
the Eyrbiggia Saga*,[121] the *Essays on Chivalry* and *on Romance*,
The Pirate, and *Letters on Demonology and Witchcraft*,[122]
however much he added from his subsequent reading in
the field. Besides acquiring a considerable knowledge of
the substance of the sagas and the eddas indirectly in the
seventeen-nineties and later, Scott is pretty certain to have
picked up a limited knowledge at least of the language of
the originals.[123] In one notebook begun in 1792, now in
the National Library of Scotland, he wrote out a table of
the runic alphabet;[124] and in the already-mentioned notebook of the same date at Abbotsford he carefully transcribed
in runic characters of the late mediaeval period the following
two lines from Gray's *Descent of Odin*:

> ' Facing to the northern clime,
> Thrice he traced the runic rhyme.'[125]

A difficulty in connection with the essay arises from
Lord Jeffrey's account to Lockhart of his first attendance
at the Speculative Society which occurred on the evening
in question. He was ' struck . . . with the singular appearance of the Secretary, who sat gravely at the bottom of
the table in a huge woollen nightcap; and when the President took the chair, pleaded a bad toothache as his apology
for coming into that worshipful assembly in such a " por-
tentous machine ".'[126] But according to Jeffrey, as reported
by Lockhart who does not appreciate the difficulty, Scott
' read . . . an essay on ballads, which so much interested the
new member that he requested to be introduced '; and
Jeffrey called the next evening at George Square where he

found Scott in his area den ' surrounded with dingy books ', and from which they adjourned to a tavern and supper.[126] But Scott never read an essay on ballads to the Speculative Society. I hazard the guess that the discussion of the essay on Scandinavian mythology may have run on longer than usual and touched on the subject of ballads and that Scott may have spoken *ex tempore* and at some length on them. Jeffrey, recalling the evening forty or more years later and having Scott and ballads firmly associated in his mind, may well have misremembered some of the details of a memorable evening.

Though Scott spoke in twenty-one of the debates while an active member of the Speculative Society, he led in only two; but that was about the average number per member, only two members leading four times during the same years and only two others leading thrice. He was always a welcome contributor, not perhaps as the orator, but as the good-humoured, sensible, and amusing talker, copiously supplied with such interesting information and apt quotation and citation as ' made him more a favourite as a speaker than some whose powers of rhetoric were far above his '.[127] Many of the questions were the stock problems of debating societies before and since—historical, moral, legal, metaphysical, or aesthetic; but not a few were topically political and suggested by the contemporary situation at home and in Revolutionary France; and none at all was frivolous or lacking the essence which alone makes for a genuine debate. The treatment, however, may be assumed to have varied with the speakers and the occasions ' From grave to gay, from lively to severe '.[128] The same questions, in the same formulas or slightly modified, tended to recur at short intervals. Capital punishment, for instance, was debated thrice, the second of the 1794-95 debates on it following a week after the first. There were likewise three debates on each of the following issues: the desirability of an established religion; divorce by mutual consent; the

English Marriage Act; the Test Act; and the maintenance of the poor.

The following is a list of the debates in which Scott took part, with the dates, the names of the openers,[129] and the voting:

18th January 1791. Ought any permanent support to be permitted for the poor?[130] Richard Fowler.[131] Affirmative carried by the casting vote of the President for the evening.[132]

25th January 1791. Ought there to be an established religion? Adam Douglas.[133] Affirmative carried by 5 to 3.

8th February 1791. Is attainder and corruption of blood ever a proper punishment? William Rae. Affirmative carried by 7 to 4.

15th February 1791. Ought the public expenses to be defrayed by levying the amount immediately from the people, or is it expedient to contract a national debt for that purpose? James Glassford. Negative carried by 8 to 4.

1st March 1791. Was the putting of Charles the First to death justifiable?[134] Walter Scott. Affirmative carried by 10 to 3.

15th March 1791. Should the Slave Trade be abolished? Francis Rigby Brodbelt.[135] Affirmative carried by 9 to 3.

13th March 1792.[136] Has the belief in a future state been of advantage to mankind, or is it likely ever to be so? John Allen.[137] Affirmative carried by 7 to 6.

4th December 1792. Is it for the interest of Great Britain to maintain what is called the balance of Europe ? Alexander Manners. Negative carried by 5 to 3.

18th December 1792. Was the death of King Charles the 1ˢᵗ justifiable?[138] David Boyle. Negative carried by 8 to 1.

8th January 1793. Ought divorces to be allowed by

mutual consent?—Johnstone.[139] Negative carried by 6 to 1. Scott teller for the Noes.

15th January 1793. Would associations be expedient with a view of counteracting the spirit of innovation in this country? John Vivian.[140] Affirmative carried by 7 to 2.

22nd January 1793. Ought there to be an established religion in this or any other country? John Boyd Greenshields. Affirmative carried by 5 to 2. Scott teller for the Ayes.

5th February 1793. Can a national debt promote the prosperity of a country? John Boyd Greenshields. Carried in the negative by 4 to 0.[141] Scott teller for the Noes.[142]

12th February 1793. Ought there to be any poors' rates in a country?—Laing.[143] Carried in the negative by 4 to 3.[144]

6th March 1793. Ought impress warrants to be issued in a free state? John Boyd Greenshields. Affirmative carried by 4 to 2.

19th March 1793. Is the personal inviolability of the chief magistrate in a monarchial government capable of becoming hostile to the liberties of the people?[145] Walter Scott. Affirmative carried by 6 to 4.

26th November 1793. Ought any crimes to be punished with death? Alexander Manners. Affirmative carried by 9 to 1.

4th February 1794. Whether a parliamentary reform would not be improper at the present period? Francis Rigby Brodbelt. Negative carried by 3 to 1.

27th January 1795. Ought there to be any bounties or restraints upon the exportation or importation of corn? Alexander Brunton.[146] Affirmative carried by 3 to 1. Scott teller for the Ayes.

17th February 1795. Is mercy incompatible with justice? John Wilson Rae.[147] " The question was understood as relating to Mercy extended to Criminals in opposi-

tion to the strict exercise of Stat^{ut} Law and was carried in favour of Mercy by a Majority of Two. Ayes Four, Noes Two. Teller for Noes Mr Jeffray, for Ayes Mr Scott."[148]
20th December 1796. Ought capital punishment to be allowed?—Colles.[149] Negative carried by 7 to 3.

I quote, for what it is worth, a passage in Allan:[150] 'The opinions which [Scott] avowed on three occasions have . . . come down to us. He maintained that a national debt can promote the prosperity of a country, and that mercy is incompatible with justice. On another occasion he argued against the expediency of divorce by mutual consent.'[151] But no evidence is given to support these assertions. The Speculative Society minutes do not state on which side of a debate the participators, even the opener, spoke; and the occasionally unconventional way of recording the divisions is confusing and ambiguous. It is also impossible to say whether the tellers were appointed, according to the parliamentary practice, to tell their opponents' side, or, contrariwise, to tell their own, or whether for that matter they were appointed without reference to sides. It is unlikely that Scott ever spoke, as is not uncommon in debating societies, ironically or from a standpoint assumed for the nonce against his own convictions. And consequently I think that some of his positions may be fairly certainly guessed or inferred from his known beliefs and loyalties, as, for example, on: the execution of Charles I and the personal inviolability of a sovereign; a provision for the poor and the abolition of the Slave Trade; the expediency of counteracting innovation by associations and the inexpediency of parliamentary reform at the particular juncture; and the necessity of an established religion and the advantage of a belief in a future life.

When the first jubilee of the Speculative Society was celebrated on 17th December 1814 with a dinner in Fortune's Tontine Tavern in Princes Street, Walter Scott was as famous a member as any on the roll. On that notable occasion Principal George Husband Baird, who was Scott's senior in the Society by seven years, occupied the chair to begin with. But after the Principal withdrew, ' Walter Scott was called to the chair, which did not impair the hilarity of a useful and interesting evening. He concluded the proceedings by the appropriate toast, " May the next half century give as much pleasure to the new members, as the last has done to the old ".'[152]

The quality of the entertainment under Scott's chairmanship may be gathered from a passage in the *Journal*. He had been, he said, ' rather felicitous ' in chairing dinners, ' not by much superiority of wit or wisdom, far less of eloquence; but by two or three simple rules which I put down here for the benefit of posterity '. And for the same laudable reason I give them in full:

' 1st Always hurry the bottle round for five or six rounds without prosing yourself or permitting others to prose. A slight fillip of wine inclines people to be pleased, and removes the nervousness which prevents men from speaking—disposes them, in short, to be amusing and to be amused.

' 2d Push on, keep moving, as Punch says. Do not think of say[ing] fine things—nobody cares for them any more than for fine music, which is often too liberally bestowed on such occasions. Speak at all ventures, and attempt the *mot pour rire*. You will find people satisfied with wonderfully indifferent jokes if you can but hit the taste of the company, which depends much on its character. Even a very high part(y), primd with all the cold irony and *non est tanti* feelings or no feelings of fashionable folk, may be stormed by a jovial rough round and ready praeses. Choose your texts with discretion, the sermon may be as you like. If a drunkard or an ass breaks [in] with anything out of joint, if you can parry it with a jest, good and well—if not, do not exert your serious authority, unless it is something very bad. The authority even of a chairman ought to be very cautiously exercized. With patience you will have the support of every one.

'When you have drunk a few glasses to play the good fellow, and banish modesty if you are unlucky enough to have such a troublesome companion, then beware of the cup too much. Nothing is so ridiculous as a drunken praeses.

'Lastly. Always speak short, and *Skeoch doch na skial*—cut a tale with a drink.

> "This is the purpose and intent
>   Of gude Schir Walter's testament." '[153]

NOTES ON REFERENCES

1. *Memoir*, I, 15. He also acquired, presumably with a like intention, Thomas Sheridan's *Course of Lectures on Elocution*.
2. Chapter XXXVI.
3. V, ii.
4. *Memoir*, I, 16. What Scott here says of his share in his literary societies generally Lockhart condenses and takes as referring to his part in the Literary Society in particular (I, 42). Cf. *The Monastery*, Introductory Epistle: Captain Clutterbuck's 'character began to dilate and expand' in consequence of his taking to antiquarian studies. 'I spoke with more authority at the club, and was listened to with deference, because on one subject, at least, I possessed more information than any of its members.'
5. Cf. *supra*, 184-85.
6. As Admiral Edward Vernon had been known as Old Grog in allusion to the grogram cloak he wore in foul weather; or as Major-General Alexander Mackay was called Buckram, not from an article of dress, however, but from his upright and stiff carriage. The bestowal of sobriquets was a common practice in Edinburgh's convivial clubs; and it continues to this day in the genial brotherhood of the Monks of St Giles. In addition to Scott's, three other Club nicknames are known: the Baronet (= William

Clerk, who had compared himself to Sir John Brute in Vanbrugh's *Provoked Wife*, and who belonged to the family of the Clerk Baronets of Penicuik); Crab (= John Irving); and Linton (= Sir Adam Ferguson, because on a boating excursion a fisherman, half-mistaking him for a friend, had called out, "Linton, ye lang bitch, is that you?").

7 Irving.

8 The survivors of the Club long continued to meet for dinner twice a year, at the close of the winter and the summer sessions, and to celebrate an appointment or a promotion. Scott gave two such dinners, one after his appointment as Sheriff of Selkirkshire in 1799 and the other in 1806 on his appointment as Clerk of Session. During forty years or more he was seldom absent from those reunions. Five members dined together on 2nd February 1829, 'a party such as the meeting of fellow scholars & fellow students alone could occasion. We told old stories; laughd and quaffd, and resolvd, rashly perhaps, that we would hold the club at least once a year, if possible twice' (*Journal*, III, 16). At a meeting in Leith on 6th July the same year Scott was in the chair. They passed, he says, 'a merry day for old fellows. It is a curious thing that only *three* have died of this club since its formation.... We took a fair but moderate allowance of wine, sung our old songs, and were much refreshd with a hundred old stori[e]s, which would have seemd insignificant to any stranger. The most important of these were old College adventurers [sic] of love and battle' (*Journal*, III, 91-2).

9 Once, when Scott woke up from a nap at a drinking party, "his friends succeeded in convincing him that he had sung a song in the course of the evening, and sung it extremely well" (Lockhart, I, 41). Cf. Francis Osbaldi-stone's confession: 'It has even been reported of me by maligners, that I sung a song while under this vinous influence; but, as I remember nothing of it, and never attempted to turn a tune in all my life before or since, I would willingly hope there is no actual foundation for the calumny' (*Rob Roy*, Chapter XII).

10   I, 43.

11   Lockhart, I, 43.

12   Even after the quorum had been reduced from nine to seven on 17th January 1792 on a motion by Scott which was hurried through by suspending a delaying regulation. Sometimes, particularly at the beginning of a new session, so few would arrive at the Hall that a meeting could not be constituted. Jeffrey and three others were summarily admitted on 11th December 1792, the night on which Scott read his third essay, without the usual interval between petition and admission; and even so, the house was so thin that no debate followed the recess (cf. *infra*, 200).

13   57.

14   *Spec. Soc.* (1845), 28.

15   This and some other quotations are from the second volume of the minutes of the Speculative Society.

16   George Husband Baird (cf. *infra*, 226, 248).

17   Creech was by this time a prosperous bookseller with the most extensive publishing business in Scotland. The most famous of his publications are his editions of Burns's *Poems, chiefly in the Scottish Dialect*, 1787, etc. Creech's numerous periodical articles were published as *Fugitive Pieces* in 1791. He was Lord Provost of Edinburgh in 1811-12.

18   Appointed in his secretarial capacity by the President, and then by a motion from the floor added to the committee *in propria persona*.

19   Scott was ordered to lay Creech's present and former accounts before the Society on 20th January. This he did and was instructed to write to Creech; but with what result does not appear. Readers of Burns's letters may recall *per contra* that the poet had to complain more than once of Creech's dilatoriness in settling.

20   *Spec. Soc.* (1845), 29.

21   Cf. Wordsworth, *French Revolution as it appeared to Enthusiasts at its Commencement*.

22   90.

23   Gillies, 36. Scott describes thus the rather similar character of his old friend George Abercromby (Lord Abercromby): ' I am entertained to see him just the same he has always been, never yielding up his own opinion in fact, and yet

in words acquiescing in all that could be said against it. George was always like a willow—he never offered resistance to the breath of argument, but never moved from rooted opinion, blow as it listed. . . . Conceive a man who always seems to be acquiescing in your sentiments, yet never changes his own, and this with a sort of *bonhommie* which shows there is not a particle of deceit intended. He is only desirous to spare you the trouble of contradiction.' *Journal*, I, 22; 28th November 1825.)

24 Later Lord Abercromby.

25 Later Lord Reston.

26 Later Earl of Selkirk.

27 Later Clerk of the Court of Session.

28 Later Sheriff of Dumbartonshire.

29 Later Lord Pitmilly.

30 Later Sir William Rae, Lord Advocate.

31 Later Lord President.

32 Clerk's elder brother John (Lord Eldin) and his kinsman James Clerk (Baron Clerk-Rattray) were members of the Speculative Society.

33 *Letters*, II, 528 (to Joanna Baillie, 4th August 1811). Scott tells in the same letter how Clerk was once utterly baffled in his efforts to engage a fellow-traveller in a stage-coach in conversation. Having in vain tried all the ordinary subjects—literature, farming, merchandise, gaming, game-laws, horse-racing, law-suits, politics, swindling, blasphemy, and philosophy—Clerk in exasperation asked, ' Is there any one subject that you will favour me by opening upon?' To which his opposite replied with a grin, ' Sir, can ye say onything clever about *bend leather*?'

34 *Journal*, I, 2 (20th November 1825).

35 When the present Old College quadrangle was built, premises for the Society had to be included in the design. They are still in use.

36 The rule did not (and does not) apply to the members of the affiliated Historical Society of Trinity College, Dublin, on the production of their credentials. An exception was made in 1770 to allow Principal Robertson, through whose favour the site for the Hall had been obtained, to attend.

37 Alexander Irving, later Lord Newton. He was the Presi-

dent for the evening.

38 Later Writer to the Signet.

39 The minute for 21st December reads: 'The meeting admits Mr Scott and Mr Greenlaw members of the Society.' The absence of their names from the list of those present was due to the lists being made up at the opening of the meeting and before the introductions. Allan, however, says that Scott was elected on 21st December, but 'took his seat for the first time' on 4th January (67). Lockhart simply says that Scott 'was admitted' on 4th January (I, 48).

40 Sometimes, when he had become Secretary, he omitted to include his own name in the list of those present; but that he was in attendance is manifest for other reasons.

41 Cf. *infra*, 223-25, for a full list of the debates in which Scott participated.

42 The minute says: 'to continue during the present session'. Scott in fact held the office for nearly five years.

43 Later Judge-Advocate for Scotland.

44 I, 48.

45 Curiously enough, though he is repeatedly referred to in the minutes as the 'late Secretary', Weir's name does not appear in the 1845 or in the 1905 *History of the Speculative Society*, either in the narrative pages or in the lists of office-bearers and members. No Secretary's name is given for the two sessions 1789-91. Thomas Smith, who graduated M.D. in 1787, is given as the Secretary in 1788-89, although he had been granted non-residing privileges on 13th November 1787.

46 Scott was not a member of it, though as acting Secretary he is likely to have attended its meetings.

47 Of six months or more.

48 Called to the Scottish Bar in 1791.

49 On the same evening, following his appointment, Scott read his first essay. There is no reference in the minutes to Weir's having resigned. Scott's election apparently meant Weir's dismissal.

50 e.g.: appology, ballance, catologue, comittee, conferr, ellected, goverment, inimicle, manny (= many), oppened, piers (= peers), previledge, previlege, priviledge, sacrafices,

scociety, Teusday, trennial (= triennial), etc. Even the names of Scott's intimate friends in the Society are often misspelled, e.g.: Abercomy or Abercromie (= Abercromby); Grinshiels (= Greenshields); Menypenny or Monnypenny (= Monypenny). Jeffrey is invariably spelled Jeffray.

51 Part of this £50 had been subscriptions paid to Weir; and the rest came from further subscriptions to the College fund collected by the committee.

52 John Boyd Greenshields, later of Drum; called to the Scottish Bar in 1793.

53 John Waugh, later bookseller in Edinburgh.

54 Alexander Manners, bookseller and publisher in Edinburgh and later also Librarian to the Faculty of Advocates.

55 Appointed on 12th April 1796 to examine the accounts and the state of the Library, and also ' for considering of and executing what might promote the interests and improvement of the Society'.

56 The ' M ' is probably an abbreviated ' Monsieur ', not the initial of a Christian name.

57 Cf. *supra*, 187, 208. On 29th January 1793 Scott proposed Wilde for honorary membership of the Society and was seconded by David Boyle.

58 His employer, Malcolm Wright, was at a slightly later date agent for the French prisoners-of-war in Edinburgh Castle. On one occasion which required the presence of the Lord President and the Lord Advocate, Fraser as deputy for his absent master not only kept their Lordships waiting, but, when he did arrive, took his place between them and arming each dignitary swaggered from the Council Chamber up to the Castle (cf. Paton, II, 12).

59 Scott was a subscriber to the Society; and, having been proposed as a member on 30th May 1793, he received his diploma on 29th November.

60 He is said to have told one visitor to Lady Yester's who, having paid for a place at the morning service, thought he was entitled to reclaim it in the afternoon, ' Oh, but I let my seats twice a day ' (Paton, I, 305).

61 By way of practice Mungo sometimes held forth from the pulpit of Lady Yester's to the vacant pews. On one

such occasion, the minister took him by surprise and bade him to come down, since 'toom [= empty] barrels make most sound'.

62   I, 305.

63   For various reasons the connection was dissolved in 1806. It was renewed in 1863 and has continued ever since.

64   So Scott spells the name. It is conceivable that it was really Tolmie.

65   On 10th December 1793 following the motion of Alexander Manners and Scott on 26th November.

66   I.e. limped.

67   Perhaps echoing David Hume's reply to his servant who was indignant at 'St David Street' being chalked up on his house: 'Never mind, lassie, many a better man has been made a saint o' before' (Graham, 57).

68   Allan, 90-91.

69   Following a motion by David Boyle and Patrick Murray on 4th January.

70   Cf. *supra*, 198-99.

71   Which, he says, was 'occasionally though not habitually the error of my youth' (*Memoir*, I, 14).

72   *Memoir*, I, 16.

73   During Scott's active membership, the numbers actually dividing in the debates rarely came to more than a dozen and sometimes fell as low as four or five. There may of course have been abstentions, and the divisions came at a late hour when the attendance may have thinned out.

74   Cf. *supra*, 200-1.

75   *Memoir*, I, 16.

76   This was also the title of one of the essays of (Sir) John Buchan Hepburn, who was Scott's senior in the Society by three years. The scroll or draft minute for 26th November 1791 has 'an essay upon the origin of the feudal system'. The fair-copy minute has 'an essay upon/ and feudal system'. In the transcription Scott may have intended to write 'an essay upon the origin of chivalry and the feudal system'.

77   After his appointment as Secretary on the same evening. He had been assigned 30th March 1791 as the date for his first essay, but had been allowed on 22nd March to

put forward as his substitute George Greenlaw, who read
an essay on 'The Olympic Games'.

78 *Letters*, I, 17.

79 Cf. *supra*, 184-85.

80 I, 47.

81 Perhaps partly due to his singing teacher, Alexander
Campbell, who could be very amusing in conversation
on the subject and very severe on Macpherson's 'inter-
polations'.

82 The authenticity of the poems of Ossian was debated
three times by the Society before Scott's admission. On
one of the occasions (2nd December 1783), the authenticity
was carried unanimously, the opener being Malcolm Laing.

83 *Letters*, I, 324 (to Anna Seward, probably September 1806).
A few years before Scott's admission to the Speculative
Society (Sir) James Mackintosh had read an essay on 'The
Omission of Religious Ideas in the Poems of Ossian';
and during his active membership John Morehead dis-
cussed 'The Religion of the Celtic Nations' on 11th
February 1792, and Francis Jeffrey 'The Authenticity of
Ossian's Poems' on 10th February 1795.

84 Home wrote his tragedy *The Fatal Discovery* 'in the false
gallop of Ossianic composition, to which we must avow
ourselves by no means partial' (*Home*, 840).

85 His son Adam was one of Scott's set, but not a member
of the Speculative Society.

86 Cf. *infra*, 280-81, note 145.

87 *Letters*, I, 319-25 (probably September 1806).

88 Henry Mackenzie, an original member of the Society,
headed the Committee. He had already written a preface
to the Society's *Transactions* which includes an interesting
account of Gaelic poetry.

89 Cf. *Essay on Amadis de Gaul* in *Essays*, 112: 'the feudal
baron believed as firmly in the exploits of Roland and
Oliver, as a sturdy Celt of our day in the equally sophisti-
cated poems of Ossian'.

90 I take Scott to mean by this that he had himself collected
these originals (whether in translation or in Gaelic), not
simply that he had Laing's *Ossian* and the Highland
Society's *Report* before him.

91 I.e. by Laing and others.
92 *Letters*, I, 321 (probably September 1806). Cf. *The Monastery*, Answer by 'The Author of Waverley' to ... Captain Clutterbuck: 'many of the most estimable [characters of Utopia], such as an old Highland gentleman called Ossian, a monk of Bristol called Rowley, and others, are inclined to pass themselves off as denizens of the land of reality'.
93 Cf. *supra*, 63.
94 *Romance*, 562.
95 Cf. *supra*, 123-24.
96 One of them may have been Professor Adam Ferguson.
97 *The Lady of the Lake*, Introduction.
98 *Waverley*, Chapter XXII.
99 Allan, 58. Allan continues, rather more arguably, as follows: 'It certainly does not appear that, with all his enthusiasm in behalf of the Gael, and all his researches into their manners and superstitions, he ever obtained a thorough knowledge of their language. His most intimate acquaintance with it never seems to have exceeded the power of quoting a few brocards, much after the fashion in which poor Burns paraded his half-a-dozen French phrases.'
100 Cf. *supra*, 46-47.
101 He refers in *Demonology*, Letter V, to Robert Kirke's translation into Gaelic, the first to be made, of the Scottish Metrical Psalms, 1684, and also to Kirke's *Essay on the Subterranean and for the most part Invisible People heretofore going under the name of Elves, Fawnes, and Fairies, or the like,* 1691. It was Kirke who superintended the printing in 1690 of the first (Irish) Gaelic Bible, as translated by Bishop William Bedell, adding a Gaelic vocabulary.
102 *Letters*, II, 411-12 (to Sarah Smith, 18th December 1810).
103 *Letters*, I, 321-22 (probably September 1806).
104 Letter III.
105 *Letters*, I, 403 (to Mrs Hughes, 15th December 1807). He later sent to Mrs Hughes 'the notes of the original Gaelic air procured [possibly from Alexander Campbell] after much enquiry and some difficulty for the character of the Highland music is so wild and irregular that it is ...

extremely difficult to render it to notes' (*Letters*, II, 67; 1st June 1808). He was also ready to find for Mrs Hughes 'more Gaelic music, for they have a tune and a song to almost everything they set about' (ibid., II, 68).

106   The passage may echo Wordsworth's *The Solitary Reaper* which was published in 1807, the year before *Marmion*.

107   *Letters*, I, 324 (probably September 1806)

108   *Farewell to Mackenzie*; *War-Song of Lachlan*; *Norah's Vow*; *Pibroch of Donuil Dhu*; *Mackrimmon's Lament* (with a Gaelic coda); *Woe! woe! Son of the Lowlander* (*A Legend of Montrose*, Introduction); *Birds of Omen dark and foul* (*ibid.*, Chapter VI); and *The Orphan Maid* (*ibid.*, Chapter IX). The second last of these poems is said to be 'a translation . . . by Secundus Macpherson, Esq., of Glenforgen, which, although submitted to the fetters of English rhythm, we trust will be found nearly as genuine as the version of Ossian by his celebrated namesake'. To the last poem, likewise 'translated' by Secundus, Scott appends a literal translation with the introductory note: 'The admirers of pure Celtic antiquity, notwithstanding the elegance of the above translation, may be desirous to see a literal version from the original Gaelic, which we therefore subjoin; and have only to add, that the original is deposited with Mr Jedediah Cleishbotham.'

109   *On the Massacre of Glencoe*; *MacGregor's Gathering*; *Lullaby of an Infant Chief* (with a Gaelic refrain); *The Maid of Isla*; and Flora MacIvor's song, which she calls a 'translation' (*Waverley*, Chapter XXII).

110   *Journal*, III, 73 (28th May 1829). Mackintosh Mackay edited the Highland and Agricultural Society's *Dictionarium Scoto-Celticum*, 1828.

111   *Journal*, III, 76 (3rd June 1829). Mackintosh Mackay edited the poetry of Robert Mackay or Rob Donn in 1829.

112   Of the Campbell set, in memory of one of his great-grandmothers.

113   I, 82-3 (27th January 1826).

114   I.e. *Vegtamskviða* in the Poetic Edda.

115   In *Antiquitatum Danicarum de Causis Contemptae a Danis adhuc Gentilibus Mortis libri tres*, 1689. Scott acquired his copy in May 1792. Cf. *Letters*, I, 23 (to William Clerk,

30th September 1792): 'I am poring over Bartholine in the long evenings, solitary enough.'

116 In William Mason's edition of *The Poems of Mr Gray. To which are prefixed Memoirs of his Life and Writings*, 1775.

117 Lockhart, I, 55.

118 *Baldrs Drammar* (= Balder's Dreams) is an alternative title of *Vegtamskviða*.

119 E.g. Thormodr Torfaeus's *Orcades*, 1697; Paul Henri Mallet's *Introduction à l'Histoire de Dannemark*, 1755-56 (translated by Bishop Thomas Percy as *Northern Antiquities*, 1770, together with a translation of the Poetic Edda). Scott dated his copy of *Northern Antiquities* 11th July 1792.

120 A second notebook, begun by Scott in 1792 and now in the National Library of Scotland, contains many notes from many sources on Scandinavian beliefs, customs, and the like. One of his acquisitions, probably made about the same time, was *A Compendious History of the Goths, Swedes, & Vandals*, the first English translation (1658) of the *Historia de Gentibus Septentrionalibus* of Olaus Magnus.

121 Contributed to Henry Weber's *Illustrations of Northern Antiquities*, 1814.

122 Letters III and IV are mainly concerned with the religion and superstitions of the Scandinavian peoples.

123 Cf. *infra*, 249-50.

124 Cf. *infra*, 250.

125 My late friend, Dr O. K. Schram, to whom I submitted a copy, was able to penetrate the little mystery for me.

126 Lockhart, I, 48-9. The nightcap was no doubt, as Lockhart surmised (I, 51), the one Scott bought with the first guinea he earned in his profession. Cf. *infra*, 243.

127 Lockhart, I, 48.

128 Pope, *An Essay on Man*, Epistle IV.

129 The opener did not necessarily speak in the affirmative.

130 The meeting on 11th January had decided on a different wording: 'Ought the poor to have any prospect of support except from their own industry?'

131 Graduated M.D. in 1793. He practised later in Salisbury and wrote several medical books and papers.

132 Crauford Tait, W.S., later of Harvieston. The number of members voting was not recorded.

133   Graduated M.D. in 1791.

134   The question had been selected from three submitted by Scott. It was something of a stock question, having been debated by the Society five times before. The general question of whether any monarch could be justifiably put to death had been debated thrice.

135   Graduated M.D. in 1794.

136   The long interval since his last debate coincides with Scott's diligence in his legal studies. On 14th February 1792, when he read his second essay, his place as opener of the debate on ' Ought the King to have unlimited power of creating peers? ' was taken by David Monypenny.

137   Graduated M.D. in 1791. He became successively Warden and Master of Dulwich College, and wrote on politics and history.

138   Lockhart was mistaken in saying in reference to this debate that this ' eternal question . . . was thus set up for re-discussion on a motion by Walter Scott ' (I, 48). Cf. *supra*, 238 note 134.

139   His Christian name is not known.

140   Later High Sheriff of Cornwall. His name as opener is given in the minutes. But the 1845 *History of the Speculative Society* gives the opener as John Smith (381). There is no John Smith in the list of members, which, however, does include John Smyth who was called to the Scottish Bar in 1793.

141   The minute confusingly says that the negative was carried unanimously with 4 Ayes and no Noes. Apparently the Ayes were those who agreed with the opener's No to the question. The 1845 *History of the Speculative Society*, however, interpreted the minute as meaning ' Carried unanimously in the affirmative ' (381).

142   The minute gives Scott as teller for the Ayes. I have altered this to conform to the normal use of Aye and No in such contexts.

143   His Christian name is not known.

144   Scott was the only speaker after the opener.

145   Louis XVI was guillotined on 21st January.

146   Later D.D. and Professor of Hebrew in the University of

Edinburgh.

147 Called to the Scottish Bar in 1795.

148 Minute. The Ayes, led by Rae, apparently voted that the extension of mercy to criminals was not contrary to ' the strict exercise of statutory law '. That is to say, they said Yes to the reworded question, ' Is mercy compatible with law? '

149 A member of the Historical Society of Trinity College, Dublin. His Christian name is not known.

150 It comes, however, from the part of the book written by William Weir who was a member of the Speculative Society and who seems to have consulted the minutes.

151 88.

152 *Spec. Soc.* (1845), 41.

153 *Journal*, II, 25-26 (22nd February 1827). The concluding couplet is a parody of the end of Robert the Bruce's ' Maxims or Political Testament ' (cf. Sir David Dalrymple, *Annals of Scotland*, ed. 1797, II, 40). Scott was reminding himself of his ' rules ' the day before he was to preside at the Theatrical Fund Dinner, the occasion on which he was induced to avow publicly his authorship of the Waverley Novels.

CHAPTER XIV

THE YOUNG ADVOCATE

I answered thus confidently, with the obstinacy often said to be proper to those who bear my surname.

The Lady of the Lake, *Introduction.*

I have the pleasure to tell you that Alan has passed his private Scots Law examinations with good approbation—a great relief to my mind; especially as worthy Mr Pest told me in my ear there was no fear of the " callant ", as he familiarly called him, which gives me great heart. His public trials, which are nothing in comparison save a mere form, are to take place, by the Honourable Dean of Faculty, on Wednesday first; and on Friday he puts on the gown, and gives a bit chack of dinner to his friends and acquaintances, as is, you know, the custom.

Redgauntlet, *Letter IX.*

And then, Alan, I thought to turn the ball our own way; and I said that you were a gey sharp birkie, just off the irons.

Redgauntlet, *Letter XIII.*

LONG before Scott's active participation in the Speculative Society ceased, his tenuous connection with the University had come to an end in the spring or early summer of 1792. He and William Clerk as ' intrants '[1] passed their Bar trials with credit on the same days—Civil Law on 30th June 1791,[2] and Scots Law on 6th July 1792.[3] More than thirty years later Scott made Alan Fairford regard his coming trials as not likely to be formidable. ' For my own part,' he writes to Darsie, ' I know there is no great difficulty in passing these formal examinations, else how have some of our acquaintance got through them? '[4] Perhaps Alan's friends had recourse in what is said to have been a not unusual practice to a private hint from the examinators as to the chapter on which the questions would be founded.[5] Scott himself, however, took no chances and worked hard at his law studies—and made the indolent Clerk do likewise. They ' both assumed the gown with all its duties and honours '[6] on 11th July 1792,[7] the day before the Court rose for the summer vacation, the ceremonial being as Scott describes it in a note to Letter I in *Redgauntlet*: ' Till of late years, every advocate who entered at the Scottish Bar made a Latin address to the Court, Faculty, and audience, in set terms, and said a few words upon a text of the Civil Law, to show his Latinity and jurisprudence. He also wore his hat for a minute, in order to vindicate his right of being covered before the Court, which is said to have originated from the celebrated lawyer, Sir Thomas Hope, having two sons on the bench while he himself remained at the bar.'

After quoting Saunders Fairford's proud letter to Darsie on Alan's success,[8] Lockhart tells how on the day of Scott's inauguration ' all things passed in due order, even as they are figured. The real Darsie[9] was present at the real Alan Fairford's " bit chack of dinner ",[10] and the old Clerk of the Signet was very joyous on the occasion. . . . I have often heard both *Alan* and *Darsie* laugh over their reminiscences of the important day when they " put on the gown ".[11] After the ceremony was completed, and they had mingled

for some time with the crowd of barristers in the Outer
Court, Scott said to his comrade, mimicking the air and
tone of a Highland lass waiting at the Cross of Edinburgh
to be hired for the harvest work: " We've stood here an
hour by the Tron, hinny, and de'il a ane has speered[12]
our price." Some friendly solicitor, however, gave him a
guinea fee before the Court rose; and as they walked down
the High Street together, he said to Mr Clerk in passing a
hosier's shop: " This is a sort of wedding-day, Willie; I
think I must go in and buy me a new nightcap." He did
so accordingly;—perhaps this was Lord Jeffrey's " por-
tentous machine ".[13] His first fee of any consequence,
however, was expended on a silver taper-stand for his
mother, which the old lady used to point to with great
satisfaction, as it stood on her chimney-piece five-and-twenty
years after '.[14]

The Latin thesis on a subject prescribed by his examinators which Scott in accordance with requirements submitted
to the Lords of Council and Session and the Faculty of
Advocates through Henry Erskine, Dean of the Faculty,[15]
was on the somewhat antiquarian title in the Pandects, *De
Cadaveribus Damnatorum.*[16] This ' very pretty piece of
Latinity '[17] with surprising references to such non-legal
authorities as the elder Pliny, Macrobius, Martianus Capella,
and Lipsius was printed, and dedicated in imposing terms
to Robert Macqueen, Lord Braxfield, the Lord Justice Clerk
of the day and the Scotts' near neighbour in George Square.[18]
The choice of dedicatee was perhaps determined, at the
shrewd suggestion of Scott's father, by political considerations, Braxfield being a stern supporter of the Government
at a time of crisis.

The literary flavour in the thesis was rather unusual;
but it does not appear to have displeased the learned judge
who soon after receiving his copy called at 25 George
Square, inquired ' very particularly ' for the absent author,
and told the elder Scott that he proposed to put work in
Walter's way.[19] As Scott was to discover, however, his

more pronounced literary bent as shown a few years later was ' unfavourable to my success at the Bar. The goddess Themis is . . . of a peculiarly jealous disposition. She will not readily consent to share her authority, and sternly demands from her votaries, not only that real duty be carefully attended to and discharged, but that a certain air of business shall be observed, even in the midst of total idleness '.[20]

However, Scott's professional life as an advocate is not part of his education and lies outside the prescribed limits of this book. His may have been a ' dry and laborious profession'[21]; but in his earlier years at the Bar he did not take it too seriously. It is his former self that he presents in the guise of young Hardie, who was likely to have ' the new novel most in repute lying on his table,—snugly entrenched, however, beneath Stair's Institutes, or an open volume of Morrison's Decisions ', and who had sometimes to rummage for his solitary legal document ' among old play-bills, letters requesting a meeting of the Faculty, rules of the Speculative Society, syllabuses of lectures—all the miscellaneous contents of a young advocate's pocket, which contains everything but briefs and bank-notes '.[22] And Scott himself was likewise the Chrystal Croftangry who ' swept the boards of the Parliament House with the skirts of [his] gown . . .—got no fees—laughed, and made others laugh—drank claret at Bayle's, Fortune's, and Walker's, and ate oysters in the Covenant Close '.[23]

NOTES ON REFERENCES

1   I.e. candidates for admission to the Faculty of Advocates.

2   Cf. *infra*, 245, note 1. Scott's petition to be examined, having been presented to the Lords of Council and Session on 13th May 1791, was remitted by Ilay Campbell the same day to the Dean and Faculty of Advocates ' to take Trial of the Petitioner's skill in Law in the Ordinary way, and to Report ' (*The Scott Exhibition, MDCCCLXXI., Cata-*

logue, 150, 163). On 11th June the Faculty authorised their Dean, Henry Erskine, to remit three petitioners, Scott, [H.] Guthrie [Wright], and William Clerk to ' the private Examinators on the Civil Law ' for their report (Faculty minutes). And on 14th June accordingly Erskine remitted Scott to the examinators, ' he having promised on his honor to give no treat or entertainment on account thereof and producing to the Examinators proper Certificates of his being twenty years of age ' (*The Scott Exhibition. MDCCCLXXI. Catalogue*, 163; cf. *supra*, 5-6).

3 Cf. *infra*, 245 note 1. On 10th July Scott, having been ' publickly Examined on Tit. [left blank] and found sufficiently qualified ', was recommended to the Dean ' to assign him a law out of the above Title for the subject of his Discourses to the Lords and to the Faculty ' (Faculty minutes). There is a similar entry under the same date for William Clerk. The Faculty appointed Scott and Clerk two of the examinators in Civil Law on 15th January 1793.

4 *Redgauntlet*, Letter VIII.

5 Cf. Gillies, 47.

6 *Memoir*, I, 17. Cf. *Redgauntlet*, Chapter I: ' the sable bombazine, which in [old Fairford's] eyes was more venerable than an archbishop's lawn '.

7 This date and the dates for Scott's examinations in Civil Law and in Scots Law, 30th June 1791 and 6th July 1792, are given in square brackets in the printed *Memoir* (I, 17). I take the brackets to indicate either Lockhart's filling-in of gaps left by Scott or Lockhart's correction of Scott's dates (cf. *supra*, 13-14). Irving, it may be added, dates Scott's admission to the Bar in June 1792.

8 *Redgauntlet*, Letter IX.

9 I.e. William Clerk.

10 *Redgauntlet*, Letter IX.

11 Cf. *Memoir*, I, 17.

12 I.e. inquired.

13 Cf. *supra*, 221.

14 Lockhart, I, 51.

15 Cf. *supra*, 5-6. Scott described Erskine as ' the bestnatured man I ever knew, thouroughly a gentleman, & with but one fault—He could not say *no*, & thus sometimes misled

those who trusted him. . . . Henry's [wit] was of the very kindest, best humourd, & gayest kind that ever cheerd Society'. (*Journal*, III, 56; 20th April 1829.) There is also a reference to ' the wittiest and best-humoured man living . . . just he—Harry—poor Harry—' by the paralysed and dying advocate in *Chronicles of the Canongate*, Chapter I (Mr Chrystal Croftangry's Account of Himself).

16 Lib. XLVIII, Tit. XXIV. The usual wording of the *titulus* is *De Cadaveribus Punitorum*.

17 As Saunders Fairford in *Redgauntlet*, Letter IX, described Alan's thesis on Lib. XVIII, Tit. VI, *De Periculo et Commodo Rei Venditae*. Allan, who can never have seen Scott's thesis, calls it a ' brief medley of indifferent Latin and common-place truisms', and says it would be unfair to hold Scott responsible since ' The whole ceremony of the composition and distribution of the thesis is, and has been so far back as the memory of man reaches, a mere farce. It is very rarely the composition of the person whose name it bears ' (92).

18 He was also the guardian of Scott's friend, John Irving.

19 Lockhart, I, 51.

20 *The Lay of the Last Minstrel*, Introduction.

21 *Redgauntlet*, Chapter I.

22 *The Heart of Midlothian*, Chapter I.

23 *Chronicles of the Canongate*, Chapter I.

CHAPTER XV

'GERMAN MAD'

Our hero was liable to fits of absence, in which his blunders excited some mirth, and called down some reproof.
Waverley, *Chapter VII*

[W]hen I first dipt my desperate pen in ink for other purposes than those of my profession . . . I was an insulated individual, with only my own wants to provide for, and having, in a great measure, my own inclinations alone to consult. . . . [M]y open interference with matters of light literature diminished my employment in the weightier matters of the law. Nor did the solicitors . . . do me less than justice, by regarding others among my contemporaries as fitter to discharge the duty due to their clients, than a young man who was taken up with running after ballads, whether Teutonic or national. My profession and I, therefore, came to stand nearly upon the footing which honest Slender consoled himself on having established with Mistress Anne Page; 'There was no great love between us at the beginning, and it pleased Heaven to decrease it on further acquaintance.'
The Lay of the Last Minstrel, *Introduction.*

Thus I was set up for a poet, like a pedlar who has got two ballads to begin the world upon, and I hastened to make the round of all my acquaintances showing my precious wares, and requesting criticism—a boon which no author asks in vain.
Essay on Imitations of the Ancient Ballads *in* Minstrelsy, *IV, 46.*

THERE remains for consideration the last chapter of Scott's pursuit of knowledge in an educational way. It began only after his admission to the Bar and towards the end of 1792. The subject of study was German.

German literature had recently and suddenly become a focus of interest, having till then not been studied and indeed having been scarcely recognised as existing, except by a few students.[1] As it happens, some of the few in Scotland who read German and were acquainted with certain departments of its literature were known personally to Scott. One was Dr John Erskine, one of the ministers of Greyfriars, which church the Scotts attended, and a particular friend of the family. He began the study of German not long before 1790, when he was nearly seventy, to help him in his correspondence with continental divines, and so rapidly acquired the language that he soon published a substantial work largely translated from it.[2] Another contemporary student of German was George Husband Baird, an able linguist who became Professor of Hebrew in 1792 and Principal of Edinburgh University in 1793 when only thirty-two. He and Scott were both members of the Speculative Society and both were advanced to honorary membership in the same session of 1793-94.[3] It was while he was still a young man that Baird 'mastered most of the European languages, and made acquaintance with their respective literatures'.[4] But we may assume that neither he nor Erskine was much concerned with German poetry and drama.

Scott traced the first interest aroused in Scotland about such German literature to Henry Mackenzie's *Account of the German Theatre*, which was read to the Royal Society of Edinburgh on 21st April 1788[5] and published in its Transactions in 1790.[6] Scott's own interest, however, seems to have been wakened two years later by the publication of a translation of Schiller's *Die Räuber* by his old History Professor, Alexander Fraser Tytler.[7] And certainly Tytler both encouraged Scott by his example to take up German and assisted him by his advice.

It says much for Mackenzie's acumen that he appreciated some of the virtues of the German stage 'although . . . at that time known to him only through the imperfect and uncongenial medium of a French translation'.[8] The *Account* caused something of a sensation and produced a powerful effect; for by it, as Scott says, 'the literary persons of Edinburgh . . . were first made aware of the existence of works of genius in a language cognate with the English, and possessed of the same manly force of expression. They learned, at the same time, that the taste which dictated the German compositions was of a kind as nearly allied to the English as their language ",[9] and as emancipated from the Neo-classicism of the French.

Scott and half a dozen of his friends (they included most of the group of young advocates dubbed 'the Mountain' or 'the Montagnards' after the extremists in the French Revolution) were encouraged by the still more obvious resemblance between German and the dialect of Lowland Scotland, with which they were all perfectly familiar as spoken all round them in the street and sometimes at them from the Bench,[10] to join a class before the Christmas of 1792 run by a German physician in Edinburgh, Dr A. F. M. Willich.[11] From it in the sessions 1792-93 and 1793-94 they derived varying degrees of profit and not a little amusement. Scott's own attack on the language, as with all the other languages he tackled except perhaps Latin, had the aim of getting as much as he needed for his own immediate purposes, not of making a critical study of it.[12] '[A]verse to the necessary toil of grammar and its rules,' he fought 'his way to the knowledge of German by his acquaintance with the Scottish and Anglo-Saxon dialects, and, of course, frequently committed blunders which were not lost on his more accurate and more studious companions.'[13]

As for the Scots dialect, it was all but his mother tongue, and he constantly resorted to its expressive phraseology in anecdotes long before he used it in the dialogue of his novels; and of course his knowledge of Scots literature from Barbour to Burns was complete. When he took an interest in Anglo-Saxon and other Teutonic languages apart from German is not certain. But according to Lockhart,[14] he was bringing lore from Anglo-Saxon sources and the Norse sagas into his contributions to discussions in the Literary Society in 1789 or 1790. The interest continued, at least till it merged in the higher interest called forth by German.[15] For in a notebook in the National Library of Scotland which Scott began in 1792, he drew up tables of the Moeso-Gothic, Anglo-Saxon, and runic alphabets, with another left blank for the German,[16] and made many notes on the beliefs, customs, institutions, and languages of the various Teutonic peoples; and in a 1792 notebook at Abbotsford, as has been noticed,[17] Scott transliterated two lines of Gray's *Descent of Odin* into runes and wrote out what appears to be material, Norse, Latin, and English, gathered for his Speculative Society essay on "The Origin of the Scandinavian Mythology".[18]

In their pursuit of German literature Scott and his friends were impatient to press on to Goethe, Schiller, and the other dramatists whose fame had been bruited by Henry Mackenzie. But their teacher, who 'predicted that Mr Scott would never succeed, as he determined at once to come to the superstructure without laying a stable foundation',[19] tried to initiate them by means of the much simpler diction of Salomon Gessner; and, to the class's great delight, Dr Willich was reduced to despair by finding it impossible to extract from lively young advocates the kind of sensibility appropriate to the beauties of *Der Tod Abels*,[20] with its 'sickly monotony and affected ecstacies'.[21] 'The pietistic style . . . was ill-adapted to attract young persons of our age and disposition,' says Scott. 'We could no more sympathise with the over-strained sentimentality of Adam and his family, than we could have had a fellow-feeling with the jolly Faun of the same author,[22] who broke his beautiful jug, and then made a song on it which might have affected all Staffordshire. . . . [W]e, with one consent, voted Abel an insufferable bore, and gave the pre-eminence, in point of masculine character, to his brother Cain, or even to Lucifer himself.'[23]   However, amid the laughter and despite the not very strenuous study, most of Scott's circle acquired enough German to select their further reading according to their differing tastes.   The companion in the class who was most serviceable to Scott in his headlong enthusiasm for German Romanticism was William Erskine (later Lord Kinnedder).   He shared with Scott a common love of English literature; but he was also a good classic and had a more impartial judgement as between classical virtues and romantic extravagances.   This 'friendly critic was just as well as delicate; and unmerciful severity as to the mingled absurdities and vulgarities of German detail commanded deliberate attention from one who admired not less enthusiastically than himself the genuine sublimity and pathos of his new favourites'.[24]   Erskine's restraining influence continued long after the first fervour of Scott's devotion to German, even although it was not always strong enough to turn him from the pitfalls of the Romantic. Indeed Erskine became one of Scott's most intimate friends from this time and through all his middle years—the one nearest to him in sympathies and loyalties, political, literary, and religious, and the one most in his confidence.

Scott was also greatly helped and encouraged in his German studies, from late in 1795, by the wife of Hugh Scott of Harden (later Lord Polwarth), to whom Walter always looked as his feudal chief and, by Scottish reckoning, his not-very-distant kinsman.   Mrs Scott of Harden was 'a lady of sixteen quarters':[25]   she was Harriet, daughter of Hans Moritz, Count von Bruhl, who was for many years the Envoy of Saxony in London;   her mother, however, was British, being Alicia Maria Carpenter, daughter of the Irish peer, Lord Tyrconnell.   Mrs Scott was much interested in her young kinsman-by-marriage's attachment to German literature, and supplied him with many standard books, including works by Goethe and Schiller and the ballads of Gottfried August Bürger which started him off on his translations.[26] Scott in fact consulted her on all his German ventures and remained on terms of intimate friendship with her and her husband and with his mother, Lady Diana Scott. He would often say that among the many ' obligations of a distant date which remained impressed on his memory, after a life spent in a constant interchange of friendship and kindness ', he counted as not the least Mrs Scott's frank correction of his Scotticisms, especially as regards rhyming.[27] Being herself English-educated and resident in London for most of her life before her marriage in 1795, she did not hesitate to point out other solecisms in language.[28]

Another who came to his help, at least in procuring an important piece of equipment for his German, was his old ally at Prestonpans, George Constable. The book was Johann Christoph Adelung's lexicon,[29] ' procured ... through the mediation of Father Pepper, a monk of the Scotch College of Ratisbon ',[30] and perhaps recommended by Dr Willich.[31]

It was probably in the same year 1795 or the next that Scott asked his friend John James Edmonstone of Newton to introduce him to James Skene of Rubislaw, having presumably heard that Skene, in the course of several years' stay in Saxony, had thoroughly mastered the language and collected more German books than Scott had hitherto been able to consult. Scott was eager to learn from a fellow-admirer of German literature whose knowledge of it was so much better than his own. The acquaintance thus begun between the two young advocates,[32] who had many tastes and traits of character in common, ripened into a close and unbroken friendship.

Scott's own knowledge of German, however hastily acquired and unscholarly, must have become reasonably good, for a while at least, though he minimised it in retro-

spect when he had largely forgotten it. At any rate it
served him well enough in his *ad hoc* purpose of getting
the substance and the spirit of whatever he read. He
became ' German-mad '[33] and ' a bold and daring reader';[34]
and inevitably he took to translating ' on all sides '[34] in
the wake of Tytler's spirited version in 1792 of Schiller's
Die Räuber.

It was naturally German balladry on which he first tried
his hand as a translator, ' less in the hope of pleasing others,
though certainly without despair of doing so, than in the
pursuit of a new and agreeable amusement to myself '.[34]
He was particularly delighted to find that ' the old English
and especially the Scottish language, were so nearly similar
to the German, not in sound merely, but in the turn of
phrase, that they were capable of being rendered line for
line, with very little variation '.[34] But, curiously enough,
Scott did not resort to the dialect of the Border ballads in
his renderings or adaptations from the German, though his
rhymes may have been affected. The reason appears to
have been the influence of certain contemporary ballads,
original or translated, in standard English.

The original ones, some of which however may have
had German antecedents, were those embedded in Matthew
Gregory Lewis's *Monk*, which was a literary *succès de vogue*
of 1795, such as *Alonzo the Brave and the Fair Imogine* and
Durandarte and Belerma. And Scott confesses that Lewis's
' possession of so much poetic reputation ' put into his head
the idea of trying to produce similar work.[35] So far as
versifying goes, he had been lying more or less fallow for
some years.[36] As Lockhart says, Scott ' was perhaps at all
times rather disposed to hold popular favour as the surest
test of literary merit, and . . . certainly continued through
life to overestimate all talents except his own '.[37] For some
years, then, he regarded Lewis as a great poet, far ahead of
himself in poetic power, though he himself was the superior
in general information. When in 1798 on his first visit to
Edinburgh, Lewis, who was anxious to meet a possible

contributor to his projected *Tales of Wonder*,[38] invited Scott to dine, the latter ' thought he had never felt such elation. . . . Since he gazed on Burns in his seventeenth year, he had seen no one enjoying, by general consent, the fame of a poet '.[39] He told Allan Cunningham that it was ' the proudest hour of his life . . .; he considered it as a sure recognition of his talents; and as he sat down at the table he almost exclaimed with Tamlane: " He's own'd amang us a'." '[40] If on the appearance of the greater Romantics Scott outgrew his regard for Lewis, he continued to believe him possessed of ' the finest ear for rhythm I ever met with—finer than Byron's '.[41]

A year or two before the publication of *The Monk*, Gottfried August Bürger's *Leonore* had enjoyed a sudden celebrity and six or seven versions of it in English were in circulation. One of the unpublished ones was by William Taylor of Norwich, who was an accomplished German scholar.[42] It electrified a party at Dugald Stewart's house in Edinburgh when it was read there in the summer or autumn of 1795[43] by Mrs Barbauld, who put the manuscript back in her pocket-book and declined to let any one take a copy.[44] Scott, who may have been ' indulging his vagabond vein ',[45] was not present on the occasion; but on his return to Edinburgh he heard rapturous reports of it from his friends, together with a broken account of the story in the ballad and a line or two of the version.[46] These secondhand descriptions were enough to fire him with the desire to translate the ballad himself. But it was some time before he could obtain a copy of the original German, probably in the spring of 1796, by which time Lewis's ballads in *The Monk* had added fuel to the fire. The reading of *Leonore* in the original ' rather exceeded than disappointed ' Scott's expectations;[47] and in the excitement of the moment he rashly promised to provide his friend, Jane Anne Cranstoun (later Countess Purgstall), with a translation in ballad verse. He began the task early in April one evening after supper and finished it about daybreak the next morning, 'having by that time', adds Lockhart, 'worked himself into a state of excitement which set sleep at defiance'.[48] The translation or adaptation deserves particular notice, for it was no less than Scott's first attempt at a piece of literary work of some importance, his earlier verses (not to mention his essays in prose) being no more than of amateur status. The next morning, even before breakfast, Scott took the manuscript translation to Miss Cranstoun, who 'was not only delighted but astonished at it.' Her prophecy, however, that 'Walter Scott is going to turn out a poet—something of a cross, I think, between Burns and Gray'[49] was not fulfilled to the letter. Still in a state of exaltation Scott the same day read the ballad to Sir Alexander Wood, who recalled to Lockhart after many years how Scott 'read it over . . . in a very slow and solemn tone, and after we had said a few words about its merits, continued to look at the fire silent and musing for some minutes, until he at length burst out with ' I wish to Heaven I could get a skull and two crossbones ".'[50] Wood at once took Scott to visit a well-known surgeon, John Bell, who allowed Scott to choose the finest *memento mori* in his professional ossuary and carry the relics home in his handkerchief to George Square. There they were set up on a bookcase in the poet's den and many years later Wood saw the same symbols of the Romantic macabre similarly displayed in Scott's dressing-room at Abbotsford.

So gratified was Scott by the reception given to his first essay in translation by his friends that he soon went on to render, with rather more freedom, Bürger's *Der Wilde Jäger*, and also 'balladized' one or two of Bürger's other pieces.[51] As he asked, when was there ever an author deaf to the wish of his friends that he should print? And in the summer of 1796 succumbing to their solicitations, and his own innocent vanity, he was prevailed on to send two ballads to the printer as his first publication, but without his name. One of the Edinburgh publishers of the ballads, Alexander Manners, had been a fellow-member with Scott of Dr Willich's class[52]; and the negotiations for the publication were carried through by another, William Erskine. The title is as follows: *The Chase, and William and Helen; Two Ballads from the German of Gottfried Augustus Bürger.*[53] Scott's name as the author of the first of the two, renamed *The Wild Huntsman*, was not given till its inclusion with revisions and additions in Lewis's *Tales of Wonder* in 1801; and his name was first attached to *William and Helen*, as he called his version of *Leonore*, in his *Ballads and Lyrical Pieces* in 1806.

In translating *Leonore*, before he had thought of publication, Scott incorporated two 'energetic and expressive lines'[54] from William Taylor's version. He retained the lines in print and sent a copy of his first publication to Taylor with a covering letter in which he asked for pardon.[55] Taylor's reply, though it contained a few points of criticism, was a generous and glowing panegyric.[56] Scott in a subsequent letter to Taylor apologised for venturing to differ with such a German expert, 'especially as I can by no means boast of my own [i.e. ability] altho it is considerably increased since I made out these translations—I was at that time but a Tyro indeed, and shall upon some future occasion avail myself of your friendly and polite criticisms to correct some of the many errors into which my ignorance has led me'.[57] The phrase 'made out' is perhaps to be noted.

Scott's friends in Scotland, among whom he 'distributed so many copies . . . as, according to the book-sellers, materially to interfere with the sale',[58] were loud in their praises.[59] Despite flaws in the texture of the translations, the freshness and vigour of them gave great delight to such friends and the sure promise of a new poet to succeed Burns, who had died in the July of the same year. But their expectations of the ballads' success in London and the South, where other versions were circulating,[60] were not realised. '[M]y efforts sunk unnoticed,' says Scott, '. . . In a word, my adventure, where so many pushed off to sea, proved a dead loss, and a great part of the edition was condemned to the

service of the trunk-maker.'[61]   Scott, however," was not
much put out by the coolness of his reception among
strangers; and ' my reputation ', he adds, ' began rather to
increase among my own friends, and, on the whole, I was
more bent to show the world that it had neglected something worth notice, than to be affronted by its indifference '.[62]

As has been stated,[63] *The Wild Huntsman* was one of
the pieces contributed by Scott[64] to Lewis's *Tales of Wonder*;
and during the long gestation of that miscellany, especially
in 1799 and 1800, Lewis was a persistent and somewhat
captious critic of *minutiae* in the poems submitted.   But
he ' found it no easy matter ', says Scott, ' to discipline his
northern recruits.[65]   He was a martinet . . . in the accuracy
of rhymes and of numbers; I may add, he had a right to
be so, for few persons have exhibited more mastery of
rhyme, or greater command over the melody of verse.   He
was, therefore, rigid in exacting similar accuracy from
others ',[66] especially as regards rhyming, maintaining that
' a bad rhyme ', in which category he included many
rhymes in common use, ' is, in fact, no rhyme at all '.[67]
But Scott ' was quite unaccustomed to the mechanical part
of poetry, and used rhymes which were merely permissible,
as readily as those which were legitimate '.[68]   Such imperfect rhyming at this period of Scott's life (for neither
before nor after could he have been accused of it) Lockhart
very reasonably attributes to his zeal during the same years
in collecting Border ballads in which assonances and jingles
were very venial licences.[69]   Though Scott does not appear
to have defended himself along these lines, he fought, to
use his own words, with ' obstinacy ', ' inflexibility ', and
' a tone of defiance to criticism ' in contests ' which were
exasperated by the pertinacity of my Mentor, who, as all
who knew him can testify, " was no granter of propositions " '.[70]   But Scott, ' severe enough, perhaps ', as was
Lewis's chiding, confessed himself as ' much indebted to
him, as forcing upon the notice of a young and careless
author hints which the said author's vanity made him un-

willing to attend to, but which were absolutely necessary to any hope of his ultimate success '.[71]

The only other surviving piece by Scott translated from Bürger is *The Triumph of Constancy*, a version of *Das Lied von Treue*. Written in 1796, it remained unpublished during Scott's life and for long after,[72] having been declined for inclusion in *Tales of Wonder* because it lacked Lewis's *sine qua non* of a ghost or a witch.[73]

In 1797 Scott began to translate some of Goethe's ballads. The first to be attempted was probably *Der Erlkönig*. He sent the version as *The Erl-king* 'to be read by a candle particularly long in the snuff' to his aunt Christian Rutherford late in October, adding 'You see I have not altogether lost the faculty of rhiming—I assure you there is no small impudence in attempting a version of that Ballad as it has been translated by Lewis '.[74] The translation was a little later passed on for anonymous publication above the signature ' Alonzo '[75] to the editor of *The Kelso Mail*, James Ballantyne. He published it in the issue of his paper for 1st March 1798, with an enthusiastic prefatory note in which he expressed ' equal pride and pleasure [at] the receipt of the . . . beautiful poem ' and the hope of being ' highly honoured by the continuance of this correspondent's favours '. *The Erl-king*, which was also printed without the author's name in *The Scots Magazine* for January 1802, was included, still anonymously, in the curious collection which Scott put out in 1799 through James Ballantyne and *The Kelso Mail* printing office, *Tales of Terror* as the first issue was entitled or *An Apology for Tales of Terror* as the second issue with a fresh title-page has it.[76] But the authorship of the version was not made known publicly till the second edition in 1806 of *Ballads and Lyrical Pieces*.

The only other Goethe original of a non-dramatic kind that Scott ' imitated, rather than translated ',[77] with alterations and additions, was a ballad from the operetta *Claudine von Villa Bella*. *Frederick and Alice*, as Scott entitled it, may have been written in 1796 or 1797,[78] and was certainly in existence by 1801 when it appeared for the first time in *Tales of Wonder* ' after some material improvements ' made by Lewis himself on its ' extremely rude state '.[79]

Probably about the same time,[80] Scott wrote *The Lamentation of the Faithful Wife of Asan Aga*, translating from the translation by Goethe of a Morlachian ballad, *Klaggesang von der edlen Frauen des Asan Aga*. It was well known to some of Scott's early friends including James Ballantyne,[81] and also to Lockhart. But it lay in manuscript till it was printed in 1924 by Mr D. H. Low as *The First Link between English and Serbo-Croat Literature*.[82]

The Noble Moringer is Scott's version of an anonymous ballad which he found in a collection of German popular songs printed in 1807.[83] He printed it for the first time in 1819.[84]

His latest ballad from a German source[85] was written in 1818 and published the same year. This is *The Battle of Sempach*, a literal translation from an ancient Swiss poem by Albert Tchudi, nicknamed the Souter.

Two other poems have German antecedents, without being translations. The one is *The Fire-King* written by Scott, late in 1799 or early in 1800, at Lewis's request for inclusion in *Tales of Wonder*, in which it was to be one of four about elemental spirits. Scott seems to have derived the partly historical story from some German source.[86] He wrote it one day after dinner with John Leyden and another friend unnamed sitting at his side; ' nor did my occupation ', he adds, ' prevent the circulation of the bottle '.[87] The other poem was suggested merely by the metre and rhythm of a German war-song, *Der Abschieds Tag ist da*.[88] It is the *War-Song of the Royal Edinburgh Light Dragoons*, written overnight in 1798[89] and forthwith adopted by the regiment.[90]

So much, then, for Scott's excursions into German balladry, which, however much separated in time, I have thought it best to keep together. But the German Romantic

drama, which owes all that is best in it to a passion for
Shakespeare, had likewise a powerful appeal for such a
lover of the Elizabethan theatre[91] as Scott was. There are
at Abbotsford the manuscripts of three closely translated
versions in prose of German prose dramas. Nothing from
these versions has been printed, except a few illustrative
quotations; nor perhaps would Scott's reputation be much
enhanced if some industrious Ph.D. researcher were to
publish them *in extenso*. The German plays are August
Wilhelm Iffland's *Die Mündel*,[92] Josef Marius Babo's *Otto
von Wittelsbach*,[93] and Jakob Maier's *Fust von Stromberg*.[94]
The translations are dated by Scott respectively 1796, 1796–
97, and 1797.[95]

Iffland specialised in sentimental domestic plays of contemporary life in prose, of which category *Die Mündel* is
a typical specimen. A *bürgerliches Schauspiel* is not the kind
of play that might have been expected to appeal to Scott;[96]
but he may have chosen it or had it recommended by Dr
Willich as affording good practice in colloquial German.
The plays by Babo and Maier are totally different and just
what Scott at the time of his ballad-collecting must have
revelled in, however much qualified is the admiration he
expresses in his *Essay on the Drama*.[97] They are both examples of *das deutsche Ritterdrama*, historical plays with a
medieval background and an abundance of knights in
armour and lawless nobles in the fashion set by Goethe's
Götz von Berlichingen. Scott must have been particularly
pleased by Maier's *Fust* which is packed with medieval detail
and has an appendix of notes longer than the play itself.

No doubt Scott began his play-translating primarily in
order to improve his German; and he clearly did so in
the process. In the first translation, there are many bad
mistakes, due largely to the kind of guessing by which he
had raised the laughter of Dr Willich's class; but the
blunders steadily diminish. The second translation is almost
free of them; and the increase again in the third translation
is due mainly to the difficulty of the German.[98] It should

perhaps be recalled that Scott acquired Adelung's lexicon during those very years. But, though the play-translating was begun, as I think, for practice in the language, the completion of so much may well indicate that some idea had occurred to him of publishing English versions of plays that had become something of a vogue.

However, he came to regard his translations as not worth printing. At least that was his opinion in 1827 when he wrote to Mrs Hughes that his translations ' are in general sad trash and if you read ever so little German you would see how inferior they are to the original '.[99] I am inclined to think, too, that long before 1827 his liking for *Sturm und Drang* dramas was considerably reduced by the brilliant parody of *The Rovers; or The Double Arrangement* by George Canning, George Ellis, and John Hookham Frere in numbers 30 and 31 of *The Anti-Jacobin* in June 1798. Even the prefatory note by the supposed author, the subversive Mr Higgins, might have given Scott food for thought. Mr Higgins called his ' a Play; which ... will ... do much to unhinge the present notions of men with regard to the obligations of Civil Society; and to substitute in lieu of a sober contentment, and regular discharge of the duties incident to each man's particular situation, a wild desire of undefinable latitude and extravagance,—an aspiration after shapeless somethings, that can neither be described nor understood,—a contemptuous disgust at all that *is*, and a persuasion that nothing is as it ought to be; to operate, in short, a general discharge of every man (in his own estimation) from every thing that laws, divine or human, that local customs, immemorial habits, and multiplied examples, impose upon him; and to set them about doing what they like, where they like, when they like, and how they like,—without reference to any Law but their own Will, or to any consideration of how others may be affected by their conduct '.[100] The drama itself, with its romantic absurdities, its confounding of the manners of the thirteenth century with those of the eighteenth, and the ludicrous mingling of stagey rhetoric and humdrum colloquialism, is only too devastatingly faithful to the victims of its caricature. Such a satiric masterpiece could not have failed to alert such a true-blue Tory and traditionalist as Scott, had he seen it, as he almost certainly had.[101]

But in 1798, possibly in the months before *The Rovers* appeared, Scott translated the first and greatest play of the *Sturm und Drang*, Goethe's *Götz von Berlichingen*. He knew perfectly well that it was infinitely superior to all its forcible-feeble imitations, including the two he had just translated. This tragedy, even though its medium throughout is prose, is rather like what Shakespeare might have written if, instead of Holinshed, the Border ballads had been his source-book. ' It is,' says Lockhart, ' a broad, bold, free, and most picturesque delineation of real characters, manners, and events. . . . With what delight must Scott have found the scope and manner of our Elizabethan drama revived on a foreign stage at the call of a real master !—with what double delight must he have seen Goethe seizing for the noblest purposes of art, men and modes of life, scenes, incidents and transactions, all claiming near kindred with those that had from boyhood formed the chosen theme of his own sympathy and reflection. In the baronial robbers of the Rhine, stern, bloody, and rapacious, but frank, generous, and, after their fashion, courteous—in their forays upon each others' domains, the besieged castles, the plundered herds, and the baffled liege-lord, who vainly strove to quell all these turbulences—Scott had before him a vivid image of the life of his own and the rival Border clans, familiarized to him by a hundred nameless minstrels.'[102]

Scott also thought better of his own translation than he did of the versions of Iffland, Babo and Maier, to the extent at least of letting Lewis see it. In January 1799 Lewis carried through the negotiations with a London publisher, inducing him to buy the copyright for twenty-five guineas and a promise of as much again if a second edition was called for. The play with the title *Goetz of Berlichingen*,

With the Iron Hand: A Tragedy. Translated from the German of Goethé, Author of 'The Sorrows of Werter' [*sic*], *etc.*, appeared in February 1799, the first publication to bear Scott's name, and the first from which he derived any profit.[103] No second edition, however, was called for, at least under the aforementioned contract.[104] 'The truth is, that, to have given Goethe anything like a fair chance with the English public, his first [important] drama ought to have been translated at least ten years before '[105]—that is, before translations of plays by more or less feeble imitators of the master had spoiled the market and provoked *The Anti-Jacobin*. Scott confessed in 1827 that he was 'ashamed' of his version 'undertaken when I did not understand German and I am not able to revise it now because I have forgotten the little I then knew '.[106]

At an uncertain date, but probably just after his *Goetz* was finished, Scott translated another of the nobler German dramas, Schiller's *Die Verschwörung des Fiesko zu Genua*, which translation he considered 'a finer thing' than his version of *Götz von Berlichingen* as late as 1827, but the manuscript of which he had given away or lost.[107] 'I remember I used to read it,' he told Mrs Hughes, 'to sobbing and weeping audiences & no wonder for whatever may be thought of the translation the original is sublime.'[108]

When Scott was still under the spell of German drama and still distrustful of his own unaided efforts, he wrote in prose *The House of Aspen, A Tragedy*. The date of composition appears to have been 1799-1800.[109] The play is not strictly a translation, but, says Scott, 'rather a rifacimento of the original . . . since the whole is compressed, and the incidents and dialogue much varied'.[110] Moreover Scott drops many of the minor characters and changes most of the names of the characters he retains.[111] The original was a long romantic drama set in 1438, *Die heilige Vehme*, which completely fills the sixth volume of Veit Weber's *Sagen der Vorzeit*.[112] *The House of Aspen*, like its original, owes its most effective scenes to the *Vehmgericht* and its awe-inspiring ritual, which Goethe's *Götz* had made familiar to Scott and which he turned once more to account near the end of his career in *Anne of Geierstein*.

Thinking well enough at the time of this piece between original work and translation,[113] Scott sent *The House of Aspen* to Lewis in London, in the hope of having it staged.[114] It was read also by Richard Heber and by him[115] submitted to John Kemble.[116] Kemble must have been favourably impressed to begin with, for he 'at one time had some desire to bring out the play at Drury Lane', with himself as the unhappy son and 'his matchless sister', Mrs Siddons, as the mother.[117] The existence of several manuscript copies,[118] some with extensive revisions and what may be the producer's notes, may indicate that the play was in fact put into rehearsal, as Lockhart believed.[119] However, as Scott himself tells us, 'great objections appeared. . . . There were dangers that the main spring of the story—the binding engagements formed by members of the secret tribunal—might not be sufficiently felt by an English audience. . . . There was also, according to Mr Kemble's experienced opinion, too much blood, too much of the dire catastrophe of Tom Thumb, when all die on the stage. It was besides esteemed perilous to place the fifth act and the parade and show of the secret conclave, at the mercy of underlings and scene-shifters, who, by a ridiculous motion, gesture, or accent, might turn what should be grave into farce'.[120] There was, besides, the fact that the taste for German drama had been laughed off the stage by *The Rovers*. Scott 'willingly acquiesced'[121] in Kemble's reasoning. But an echo of his disappointment can, I think, be detected in his *Essay on the Drama*, where he remarks that the very numbers of the plays thrust on theatrical managers 'must prevent their doing equal justice to all; and must frequently deter a man of real talents either from pride or modesty, from entering a competition, clogged with delay, solicitation, and other circumstances, *haud subeunda ingenio suo*'.[122]

It must have been while the manuscript of *The House of Aspen* was still in London that it was seen late in 1801 by no less critical a reader of German drama than George Ellis, one of the collaborators in *The Rovers*, with whom Scott had been corresponding for some months about *Sir Tristrem* and other medieval literature.[123]   Ellis and also his wife, he politely told Scott, had derived pleasure from reading *The House of Aspen*; but in his opinion the fifth act would have to be thoroughly revised before production or publication.   By this time, however, Scott was 'entirely out of conceit with my Germanized brat'[124] which compared so unfavourably with the plays of his countrywoman, Joanna Baillie.[125]   *The House of Aspen*, he said, was but 'a very hurried dramatic sketch; . . . At one time I certainly thought, with my friends, that it might have ranked well enough by the side of the Castle Spectre,[126] Bluebeard, and the other drum and trumpet exhibitions of the day; but . . . should I ever again attempt dramatic composition, I would endeavour after the genuine old English model',[124] a resolution to which he adhered in such plays as he wrote later, except perhaps in the somewhat Germanized *Doom of Devorgoil*.

The manuscript of *The House of Aspen* lay long among Scott's papers.   He proposed to publish it in 1806 along with *Ballads and Lyrical Pieces*,[127] and then on reflection decided not to.   Many years later, on 27th February 1829 to be exact, he decided to send 'the old drama of *The House of Aspen* '[128] to Charles Heath and F. M. Reynolds[129] for the 1830 *Keepsake*,[130] in order to clear himself of the residue of an obligation.[131]   'This will make up my contribution,' he confides to his *Journal*, 'and a good deal more, if as I recollect there are five acts.   Besides it will save me further trouble about Heath and his Annual.   2dly, There are several manuscript copies of the play abroad, and some of them will be popping out one of these days in a contraband manner.   3dly, If I am right as to the length of the piece, there [is] £100 extra work at least which will not be evil

convenient at all.'[132]   It was not, however, till 12th April
that he despatched the play, the preface or Advertisement
following on the 18th.   That preface is far from being a
recommendation of the play to the readers of *The Keepsake*.
The author, said Scott in it, had lately chanced to look
over the following scenes ' with feelings very different from
those of the adventurous period of his literary life during
which they had been written, and yet with such as perhaps
a reformed libertine might regard the illegitimate production of an early amour.   There is something to be ashamed
of, certainly; but, after all, parental vanity whispers that
the child has a resemblance to the father '.   Scott's reason
for looking over his own play was that from the autumn
of 1828 till the end of April 1829 he was engaged on *Anne
of Geierstein* and wanted to bring into it the *Vehmgericht*
which had so thrilled him in Goethe's *Götz* and which he
had met again in his model for *The House of Aspen*.   He
actually refers once in the *Journal* to his play as ' the Secret
Tribunal '.[133]   On 17th December 1829 *The House of Aspen*
was staged in Edinburgh and was given a mixed and mostly
unfavourable reception.

When Scott wrote his admirable *Essay on the Drama*
in 1819, the taste which he had shared for the German
theatre had passed away and he himself had come to take
a more objective and comparative view of it.   Some of
his opinions echo or coincide with the dramatic criticism
of A. W. von Schlegel and Coleridge.   Scott rightly considered that German drama reached its zenith in ' the
sublimity of Goethe, the romantic strength of Schiller, or
the deep tragic pathos of Lessing ',[134] not in ' the wretched
pieces of Kotzebue '.[135]   But at the same time he realised
that even the greater German dramatists had the defects of
their qualities, that those defects were often carried to
absurdity by their imitators, and that unfortunately it was
on the whole the poorer specimens of cloak-and-dagger
romance on the one hand and of mawkish sentimentality
on the other which had ' found a readier acceptance, or

more willing translators '[136] in Britain. Nevertheless he
believed that English dramatic literature towards the end of
the eighteenth century had required 'a new impulse from
some other quarter—a fresh turning-up of the soil, and
awakening of its latent energies by a new mode of culture '.[137]
The impulse came 'from Germany, where literature was
in the first luxuriant glow of vegetation with all its crop of
flowers and weeds rushing up together. There was good
and evil in the importation from this superabundant source.
But the evil was of a nature so contrary to that which had
long palsied our dramatic literature,[138] that, like the hot
poison mingling with the cold, it may in the issue bring us
nearer to a state of health '. [139]

My main purpose in this chapter has been, not to trace
the influence of German on the mature Scott, though I
have referred occasionally to his middle and later years, but
to explore the subject of Scott's study of the German
language and its literature when he was still in his educational phase and had not yet realised his own potentialities
as a creative writer. Precocious as he was in his outlook
on life, in the variety of his interests, and in his acquisition
of knowledge, and passionate as was his love of literature,
he was not creatively precocious, mainly because he was
too modest and unsure of himself to try, except in the very
minor way of anybody who has ever contributed to a school
or college magazine or sent a copy of verses to a local
newspaper or scribbled doggerel when he first fell in love.
Wordsworth and Coleridge, Byron, Shelley, and Keats
versified voluminously while still in their 'teens; but Scott
was twenty-eight before he wrote *Glenfinlas*, which, ignor-
ing anything earlier, he called 'the first original poem which
I ventured to compose '.[140]
And it may be said that German literature was the
catalyst. The years when Scott was 'German mad '[141]
were from 1792 to 1800 and more particularly somewhere
between, after he had made sufficient progress in the language

to read the literature fairly easily and before the waning of his first enthusiasm. During those years he read far more German works than those I have named; in fact he is likely to have read, as he did in English, with an ardent and indiscriminate omnivorousness, limited only by the impossibility of getting the books he wanted or by his finding what he got uncongenial. He probably read comparatively little German after 1800, and less and less later until he dropped it altogether and, in his own opinion, could no longer understand it,[142] though he still occasionally quoted it.

But he did not forget the substance of what he had read: it went, like all that he read in English or in any other language, into the capacious reservoir of his memory. What he wrote by way of translation from, or direct imitation of, German ballads, plays, and romances, is far from exhausting the influence of German literature on his work. In many of the poems and novels of his maturity parallels, more or less convincing, have been found to passages in his German predecessors.[143] But such echoes and recalls are like his reminiscences from any other item in his reading—medieval romance, Shakespeare and the Elizabethan drama, Scottish national or local or family history, and so on. They are of quite a different kind, caught up as they are and carried along in a larger creative purpose like straws on the surface of a stream, from the debts with which I have been concerned.

The point I would stress is that it was Scott's dabbling in German and still more his translating and imitating therefrom that lured him on into creation; or, as Sir Herbert Grierson puts it, ' it was from German literature that the impulse came, which made of the young antiquary and omnivorous reader a creative writer, supplied the spark which fused the love of history and antiquities with the love of poetry and romance '.[144] It was in the summer of 1799 that he passed on to his first ventures in original composition. But in them he was still less than self-reliant, like a learner on the ice. For in *Glenfinlas, The Eve of St*

John, and *The Gray Brother* he was leaning heavily on the supporting tradition of the Border ballads,[145] which the antiquary in him, as distinct from the creative writer, was editing at the same time. It was not till *The Lay of the Last Minstrel* in 1805 that Scott took off on a bolder flight.

> ' For his was minstrel's skill, he caught
> The art unteachable, untaught.'[146]

NOTES ON REFERENCES

1 Cf. *Drama,* 614: ' a country whose literature had hitherto scarce been known to exist '.

2 *Sketches and Hints of Church History, and Theological Controversy. Chiefly translated or abridged from Modern Foreign Writers,* vol. I, 1790; vol. II, 1797.

3 Cf. *supra,* 211-12. He was one of the clergy who officiated at Scott's funeral.

4 Paton, II, 411-12.

5 W. C. van Antwerp is mistaken in stating that Scott was present (*A Collector's Comment on his First Editions of the Works of Sir Walter Scott,* 4). An essay on ' The Present State of the German Stage ' was read to the Speculative Society in 1795 by Alexander Brunton, later Professor of Hebrew in the University of Edinburgh.

6 *Imitations,* IV, 26.

7 In *Intro. Note,* 652, Scott describes himself as ' one whose early attention to the German had been arrested by Mackenzie's Dissertation, and the play of *The Robbers* '. He bought Fraser Tytler's translation of the latter on 30th July 1792.

8 *Imitations,* IV, 26.

9 *Imitations,* IV, 25.

10 Lords Braxfield, Polkemmet, and Balmuto often addressed counsel in broad Scots, continuing what had been the common idiom of the Court fifty years before. Lord Balmuto retired only in 1822. Cf. *Rob Roy,* Chapter XXIII: ' the Scottish brogue, with its corresponding

dialect and imagery, which, although he possessed the power at times of laying them aside, recurred at every moment of emotion, and gave pith to his sarcasm, or vehemence to his expostulation'.

11 Dr Willich's Christian names were Anthony Florian Madinger. He wrote on education, philology, and philosophy as well as on medicine. The following friends of Scott were members with him of Dr Willich's class: William Clerk; George Cranstoun (Lord Corehouse); William Erskine (Lord Kinnedder); John Macfarlane of Kirkton; Alexander Manners; Thomas Thomson; and H. Guthrie Wright, with the almost certain addition of John Boyd Greenshields.

12 Cf. Lockhart, I, 36: ' In [the foreign languages he studied] he sought for incidents, and he found images; but for the treasures of diction he was content to dig on British soil [in English literature and in] that sister idiom which had not always, as he flattered himself, deserved the name of a dialect.'

13 *Imitations*, IV, 27.

14 I, 42.

15 There is a brief reference in *Romance* (557) to *The Battle of Brunanburgh* in the *Anglo-Saxon Chronicle*.

16 Cf. *supra*, 220-21.

17 Cf. *supra*, 221.

18 The following other items in the Abbotsford notebook may also be mentioned in this connection: the original and the Latin translation of the introduction, not translated by Thomas Gray, to *Vegtamskviða*; transcriptions (with notes) of *Sumer is icumen in* and *Merie sungen the muneches binnen Ely*; an English poetical version ' by a gentleman in Devonshire' (possibly the Rev. Richard Polwhele) of ' A part of the Epicedium or death Song of Regnar Lodbrog ', with a prose introduction by Scott; Scott's translation in verse of the song or carol for St Edmund's Day; and etymologies from Du Cange's *Glossaria*.

19 Gillies, 71. Dr Willich ' wished to make his pupils *au fait* of what he called the *geheimnissvolle Tiefe* . . . of his native language, which, as he well knew, could only be

mastered by patient submission to grammatical exercises '.

20   As a child Scott had read an English translation (cf. *supra*, 55).

21   *Imitations*, IV, 28.

22   *Der zerbrochene Krug* in *Idyllen*, I, x.

23   *Imitations*, IV, 27-28. Byron's *Cain*, which was dedicated to Scott and pronounced by him to be 'very grand and tremendous' (*Letters*, VII, 37; to John Murray, 17th December 1821), was more to his taste. But *Cain*, though so different in treatment and effect, echoes *Der Tod Abels* much more than Byron realised. His own statement is that he had not re-read Gessner since he was a child of eight at Aberdeen (*The Works of Lord Byron: Poetry*. Edited by E. H. Coleridge, V, 200-1, 208-9).

24   Lockhart, I, 56. Lockhart alludes to another member of the German class, without naming him, whose influence combined with Erskine's but did not continue so long. He was probably John Boyd Greenshields.

25   *Letters*, I, 42 (to William Clerk, 23rd August 1795).

26   He could not have received through Mrs Scott of Harden at this time, as Allan states (152), any works by De La Motte Fouqué, none of which appeared till 1804. But he may have obtained some of the forgotten romances of Christian Heinrich Spiess, of whose *Geistergeschichte*, *Das Peter Männchen*, Gillies heard him speak 'with peculiar interest' (72). Curiously enough, in Note XI of *The Monastery* he misattributes Spiess's ghost-story to Johann Ludwig Tieck.

27   Lockhart, I, 69.

28   She also constituted herself a social mentor. 'He used to say, that she was the first *woman of real fashion* that *took him* up; that she used the privileges of her sex and station in the truest spirit of kindness; set him right as to a thousand little trifles, which no one else would have ventured to notice; and, in short, did for him what no one but an elegant woman can do for a young man, whose early days have been spent in narrow and provincial circles' (Lockhart, I, 69).

29   *Neues grammatisch-kritisches Wörterbuch der englischen Sprache für die Deutschen . . . ausdem . . . Werke des Hrn. S. Johnson*

. . . gezogen, und mit vielen Wörtern . . . vermehrt, 1786, etc.

30 *Intro. Note,* 652. Dr Dryasdust obtained some particulars about Redgauntlet's later history ' from an excellent person, who was a priest in the Scottish Monastery of Ratisbon before its suppression ' (*Redgauntlet,* Conclusion).

31 Dr Willich published in 1798 *Three Philological Essays . . .; chiefly translated from the German of J. C. Adelung.* One of the essays is *On the Relative Merits and Demerits of Johnson's English Dictionary.* Scott also acquired Christian Ludwig's *Deutsch-Englisches Lexicon* and his *Dictionary English, German, and French* (revised by J. B. Rogler).

32 Skene was admitted to the Bar in 1797.

33 *Letters,* X, 331 (to Mrs Hughes, 13th December 1827).

34 *Intro. Note,* 652.

35 *Intro. Note,* 650. Cf. Lockhart, I, 81: Lewis's ballads ' had rekindled effectually in his breast the spark of poetical ambition '.

36 Cf. *supra,* 128–29; and Lockhart, I, 68.

37 I, 80.

38 William Erskine had already shown to Lewis in London some of Scott's translations and mentioned others; and Lewis had invited Scott's help in a way which he (Scott) regarded as highly flattering.

39 Lockhart, I, 81.

40 Allan, 116. The words from *The Young Tamlane* in *Minstrelsy* are: ' He's won amang us a " (II, 403).

41 Lockhart, I, 81.

42 It was printed in *The Monthly Magazine* for March 1796 (cf. *infra,* 273, note 49). Lewis preferred it to Scott's version and reprinted it the same year.

43 Scott himself dates the occasion ' About the summer of 1793 or 1794 ', (*Intro. Note,* 650). But on the same page he states that Lewis's ballads, which were not published till 1795, had already suggested a translation to him and that the translation was only ' hurried into execution, in consequence of a temptation, which others, as well as the author, found it difficult to resist '.

44 Cf. Allan, 114.

45 Lockhart, I, 65.

46 Remembered and quoted by George Cranstoun (later

Lord Corehouse), who was a brother of Mrs Dugald
Stewart and Jane Anne Cranstoun and a member of Dr
Willich's German class.

47   *Intro. Note*, 651. When Paymaster of the Royal Edinburgh Light Dragoons a few years later, Scott named his
first charger Leonore.

48   I, 66.

49   Lockhart, I, 66. Later, on 18th April 1796, the enthusiastic
Miss Cranstoun wrote to Scott: ' Be it known unto thee
that Will. Taylor's translation of yr. ballad is published
[in the March *Monthly Magazine*] & so infinitely inferior
is it in every respect I wonder how we could tolerate it.
—Dugald Stewart read yours to Greenfield [William
Greenfield, Blair's successor as Professor of Rhetoric and
Belles Lettres] the other day. When he came to the
fetter dance, he look'd up & poor G. was sitting with
his hands nail'd to his knees & the big tears rolling down
his innocent nose in so piteous a manner that Mrs S.
burst out laughing, an angry man Greenfield at such a
cruel interruption. I have Stanley's addition to it, but
it is below contempt . . . so that every day adds to your
renown' (Grierson, 35).

50   Lockhart, I, 66.

51   *Intro. Note*, 651. The only other surviving piece from
Bürger is *The Triumph of Constancy* (cf. *infra*, 258).

52   Manners was also a member of the Speculative Society.

53   According to Lockhart, Miss Cranstoun at a date not
long after the beginning of April 1796 thought that she
might help Scott in his courtship of Williamina Belsches
' by presenting him in the character of a printed author.
William Erskine being called in to her counsels, a few copies
of the ballads were forthwith thrown off in the most
elegant style, and one, richly bound and blazoned,
followed Scott in the course of a few days to the country.
The verses were read and approved of, and Miss Cranstoun
at least flattered herself that he had not made his first
appearance in type to no purpose' (I, 66). Basil Hall
was told the same story by Countess Purgstall (as Miss
Cranstoun became by her marriage) when he visited her
in 1834; and he mentions it in his *Schloss Hainfeld, or A*

Winter in Lower Styria of 1836 (cf. Grierson, 32 note 1).
But no specimen of the alleged special edition exists,
though no doubt Scott's resolve to print was with some
idea of presenting a copy to Miss Belsches in due course.
Lord Sands says that the ballads were in print by 20th
August (*Sir Walter Scott's Congé*, 126); but Miss Cranstoun
says they were only ' in the press ' in September (Grierson,
38, note 1), and Ruff dates their publication in October
(I, 116). As for the favour said to have been won by
the presentation copy, Miss Belsches had given her heart
to young William Forbes by the autumn of 1796 (cf.
Grierson, 32).

54 *Letters*, I, 59 (to William Taylor, 25th November 1796).

55 *Letters*, I, 59-61 (25th November 1796).

56 Cf. Lockhart, I, 71.

57 *Letters*, I, 62-63 (22nd January 1797).

58 *Intro. Note*, 651.

59 Cf. Lockhart, I, 70-1, for the letters to Scott of Dugald
Stewart and John Ramsay of Ochtertyre, ' two of Burns's
kindest and warmest friends '; and for the opinion of
the expatriated antiquary, George Chalmers, with whom
Scott had been in correspondence from the beginning of
1796 about Scottish ballads.

60 E.g. those by William Taylor, William Robert Spencer,
and even the Poet Laureate of the day, Henry James Pye.

61 *Intro. Note*, 651-52.

62 *Intro. Note*, 652.

63 Cf. *supra*, 256.

64 The others were: *The Fire-King* (cf. *infra*, 259); *Glenfinlas*
(cf. *supra*, 215; *et infra*, 268-69); *The Eve of Saint John*
(cf. *infra*, 268-69); and *Frederick and Alice* (cf. *infra*, 258-59).

65 I.e. himself and John Leyden.

66 *Imitations*, IV, 48-49.

67 Ibid., I, 54.

68 Ibid., IV, 49.

69 I, 84.

70 *Imitations*, IV, 49.

71 Ibid., IV, 53-54.

72 It was printed for the first time from the MS. at Abbotsford
by C. O. Parsons in *Scott's Translation of Bürger's ' Das*

Lied von Treue' in *The Journal of English and Germanic Philology*, XXXIII (1934).

73 Cf. Lockhart, I, 81.

74 *Letters*, I, 76-77.

75 After Lewis's lover of the fair Imogine.

76 Both issues, identical but for the title-pages, include also *The Chase* and *William and Helen*, in addition to matter not by Scott; and both appear to have been for private circulation. Ruff was aware of only one copy of the first issue, and of only three of the second (I, 121-22). Lockhart knew only the second (I, 87). Lewis had originally intended to call *Tales of Wonder Tales of Terror*. Countess Purgstall in Styria may have been confused in consequence. She wrote on 26th July 1799 urging Scott to give his name to his part of an unnamed forthcoming collection: ' A very pretty thing indeed when a man has real genius to let another get the credit of it . . . Mr Lewis has great merits, but I have also seen things written by him which were not fit to wipe your worst Poetical Pen withal ' (Wilfred Partington, *Sir Walter's Post-Bag*, 8).

77 *P.W.*, 653.

78 Cf. Lockhart, I, 69.

79 *P.W.*, 653.

80 Cf. Lockhart, I, 69. There is some doubt, however, about the date. One of the two manuscripts is dated 1807 (National Library of Scotland); the other is undated (Edinburgh University Library).

81 In 1799 Scott supplied Ballantyne with some paragraphs on a legal question for *The Kelso Mail*. When delivering his copy, he took with him some recent verses designed for Lewis's *Tales of Wonder* in the main. Ballantyne was delighted with them, especially the Morlachian ballad. Scott ' talked of Lewis with rapture ' and depreciated his own work in comparison, dissenting from Ballantyne's opinion that his verses ' were far above what Lewis could ever do ', yet seeming ' pleased with the warmth of my approbation ' (Lockhart, I, 87; cf. ibid., I, 69).

82 *The Slavonic Review*. John Boyd Greenshields, Scott's contemporary in the Speculative Society, included a translation of the ballad in *Selim and Zaida, with other*

Poems, 1800, done in the main from Goethe but incorporating some passages from the Abate Alberto Fortis's version in his *Viaggio in Dalmazia*, 1774. W. E. Aytoun did a more literal translation for his and (Sir) Theodore Martin's *Poems and Ballads of Goethe*, 1859.

83 *Sammlung Deutschen Volkslieder.*

84 In *The Edinburgh Annual Register* for 1816. Scott quotes fifteen of his stanzas in summarising the ballad for the Introduction to the 1832 edition of *The Betrothed*, and says, ' The song is supposed to be extracted from a manuscript chronicle of Nicolas Thomann, chaplain to St Leonard in Wiessenhorn, and dated 1533.'

85 Two stanzas in Chapter XI of *The Talisman*, said to be translated from ' high German ', seem to be a revision of earlier work found by Dr J. C. Corson in a commonplace book at Abbotsford which Scott began in the seventeen-nineties.

86 Cf. *P.W.*, 653.

87 *Imitations*, IV, 57. Cf. ibid., IV, 58, for Lewis's mingled praise and criticism in a letter of 3rd February 1800.

88 Recited by James Skene of Rubislaw (cf. Lockhart, I, 81).

89 According to Lockhart, I, 81. But in *P.W.*, 701, it is dated 1802.

90 Scott's military education had long been pursued by him in the inactive but by no means uninterested way of a reader of military history and a student of fortification and tactics (cf. *supra*, 51, 107, 138-39). From 1794, when a volunteer infantry was embodied in Scotland, Scott was full of enthusiasm, though condemned to be only a spectator of the drill. But a plan was proposed, by Scott himself according to James Skene of Rubislaw, for a volunteer corps of light horse. Its formation was delayed till 1797, when Scott became Quartermaster and Secretary, and also for a short time Paymaster. Skene, who was a Cornet in the corps, admired Scott's horsemanship and his fearless and tireless energy. ' [H]is zeal and animation served to sustain the enthusiasm of the whole corps, while his ready *mot à rire* kept up, in all, a degree of good humour and relish for the service, without which the toil and privations of long *daily* drills would not easily have been

submitted to by such a body of gentlemen. . . . He took his full share in all the labours and duties of the corps, had the highest pride in its progress and proficiency, and was such a trooper himself, as only a very powerful frame of body and the warmest zeal in the cause could have enabled any one to be' (Lockhart, I, 72). This passage sufficiently disproves Allan's assertion that the description of Edward Waverley's military apprenticeship in Chapter VII of the novel 'has every feature of a picture from the life' (134), however closely parallel to Scott's own was his hero's bookish education in Chapter III (cf. *supra*, 100, 139-41). Scott has in fact attributed to Waverley in regard to things military the wandering attention and fluctuating interest that he himself had given to things pedagogic during his days at school and college and also at his German class. But Scott was far too keen to be a soldier ever to have been bored by or to have neglected any military detail however ' dry and abstract ' or any ' technical phrases, and minute points of etiquette or field discipline ' (*Waverley*, Chapter VII).

91 And of the contemporary theatre, too (cf. Lockhart, I, 79).

92 Scott, translating from the 1785 title-page, calls his version *The Wards from the German of Will. Augustus Iffland. Acted for the first time at Manheim 25 October 1784.* For *Wards* he had at first written *Pupils*.

93 Scott originally called his translation *Otho of Wittelsbach a Tragedy From the German of Steinsberg*. But subsequently he stroked out the last two words and added *adapted to the Stage by Steinsberg*, having in fact used the stage edition of Babo's play by Karl Friedrich Guolfinger, Ritter von Steinsberg.

94 Scott calls his translation *Wolfred of Stromberg A Drama of Chivalry from the German of Meier*. He chose to use Fust's second Christian name Wolfried (in an anglicised spelling).

95 On 24th April 1796 Scott asked William Erskine, wrongly assumed to be in London, 'to pick up a few German books—& remember *Agnes Bernauerinn*' (*Letters*, I, 47). This was a play by Josef August, Graf von Törring. In a 1797 notebook Scott records his reading in June and July of that year two other German plays, Lessing's

Nathan der Weise and Heinrich Wilhelm von Gerstenberg's *Die Braut.*

96   Cf. *Drama*, 614, for his mature and very unfavourable opinion of German ' pathetic comedy, which might rather be called domestic tragedy' with its ' demoralising false-hood' and 'intellectual jacobinism'.

97   613-14.

98   Cf. D. M. Mennie, *Sir Walter Scott's Unpublished Translations of German Plays* in *The Modern Language Review*, XXXIII (1938), 236.

99   *Letters*, X, 331 (13th December 1827).

100   *The Anti-Jacobin*, ed. 1799, II, 416-17.

101   He cites *The Rovers* in his *Journal*, I, 56 (23rd December 1825). Cf. Advertisement to *The House of Aspen* in *The Keepsake for* 1830: ' The effect of their singularly happy piece of ridicule . . . was, that the German School, with its beauties and defects, passed completely out of fashion'.

102   I, 82. Cf. Gillies, 72-3.

103   The printer ran off some copies as ' By William Scott, Esq. Advocate, Edinburgh' before the mistake was noticed.

104   A pirated edition was published at Paris in 1826.

105   Lockhart, I, 82. Rose Lawrence published a translation in 1799 with the title *Gortz of Berlingen with the Iron Hand*.

106   *Letters*, X, 283 (to Mrs Hughes, 20th September 1827). Mrs Hughes had made a copy of ' old Goetz ' (ibid., X, 331; to Mrs Hughes, 13th December 1827).

107   *Letters*, X, 331 (to Mrs Hughes, 13th December 1827).

108   *Letters*, X, 283 (20th September 1827). A translation of the play by Georg Heinrich Noehden and (Sir) John Stoddart was published in 1796.

109   In the Advertisement to the play in *The Keepsake for* 1830 Scott says it was ' executed nearly thirty years since '; and two songs from it, *A Song of Victory* and *Rhein-Wein Lied*, and the first version of a third, *The Maid of Toro*, are dated 1800 (*P.W.*, 699-700, 705-6). The revision of the third song is dated 1806. Lockhart dates the play more vaguely at ' about the same time ' as the translation of *Götz* (I, 82); but later he is inclined to date it after Scott's return from London in late April or early May 1799 (I, 83). By the kindness of Dr Isabel M. Brown I have been able

to examine a manuscript copy of the play dated 1809 in which *The Mother and the Son* is given as an alternative title.

110 Advertisement.

111 Aspen itself is abbreviated from the original Aspenau. As it happens, Aspen is the name of a character in (?) Richard Savage's *The School for Mirth; or, Woman's a Riddle*, which was acted in Edinburgh in the seventeen-eighties.

112 Published in 1795. Veit Weber is said to be a pseudonym. It is interesting to notice that Scott in the 1830 Advertisement falls into two blunders owing to the decay of his German: he makes *Vehme* masculine instead of feminine; and, though he reads correctly the German-text capital V in *Vehme* and *Vorzeit*, he misreads it as B in *Veit*, which he gives as *Beit*.

113 Cf. Allan, 161.

114 Cf. *Journal*, III, 26 (27th February 1829): 'the old drama of the *House of Aspen*, which I wrote some thirty years [ago], and offerd to the stage'.

115 Heber admired the play and was surprised at its being dropped by Kemble. Scott thanked Heber for his help on 5th April 1800 (*Letters*, XII, 157).

116 But according to Lockhart, who does not mention Heber in this connection, the play, 'having first been read and much recommended by the celebrated actress, Mrs Esten, . . . was taken up by Kemble, and I believe actually put in rehearsal for the stage' (I, 82).

117 Advertisement.

118 One, on paper watermarked 1809, is entitled *The Mother and the Son*.

119 I, 82.

120 Advertisement.

121 Ibid.

122 615. Cf. *supra*, 174, 181, note 83.

123 Ellis published his *Specimens of Early English Poets* in 1790 and with additions in 1801. His *Specimens of Early English Metrical Romances* appeared in 1805. He also edited G. L. Way's *Fabliaux or Tales, abridged from French Manuscripts of the XII and XIII Centuries*, 1796.

124 *Letters*, I, 124 (to George Ellis, 7th December 1801).

125   *A Series of Plays in which it is attempted to delineate the Stronger Passions*, 1798. A second series followed in 1802, and a third in 1812.

126   A melodrama by Lewis of which there were eight editions in 1798 and another in 1799.

127   It was probably for this intended edition that Scott revised *The Maid of Toro* (cf. *supra*, 278, note 109), perhaps making other changes at the same time.

128   *Journal*, III, 26 (27th February 1829).

129   Scott became rather annoyed at Heath, the editor-publisher of *The Keepsake*, and still more at Reynolds, his assistant.

130   An annual ' of which the plates are beyond comparaison [sic] beautiful. But the letter-press indifferent enough ... a New-Year Gift-Book ' (*Journal*, II, 181, 30th January 1828). A little later Scott refers contemptuously to ' Heath's what-dye-call-it ' (ibid., II, 224, 13th April 1828).

131   ' [A]s he [i.e. Heath] says I am still in his debt ' (*Journal*, III, 26). Scott had contributed *The Tapestried Chamber, My Aunt Margaret's Mirror*, and *The Laird's Jock* to the 1828 *Keepsake* under an arrangement as to reprinting. But it is not clear why he let Heath have *The House of Aspen* as well, for his 1830 issue.

132   *Journal*, III, 26 (27th February 1829).

133   III, 62 (6th May 1829).

134   614.

135   Ibid.

136   *Drama*, 614.

137   Ibid., 613.

138   I.e. the long French vogue.

139   *Drama*, 613.

140   *Imitations*, IV, 44.

141   Cf. *supra*, 253.

142   Cf. *supra*, 263.

143   Cf. William Macintosh, *Scott and Goethe. German Influence on the Writing of Sir Walter Scott*, 1925.

144   24.

145   He says himself, however, of *Glenfinlas* (cf. *supra*, 215) that ' As it is supposed to be a translation from the Gaelic, I considered myself as liberated from imitating the anti-

quated language and rude rhythm of the Minstrel ballad. A versification of an Ossianic fragment came nearer to the idea I had formed of my task' (*Imitations*, IV, 44).

146   *Rokeby*, Canto First.

CHAPTER XVI

CONCLUSION

What a life mine has been! half-educated, almost wholly neglected or left to myself, stuffing my head with most nonsensical trash and undervalued in society for a time by most of my companions—getting forward and held a bold and clever fellow contrary to the opinion of all who thought me a mere dreamer.

Journal, I, 50 (18th December 1825).

Ay, ay, I kend Alan was the lad to make a spoon or spoil a horn.

Redgauntlet, *Chapter I.*

I would rather have it written on my monument that I died on the desk than live under the recollection of having neglected it.

Journal, II, 128 (5th November 1827).

IF the University of Edinburgh owes some of its glory to having had Scott as an alumnus, it must be admitted that Scott owed little of his achievement to the University. He learned none of his mighty magic within its walls; and in all the essentials of his art he was, as has been said,[1] self-educated, but without a trace of the usual self-satisfaction, not to say arrogance, of the automath and with too ready an admission that all his acquirements were eccentric and of little account in comparison with the regular studies of his day. Though his attendance at the University coincided with the formative period of his life, it was not the professoriate or the curriculum that left their mark on Scott the poet and novelist, but rather the accidentals and incidentals of his academic career, his friendships, and his extramural activities. Except for inevitable references in his *Memoir*, there is nothing in any of his works which might not have been there had he never attended a single class. He has schoolmasters and pedants, scholars and antiquaries, but no professors, in his gallery. He has episodes in innumerable settings, but none in a university. He has much to say about the education of his heroes; but except Captain, nay, Major Sir Dugald Dalgetty, Alan Fairford, and Darsie Latimer, none of them was academically trained. He took no degree by examination, and he was offered none *honoris causa*.[2] He presented but one of his works to the University Library, his edition of *Sir Tristrem* (1804); sent his son Charles to Oxford; and was ' rather surprised ' on being nominated by Lord Melville and Peel a member of the first Royal Commission on the Scottish Universities. ' I know little of the subject,' he wrote in his *Journal*, ' but I dare say as much as some of the official persons who are inserted of course. The want of efficient men is the reason alleged. I must of course do my best, though I have little hope of being useful.'[3] Though, as we have seen,[4] Scott had valuable and fruitful ideas for changes in the scholastic curriculum, the only idea that occurred spontaneously to him with respect to the Scottish Universities had no reference

at all to the academic curiculum and was only the belief
that bursaries and scholarships should not be awarded except
on merit.[5] No doubt he attended meetings of the Commission; but he thought of recording in his *Journal* only
the first informal one at Melville Castle [6] and a formal one
at the University—which nobody attended except himself.[7]

The nearest Scott was carried to academic honour in
Scotland was when he was nominated on four different
occasions by bodies of students who wanted him as their
Lord Rector, not at his own University of Edinburgh, but
three times at Glasgow and once at St Andrews. One can
hardly describe him as having been a candidate, for it was
no wish of his to stand and no ambition to be elected; and
indeed it is more than likely that the first intimation he
would receive of his nomination was in every case too late
to leave him any choice. On the first two occasions at
Glasgow, in 1822 and in 1824, he was defeated, as perhaps
might have been expected in the political climate of the
time and place, by two Whigs in turn, Sir James Mackintosh
and Henry Brougham. In 1825 the St Andrews students
did elect him and that unanimously; but Principal Francis
Nicoll had reluctantly to declare the election void, because
the statutes of the University, to say nothing of precedents
going back four hundred years, limited the choice of a
Lord Rector to one of its own officials.[8] In the circumstances Scott could do no other than decline to assert what
his student supporters called his ' right ' to the office—which
assertion by him, they assured him, would at the same time
be ' all that is necessary for eliciting the fact of our full
right to vote for whom we will and for securing to us in
all time coming the privilege and distinction which the
other Scottish Universities have succeeded in acquiring, of
never wanting at the head of our Institution a man of literary
eminence and public character '.[9] In any case Scott was
a very busy man and by 1825 beginning to want to demit
offices rather than to assume them, even if the formal duties
of the Lord Rector at St Andrews could be discharged, as

the students told him, by a deputy. In the 1828 election at Glasgow, Scott was more popular with the voters than in 1822 or in 1824, probably because he now stood revealed as the Author of *Waverley*. The other candidate was Scott's friend and brother in literature, Thomas Campbell, who was a Whig and who had held the office of Lord Rector for the two previous years. On 13th November, only two days before the election but as soon as he had heard of his nomination, Scott wrote to Principal Duncan Macfarlane, asking to have his name withdrawn from the contest. Scott's letter,[10] however, arrived too late. The election took place on 15th November as arranged; the result was a tie; and the issue was decided by the Vice-Rector, Dr Gavin Gibb, giving a casting vote in favour of Scott. The same day the Principal wrote to tell him he had fourteen days for deliberation and to entreat him not to send his decision till they could meet and talk over the matter. The Whig placard, which one of the opposition had sent to Scott and which seems to have led him to believe that the contest had more of a political character than he relished, the Principal dismissed as 'absolute nonsense'; and, with perhaps more friendship than accuracy, he assured Scott 'that there is not a particle of Whig or Tory in the business' and that it was simply a struggle between the Glaswegians determined to keep their fellow-townsman for a third year 'in spite of all precedent or even decency', and 'a Muster of the Caledonian youth of all parties and from all quarters of the Country' equally determined to resist 'and to pay the tribute of their respect where they conceived it to be most justly due'.[11] But Scott wrote again to Macfarlane on 16th November, as soon as he had received the latter's persuasive letter and before a deputation of disappointed Campbellites could wait on him to state their case.[12] While he was anxious that his 'declining this high situation' should not be 'thought or represented as an ungrateful indifference' to his young friends who had esteemed him worthy of it, he was gently and courteously firm in his refusal, on the score of 'increasing age and numerous avocations', of reluctance to take on new duties even when accompanied with new honours, of the inconsistency and lack of respect if he were to accept from Glasgow a distinction which he had not accepted from St Andrews, and of the mischief of a disputed election 'in the bosom of a Seat of learning and that too by a competition with my old friend Mr Thomas Campbell'.[13]

The fact has to be recognised, I think, that Scott and his Edinburgh contemporaries had less devotion to their *alma mater* than to the High School—'the pride and boast of our city', as he called it, at the same time avowing himself 'not capable of entertaining a thought to the prejudice of that seminary'.[14] He recalled with fondness 'the forms of the little republic',[15] the schoolboy slang,[16] the schoolboy exploits, the schoolboy code of honour,[17] and the honoured and well-beloved headmaster, 'Dr Adam, to whose memory the author and his contemporaries owe a deep debt of gratitude'.[18] But Scott does not write of the University with the same affection or with a similar sense of belonging. He took a lively interest in the transfer in 1825 of his own old school to a new site and an impressive new building, but none, it would appear, in the rehousing of the University, not even casually alluding in his *Memoir* to the great ceremony of the laying of the foundation-stone of Robert Adam's magnificent quadrangle on 16th November 1789, when he had himself just returned for his second academic spell and when all the students with their hats garnished with laurel walked in the procession. Nevertheless Scott's undemonstrative and tepid attachment to it cannot lessen the pride which the University must ever take in him who was unquestionably the greatest son of her greatest age.

NOTES ON REFERENCES

1   Cf. *supra*, 2, 46, 114, 117-18.
2   I.e. by his own University. But he was made 'D.LL. and A double S', as he puts it, by Trinity College, Dublin, in

1825 (*Letters*, IX, 188; to Sir Adam Ferguson, 18th July 1825).

3   I, 231 (17th September 1826).

4   Cf. *supra*, 83-94.

5   Cf. *Journal*, I, 235 (24th September 1826): 'I wonder what I can do or say about these Universities. One thing occurs —the distribution of bursaries only *ex meritis*. That is, I would have the presentations continue in the present patrons, but exact that those presented should be qualified by success in their literary attainments and distinctions acquired at school to hold these scholarships. This seems to be following out the ideas of the founders, who, doubtless, intended the furthering of good literature. To give education to dull mediocrity is a flinging of the children's bread to dogs—it is a sharping a hatchet on a razor-strop, which renders the strop useless, and does no good to the hatchet. Well, something we will do.'

6   Where Lord Melville, Scott, and Principal Francis Nicoll of St Andrews University 'spoke of the visitation [i.e. by the Royal Commission], of granting degrees, of publick examinations, of abolishing the election of professors by the Senatus Academicus (a most pregnant source of jobs), and much beside—but all desultory' (I, 235-6, 25th September 1826).

7   I, 294 (18th December 1826).

8   Principal Nicoll was himself elected Lord Rector in 1822.

9   *Post-Bag*, 264 (7th March 1825).

10   It seems to have disappeared.

11   *Post-Bag*, 262.

12   It seems to have been that Gibb had not been present 'during the statutory solemnities of the election' (*The Caledonian Mercury*, 22nd November 1828) and that in any case it was doubtful if he had the right to a casting vote at all. William Beattie is mistaken in saying that in consequence of the representations of the deputation 'Sir Walter sent word to the Professors that he declined the proffered honour' (*The Life and Letters of Thomas Campbell*, III, 39-40).

13   *Letters*, XI, 41. At the new election which took place shortly after, Campbell was re-elected, defeating the Tory

candidate, Sir Michael Shaw Stewart.

14 Lockhart II, 526. The words are from Scott's speech at the opening of Edinburgh Academy in 1824 (cf. *supra*, 93-94).

15 *Redgauntlet*, Letter I.

16 Cf. *Redgauntlet*, Letter I: ' And who taught me to smoke a cobbler, pin a losen, head a bicker, and hold the bannets?'

17 Cf. *Redgauntlet*, Letter I: ' You taught me to keep my fingers off the weak, and to clench my fist against the strong; to carry no tales out of school; to stand forth like a true man, obey the stern order of *Pande manum*, and endure my pawmies without wincing, like one that is determined not to be the better for them.'

18 *Redgauntlet*, Letter I, note.

I have said enough to intimate that I talk not without book.
The Monastery, *Chapter XIII.*

PRINCIPAL EVENTS AND DATES IN
SIR WALTER SCOTT'S LIFE

The list of publications below is not a complete one. The dates given for the works are those on their title pages; but some of the works were in fact published towards the ends of the years preceding the dates borne by them. Subsequent editions and collections of previously published works are not included.

1770 (not 1771) Birth in College Wynd, Edinburgh (15th August).
1772 Illness resulting in lameness for life.
1773-76 Resides mainly at Sandy-knowe with intermediate stay at Bath.
1776 Rejoins family at George Square, Edinburgh.
1776-79 Schooling under John Leechman and others.
1779-83 Attends High School of Edinburgh and concurrently (for part of time) writing-and-arithmetic school of John Morton.
Receives tutoring also in school subjects and French from James Mitchell, in singing from Alexander Campbell, and perhaps in dancing or deportment from one Wilson.
1783 Attends Grammar School of Kelso.
1783-86 Attends classes at Edinburgh University.
1785 Begins to take lessons in sketching.
1785-86 Serious haemorrhage and protracted convalescence.
1786 Begins W.S. apprenticeship (31st March).
1787 Meets Robert Burns at house of Professor Adam Ferguson.
Has boyish love affair with Jessie —— of Kelso.
Takes first longer excursions, in Borders and to Highlands.
1789 Decides to read for Bar.
1789-92 Attends classes at Edinburgh University.
1790-95 Active membership of Speculative Society.

1792   Called to Bar along with William Clerk (11th July).

Makes first 'raid' into Liddesdale.

Falls in love with Williamina Belsches.

1792-1800   Is 'German mad' and translates German poems and plays.

1796   First publication, issued anonymously: *The Chase, and William and Helen*, translated from Bürger.

Is disappointed in love.

1797   Becomes Quartermaster, Secretary, and (for a time) Paymaster of Royal Edinburgh Light Dragoons.

Marries Margaret Charlotte Carpenter or Charpentier (24th December).

1798   Takes up house at 39 Castle Street, Edinburgh.

1799   First publication under own name: *Goetz of Berlichingen*, translated from Goethe.

Death of Walter Scott (father).

Takes cottage at Lasswade as country house.

Contributes to *Tales of Terror*.

Appointed Sheriff-Depute of Selkirkshire (16th December).

1800   *The Eve of St John.*

1801   Contributes to M. G. Lewis's *Tales of Wonder*.

1802   *Minstrelsy of the Scottish Border*, vols I and II.

1803   *Minstrelsy of the Scottish Border*, vol. III.

Begins contributions to periodicals.

1804   Edits *Sir Tristrem*.

Removes country quarters to Ashestiel.

1805   *The Lay of the Last Minstrel.*

Enters into partnership with James Ballantyne and Company, printers.

1806   Appointed one of Principal Clerks of Court of Session.

Ballads and Lyrical Pieces.

Edits *Original Memoirs written during the Great Civil War*.

1807   Appointed Secretary to Parliamentary Commission for Improvement of Scottish Jurisprudence.

1808 *Marmion.*
Edits *The Works of John Dryden . . . with Notes,
. . . and a Life of the Author.*
Edits Joseph Strutt's *Queenhoo Hall, . . . and
Ancient Time.*
Edits *Memoirs of Capt. George Carleton.*
Edits *Memoirs of Robert Carey, and Fragmenta
Regalia . . . by Sir R. Naunton.*
One of the organisers of *The Quarterly Review*
(begun 1810).
Enters into partnership with John Ballantyne
and Company, booksellers and publishers.
Projects *The Edinburgh Annual Register* (begun
1810).

1809 Edits *A Collection of Scarce and Valuable Tracts*
(Somers Tracts), vols I-III.
Edits *The Life of Edward, Lord Herbert of Cherbury.*
Contributes to Arthur Clifford's edition of *The
State Papers and Letters of Sir Ralph Sadler.*

1810 *The Lady of the Lake.*
Edits *English Minstrelsy.*
Edits *The Poetical Works of Anna Seward.*
Contributes *Essay on Judicial Reform* to *The
Edinburgh Annual Register.*

1811 Edits *Memoirs of Count Grammont.*
Edits Horace Walpole's *The Castle of Otranto.*
Purchases Clarty Hole, nucleus of Abbotsford
estate.
The Vision of Don Roderick.
Edits *Secret History of the Court of James the First.*

1812 Edits *A Collection of Scarce and Valuable Tracts*
(Somers Tracts), vols IV-X.
Removal from Ashestiel to Abbotsford.

1813 *Rokeby.*
The Bridal of Triermain.
Financial embarrassment of John Ballantyne
and Company, and negotiations for help from
Archibald Constable and Company.
Edits Sir Philip Warwick's *Memoirs of the Reign
of King Charles I.*

	Adds to Abbotsford estate.
	Declines offer of Poet Laureateship.
	Accepts Freedom of City of Edinburgh.
1814	Contributes to H. W. Weber's *Illustrations of Northern Antiquities*.
	Edits *The Works of Jonathan Swift . . . with Notes and a Life of the Author*.
	Waverley.
	Contributes *Essays on Chivalry* and *on the Drama* to *Encyclopaedia Britannica*.
1814–17	*The Border Antiquities of England and Scotland*.
1815	Edits *Memoirs of the Somervilles*.
	Edits Samuel Rowland's *The Letting of Humours Blood in the Head Vaine*.
	The Lord of the Isles.
	Guy Mannering.
	First continental visit (Waterloo, Paris, etc.).
	The Field of Waterloo.
1816	*Paul's Letters to his Kinsfolk*.
	The Antiquary.
	Tales of my Landlord, first series consisting of *The Black Dwarf* and *Old Mortality*.
1817	*Harold the Dauntless*.
	First attack of cramp in stomach.
	Adds to Abbotsford estate.
1818	*Rob Roy*.
	Tales of my Landlord, second series consisting of *The Heart of Midlothian*.
	Is offered and accepts Baronetcy (gazetted 30th March 1820).
	Edits with Robert Jamieson *Burt's Letters from Scotland*.
1819	Recurrences of cramp in stomach.
	Tales of my Landlord, third series consisting of *The Bride of Lammermoor* and *A Legend of Montrose*.
	Death of Mrs Walter Scott (mother).
	The Bridal of Triermain.
1819–26	*Provincial Antiquities of Scotland*.
1820	*Ivanhoe*.

The Monastery.
Marriage of elder daughter Sophia and J. G. Lockhart.
The Abbot.
Elected President of Royal Society of Edinburgh.

1821 *Kenilworth.*
Edits Richard Franck's *Northern Memoirs.*

1821-24 Contributes *Lives of the Novelists* to Ballantyne's *Novelist's Library.*

1822 Edits *Chronological Notes of Scottish Affairs from 1688 to 1701.*
Edits *Military Memoirs of the Great Civil War.*
The Pirate.
The Fortunes of Nigel.
Halidon Hill.
George IV's visit to Scotland.
Contributes *Essay on Romance* to *Encyclopaedia Britannica.*
Peveril of the Peak.

1823 First apoplectic symptoms.
Founds and becomes President of Bannatyne Club.
Elected Chairman of Edinburgh Oil Gas Company.
Quentin Durward.

1824 *St Ronan's Well.*
Redgauntlet.
Contributes *Character of the late Lord Byron* to *The Pamphleteer.*
Co-founder of Edinburgh Academy.

1825 Marriage of elder son Walter to Jane Jobson.
Tales of the Crusaders, consisting of *The Betrothed* and *The Talisman.*
Begins *Journal.*

1826 Bankruptcy as result of financial collapse of three firms: John Ballantyne and Company, Archibald Constable and Company, and Hurst and Robinson
Contributes letters as by Malachi Malagrowther

to *The Edinburgh Weekly Journal.*
Departure from 39 Castle Street, Edinburgh.
Death of Lady Scott (15th May).
Woodstock.
Appointed member of Royal Commission on Scottish Universities.
Second continental visit (Paris).

1827 Avowal of authorship of Waverley Novels at Theatrical Fund Dinner (23rd February).
The Life of Napoleon Buonaparte.
Chronicles of the Canongate, first series consisting of *The Highland Widow, The Two Drovers*, and *The Surgeon's Daughter.*
Contributes *Memoirs of the Marchioness de la Rochejaquelin* to *Constable's Miscellany.*

1828 *Tales of a Grandfather*, first series.
Religious Discourses.
Contributes *My Aunt Margaret's Mirror, The Tapestried Chamber*, and *The Laird's Jock* to *The Keepsake.*
Chronicles of the Canongate, second series consisting of *The Fair Maid of Perth.*

1829 Edits *Memorials of George Bannatyne.*
Anne of Geierstein.
Tales of a Grandfather, second series.

1829-30 Contributes *History of Scotland* to *Lardner's Cabinet Cyclopaedia.*

1830 Contributes *The House of Aspen* to *The Keepsake.*
Tales of a Grandfather, third series.
The Doom of Devorgoil, A Melo-drama. Auchindrane; or, The Ayrshire Tragedy.
Essays on Ballad Poetry added to 1830 edition of *Minstrelsy of the Scottish Border.*
Paralytic seizure.
Resigns Clerkship of Court of Session.
Declines offer of State pension and of Privy Councillorship.
Apoplexy.
Letters on Demonology and Witchcraft.

1831 *Tales of a Grandfather*, fourth series.

Apoplectic paralysis.

Voyage to Mediterranean on H.M.S. *Barham*.

1823 *Tales of my Landlord*, fourth series consisting of *Count Robert of Paris* and *Castle Dangerous*.

Residence in Italy and journey home via the Rhine.

Death at Abbotsford (21st September).

ERRATUM

p. 297, 1823 *should read* 1832

INDEX

Owing to the printing of the Notes on References after the chapters of the book, it has been thought advisable to give in the Index not only pages where persons, places, etc. are actually named, but also pages where they are alluded to without being named. Only certain books published after 1832, the year of Scott's death, are listed in the Index. Their authors' names, however, will serve as keys to any citations of them in the text.

INDEX

INDEX

INDEX

INDEX

303

INDEX

INDEX

Gerstenberg, H. W. von, 277-278
Gessner, Salomon, 55, 74, 250-251, 271
Gibb, Dr Gavin, 286, 288
Gibson, John, 153
Gil Blas, 123
Gilbertfield, 60
Gillies, R. P., 7, 18, 20, 36, 40-41, 43,
    54, 73, 94, 153, 201, 203, 209, 245,
    250, 270-271, 278
Gilman's Cleuch, 73
Gipsies, 65
Glasgow, 75
Glasgow University, 171, 187, 285-289
Glassford of Dugalston, James, 171,
    203, 223, 230
Glencoe, 217
Glendearg (*Monastery*), 176
Glendinning, Edward, 163
Glendinning, Halbert, 23
Glenforgen (*Legend of Montrose*), 236
Glennaquoich (*Waverley*), 153
Glenorchy, Viscountess, 41
Glossaria (Du Cange), 270
Godwin, (*née* Wollstonecraft) Mrs, 84
Goethe, Johan Wolfgang von, 252,
    258-260, 262-264, 266, 270, 275-276,
    278, 280
Goldsmith, Oliver, 13, 60, 62, 157, 173
Good-natured Man, 13
Gordon, Jean, 65, 76
Gordon, Madge, 65
Gortz of Berlingen, 278
Götz von Berlichingen, 260, 262-264,
    266
Gourlay, Ailsie, 2
Govan, 75
Graham, Dugald, 75
Graham, H. G., 40, 77, 109-110, 194,
    233
Graham, Dr James, 6
Graham (Marquis of Montrose), James,
    27
Grammar and Composition, 13, 18,
    38, 84, 94, 198-199, 270-271
*Grammatica Minora, see Rudiments of
    the Latin Tongue*
Grampians Desolate, 42
Granada, 128
Grant, Principal Sir Alexander, 101,
    108, 191
Gray, Thomas, 93, 96, 220-221, 237,
    255, 270
Grecian History, 62
Grecian, *see* Williams, H. W.
Greece, 94, 105
Greek, *see* Languages

Greek Blockhead, 103
Greenbreeks, 39
Greenfield, Professor William, 102,
    119, 273
Greenlaw, George, 204, 231, 234
Greenshields of Drum, John Boyd,
    207, 224, 232, 270-271, 275-276
Gregory, Professor James, 214
Grierson, Sir Herbert, 34, 72-73, 77,
    92, 96, 126, 154, 178-179, 181, 193,
    268, 273-274
Grierson of Lag, Sir Robert, 61, 75-76
Griffith, Richard, 73
Guerras Civiles de Granada, 123, 128
Guildbert (teacher of French), 125-126
Guiscard, Robert, 128, 131

Hailes, Lord, *see* Dalrymple (Lord
    Hailes), Sir David
Haliburton, Barbara, *see* Scott (grand-
    mother, *née* Haliburton), Mrs
Halket, Elizabeth, *see* Wardlaw (*née*
    Halket), Lady
Halket of Wardlaw, Mrs, *see* Wardlaw
    (*née* Halket), Lady
Hall, Captain Basil, 273-274
Hall, Rev. James, 5
Hamilton, Professor Sir William, 191
Hamilton of Gilbertfield, William, 60,
    75
Hamlet, 198
Hanoverians, 25-26, 66-68, 77-78
Harden, 50, 76, 180, 251, 271
Hardie (*Heart of Midlothian*), 244
Hardie, C. M., 176
Hardyknute, 51-52
Harley (in *The Man of Feeling*), 194
Harry, Blind, *see* Henry the Minstrel
Harry and Lucy Concluded, 86
Hartley, David, 184
Harvieston, 237
Hastings (*Jane Shore*), 57
Hawkins, Sir John, 155
Hay (Lord Newton), Charles, 193
Hayley, William, 155
*Heads of Lectures for . . . Students in
    Humanity*, 108
Heath, Charles, 265, 280
Heber, Richard, 116-117, 120, 264, 279
Heineccius, J. G., 187-188, 194
Henry IV, 27, 57, 179
Henry the Minstrel, 60, 87
Hepburn, Sir John Buchan, 233
Heberay des Essarts, Nicolas de, 120
Hercules, *see* Alcides
Hermitage Castle, 130-131

306

INDEX

Herodotus, 110
Herries of Birrensworth, see Redgauntlet, Mr
Hexham, 132
Higgins, (*Anti-Jacobin*), Mr, 261
Highfliers, see Church of Scotland
Highlands and Highlanders, 27, 45, 51, 66-68, 70, 151-153, 155, 216-220, 243
Highland and Agricultural Society, 236
Highland Society, 215, 234
Hill, Professor John, 98-99, 103, 107
Histoire des Chevaliers ... de ... Malte, 54, 114, 138-139, 143
Historia de Gentibus Septentrionalibus, 237
Historia de las Guerras Civiles de Granada, 123, 128
Historical Society (of Trinity College, Dublin), 209-211, 230, 233, 239
History of Automathes, 53, 73
History of Buckhaven, 59, 75
History of England (Goldsmith), 62
History of Scotland (Buchanan), 104
History of Scotland (Laing), 215
History of Scotland (Lindsay of Pitscottie), 155
History of Scotland (Robertson), 62, 155
History of ... the British ... in Indostan, 139
History of the Buchanites, 61, 75
History of the Peninsular War, 119-120
History of the Rebellion, 1688, 77
History of the Rebellion in 1745, 77
History of the Royal Society of Edinburgh, 192
History of the Speculative Society (1845), 201-202, 229, 231, 238-239
History of the Speculative Society (1905), 231
History of the University of Edinburgh, 109
History of the World, 62
Hogg ('Ettrick Shepherd'), James, 73, 115, 120
Hogg (law tutor), James, 94
Holinshed, Raphael, 262
Home (Lord Kames), Henry, 147, 192, 214
Home, John, 28, 41, 66-67, 77-78, 135, 137, 142, 157, 160, 175, 214, 234
Homer, 55-56, 103, 105, 110, 115, 117
Homeri Vita, 110
Hood, Robin, 50, 60, 85

Hoole, John, 63, 122-123
Hope, Sir Thomas, 242
Hope, Professor Thomas Charles, 3
Hope-Scott of Abbotsford, J. R., 13
Horace, 19, 21, 89, 157
Horner, Leonard, 92
Hotspur, see Percy, Henry
Howie of Lochgoin, John, 76
Hughes, John, 126
Hughes (*née* Watts), Mrs, 23-24, 39, 42, 68, 74, 78, 82, 90, 94, 96, 126, 132, 192, 235-236, 261, 263, 272, 278
Humanity, see Languages (Latin)
Hume, David, 2, 189, 214, 233
Hume (Baron Hume), Professor David, 189-190, 194-195
Hunter, Professor Robert, 101
Hunter, Tibby, 10
Hutchison, Judge-Advocate Gilbert, 205, 231
Hutton, Dr James, 160, 199
Hutton, R. H., 115

Iaen, 120
Idyllen, 271
Iffland, A. W., 260-262, 277
Illustrations of Northern Antiquities, 237
Inchcape Rock, 73
India, 111, 139
Innes, Cosmo, 109
Institute of the Law of Scotland, 187-188, 193-194
Institutes, 187-188
Introduction à l'Histoire de Dannemark, 237
Introduction to the History of Poetry in Scotland, 42
Inveresk, 67
Invermay, 193
Invernahyle, 67-68, 152
Invernenty, 156
Ireland, 37, 167
Irving (schoolmaster), 75
Irving (Lord Newton), Alexander, 204-205, 230-231, 246
Irving, John, 4, 6, 37, 74, 122-125, 132, 139, 151, 155, 163, 169, 171, 175, 177, 179, 192, 199-200, 204, 228, 245
Irving, Mrs, 74
Istoria delle Guerre Civili di Francia, 125
Italian music, 31
Italy, 128

Jack the Giant-killer, 59
Jacobite Relics of Scotland, 120

307

INDEX

INDEX

INDEX